MYTHOLOGIES OF THE WORLD

Mythologies of the World:
A Concise Encyclopedia

Max S. Shapiro, *Executive Editor*

Compiled by **Rhoda A. Hendricks,** *Research Editor*

Doubleday & Company, Inc., Garden City, New York 1979

NOTE: A portion of the material in this book, also prepared by Rhoda A. Hendricks, has appeared in the *Cadillac Modern Encyclopedia,* copyright © 1973 by Cadillac Publishing Co., Inc., St. Louis, Missouri.

Genealogical charts drawn by John Morris

Library of Congress Cataloging in Publication Data
Main entry under title:

Mythologies of the world.

Bibliography: p. 217
1. Mythology—Dictionaries. I. Shapiro, Max S
II. Hendricks, Rhoda A
BL303.M95   291.1′3
ISBN 0-385-13667-6
Library of Congress Catalog Card Number 78–1221

CONTENTS

KEY TO ABBREVIATIONS

vii

PRONUNCIATION GUIDE

ix

INTRODUCTION

xi

GENEALOGICAL TABLES

xix

1 The Olympian Gods   xix
2 House of Atreus   xix
3 The Family of Helen of Troy   xx
4 House of Troy   xx
5 House of Cadmus   xx
6 Egyptian Creation Deities   xxi
7 Assyro-Babylonian Creation Deities   xxi
8 The Volsunga Saga   xxii

CONCISE ENCYCLOPEDIA
A through Z

I

BIBLIOGRAPHY

217

85275

KEY TO ABBREVIATIONS

Af	African	M	Mayan
A-B	Assyro-Babylonian	NA	North American
Az	Aztec	O	Oceanian
Ce	Celtic	Pe	Persian
Ch	Chinese	Ph	Phoenician
E	Egyptian	R	Roman
F	Finnish	Sc	Scandinavian
G	Greek	Sl	Slavic
I	Indian	SA	South American
J	Japanese	T	Teutonic

PRONUNCIATION GUIDE

Pronunciation keys appear within parentheses following the last element of the entry heading. In order to avoid using intricate symbol systems which are less familiar, a system of phonetic keys was devised using only the standard letters of the alphabet. Combinations of silent letters are used where necessary to make the pronunciation clear. Below are the phonetic keys used, accompanied by a brief indication of how they are intended to be pronounced.

Vowels

ay	pay
a	pat
ahr	ark
ah	father, Maria, pot, hot
e	pet
ehr	care, air
ee	be, real
i	ih pit
ahy	pie, buy
o or oh	no, toe
aw	paw, for
oi	noise, boys
au	out, about
oo	boot, new
uh	took, should
u	cut, about, item, nation
ur	urge, serge, firm

Consonants

k	come
ch	church
g	gag
j	judge
s	cellar
sh	shell (unvoiced)
zh	pleasure (voiced)
th	thin, then (both voiced and unvoiced)

Foreign Sounds

ah	Fr. ami
uh	Fr. feu, Ger. schön
Kh	Ger. ich, Scot. loch
ur	Fr. soeur
n	Fr. bon, Port. são (saun)
oo	Fr. tu, Ger. über

NOTE   Cross references are in SMALL CAPITAL LETTERS

INTRODUCTION

The term "mythology" refers both to the study of myth, the literal meaning of the word, and to the corpus of the myths and legends of any particular culture viewed collectively, as, for example, the mythology of ancient Greece.

Most myths had the purpose of explaining something in nature, such as how the universe came into existence or the origin of thunder, earthquake, storm, tree, or flower. From this rudimentary, elemental scientific approach to the world around him, man's need for some control over his environment and existence led to a fundamental worship, frequently with the aid of shamans, priests, or medicine men, and the propitiation of those who might influence his life or his surroundings.

Other myths explained social traditions, customs, religious practices, and the mysteries of life and death. Imagination, superstition, and embellishment mingled freely with observation. Some myths were used to teach; some had no purpose other than entertainment and storytelling.

Legends are stories embedded in some elements of fact and history, however tenuous, concerning heroes and events. They overlap with myths in that fancy and exaggeration tended to elevate the heroes to superhuman status. In addition, the gods often played a role, sometimes major, sometimes minor, in the legends, as in the tales of the Trojan War. Also, the central figures of legend, in many cases, assumed divine powers.

Myths and legends, handed down from generation to generation, enriched the lives of all who listened, giving them value and a sense of security, linking them with the heroic and divine wisdom that seemed so real to them. In this way, they became traditional stories, with changes due to the passage of time and variations given them by the narrators, resulting, in many cases, in modifications and in different versions, many quite divergent, but always with the same purpose—to clarify and explain the narrative.

In primitive cultures, respect and amazement before the world around them was expressed in simple terms. With developing civilizations the myths became more complex over the years because of the interpretations and details added by successive generations.

As the mythology of the ancient peoples intermingled with their religious beliefs, it became a civilizing influence, giving rise to various forms of worship, from those involving superstition and magic to the building of fine temples and the creation of beautiful statues in honor of the gods.

Mythological material surrounding actual religious leaders, such as Zoroaster or Buddha, is not true myth in the strictest sense, but forms a part of the entire corpus of mythology in which these religious personages had their tradition, the framework they used to explain, illustrate, and teach new doctrines.

Although a number of the more advanced tribes in the Americas recorded their mythology before the Spanish conquest, this information was almost totally destroyed by the invading Europeans, leaving only glyphs, as yet undeciphered, a paucity of written material in the form of picture writing, and an oral tradition to go by. Among the Teutonic peoples, Celts, and Slavs, the advent of Christianity relegated the mythology of their past to a position of little importance, setting down in writing myths and legends so mixed with other material and viewpoints as to change their whole complexion. The same process evolved wherever missionaries preceded the skill of writing or where that art was underdeveloped, as in Polynesia and Africa. Conversely, the extensive literature of Greece and Rome and the *Eddas* of Scandinavia are storehouses of the mythologies of those cultures as they were recorded without adulteration.

There is much waiting to be deciphered and translated, but new discoveries and continuing investigation by anthropologists, archaeologists, linguists, historians, and others constantly shed new light on the reconstruction of mythology.

There is a universality of certain themes and motifs running through the mythologies of all cultures, even though these are found among peoples living in different parts of the world and developing at various points in history. We can only speculate on the reasons for this likeness, both striking and surprising, but a logical thesis is that the basic nature of man, wherever and whenever he exists, gives him the need to ask and answer the same questions relating to the tangible and intangible, the visible and invisible.

Most cultures had their cosmological myths, dealing with the creation and origin of the universe and mankind. In some instances, a second creation followed some natural calamity, generally a great flood, but sometimes earthquake or fire, usually brought about when the people incurred the anger of the gods at some point after the early creation and were punished accordingly. This new creation and rebirth was often due to the survival of a human pair, animals, and seeds of the new world.

The dualistic principle of opposing forces and the struggle and conflict between good and evil, light and dark, or heaven and earth appears in many myths. This dualism was frequently represented by twins.

The mother figure, or Great Mother, is found in a great number of cultures, especially among those peoples who did not hold women in a position subordinate to men. At times a daughter shared the mother's prominence, as in the case of Demeter and Persephone.

Mythological pairs and triads occur in almost all mythologies. The pairs were usually brother and sister, who were in many instances also husband and wife, or twins, often, but not necessarily, dualistic in nature. The triads were generally composed of father, mother, and son.

Most beliefs surrounding death show fundamental similarities in that the dead went to an afterworld, which might be an underworld beneath the earth, an island paradise, a Valhalla, or the moon, and a number of mythologies linked death to a cycle of rebirth, somewhat parallel to that occurring in vegetation.

The theme of the exploits of heroes, performing great feats or bringing the skills of culture to their people, appears in all legends. The heroes, modeled after the gods, displayed superhuman characteristics, and many were of semidivine origin.

Foremost among the processes at work in mythology are those relating to cosmogony, the creation of the universe or the earth with its solar system, and the theory of their origin; to theogony, the origin of the gods, and their genealogy; and to etiology, the study of causes and beginnings in general.

Myths were also shaped by personification, the endowment of aspects of nature, inanimate objects, or qualities and abstractions with human form, attributes, and characteristics. Another and similar factor was anthropomorphism, the assigning of human shape, qualities, and concepts to a deity, or to an animal, plant, or other object. By means of deification, humans and personifications were elevated to the position of a deity.

All of these elements are present in the myths and legends of peoples around the world as essential components in their development.

The early Egyptians worshiped local, tribal gods, more like animals and birds than humans. In the process of anthropomorphism, at work through the centuries, some deities became more humanized than others, but few were represented with human heads. The regional worship of certain deities led to local cult centers, such as those at Memphis, Thebes, Busiris, and Heliopolis. Temples were erected, and a large priesthood to carry out the required ritual, offerings, and sacrifice developed. With time, many local gods became national deities, often taking on new characteristics and names.

The Nile, the cycle of vegetation, and the power of nature shaped Egyptian mythology, raising those gods concerned to a position of supremacy. An equally dominant factor was the Egyptians' belief in an afterlife modeled on that led on earth.

Egyptian myths were handed down by oral tradition. Other than the Pyramid Texts, concrete remains, mainly wall paintings, statuary, and reliefs on temple walls, are fragmentary and must be pieced together, aided by the records of Greek travelers, geographers, and writers, such as Herodotus, Plutarch, and Strabo.

In the rest of Africa, with its myriads of tribes and languages, the mythology remained uncomplicated, peopled with nature deities, spirits, and heroes, without any real pantheons or series of myths and legends. Common features, however, varying somewhat among different tribes, reveal a concern for creation, the world of nature, and certain gods who fulfilled the role of culture heroes. A supreme being, with a priesthood of medicine men, ruled over other deities of less importance, each functioning in his own sphere. The supreme god was viewed as the creator and all-powerful, controlling the world, mankind, and events. Personification and belief in the divine power of natural phenomena, the force of magic, fetishes, sorcerers, and ancestor worship are evident throughout African mythology.

The Tigro-Euphrates Valley was the homeland of peoples contemporary with those of Egypt, but it was a place of struggle, invasion, and conquest. The Sumerians and Akkadians, entering the valley at an early date, built a number of cities and developed to a high point of civilization. When the Assyrians and Babylonians entered Mesopotamia, bringing their own gods with them, they adopted features of the mythology they found there.

Assyro-Babylonian mythology was peopled with beings resembling beasts and represented as creatures that could exist only in the imagination, similar to men in shape, but given the heads of animals or birds, and often winged. The deities were chiefly male; the female deities, with a few exceptions, were cast in minor roles.

Sumerian and Akkadian myths and legends had given way to the Assyro-Babylonian by about the second millennium B.C. Cuneiform tablets preserved at Nineveh in the library of King Ashurbanipal present myths as they existed in about the eighth century B.C. Most cuneiform records on mud brick, however, have disappeared with the crumbling bricks themselves. Further documentation has survived in the *Gilgamesh Epic* and the *Epic of Creation,* giving us details about the hero Gilgamesh and Marduk, the chief deity of Babylon.

The mythology of the Phoenicians, who were Semitic in origin, is not as well documented as most other eastern Mediterranean mythologies. Our information is compiled chiefly from epigraphic and literary sources, including the Ugarit Tablets. The Phoenicians were active traders who established colonies throughout the Mediterranean area, the most important of which was Carthage, whose legendary founder was Queen Dido, taking their mythological beliefs with them and absorbing some of the beliefs of the peoples with whom they came into contact.

The Persians, Indo-Europeans of Aryan stock, and under strong Assyro-Babylonian influences during their early period, achieved a state of highly developed religious and philosophical thought, as marked by the *Avesta,* whose roots were buried in the mythology of ancient Persia, but their deities were somewhat ill defined in character.

The principle of dualism was in operation, exemplified by the conflict between good and evil, light and darkness, as Ahura Mazda struggled with, and was ultimately victorious over, Angra Mainyu. There are very few visible signs of Persian mythology in the form of art and architecture. The *Zend-Avesta,* almost the sole written source, dates from the time when changes in the development of their mythology had already taken place.

The extremely full and complex mythology of India contains ancient native elements affected by incursions of Aryans, who introduced their own beliefs and gods. The god Indra is an example of this. It is complicated further by a mingling of mythology and religion to a degree that one can scarcely be extricated from the other.

The Vedas contain a mythology belonging to the period of the early history of the people of India before it branched out and away from the Persian. As they went from the Vedic period to the Brahmanic and the Buddhist, much of the early Indian myth and legend was retained in the process of transition and was incorporated into the newer beliefs.

Greek mythology has come to us through a wealth of literature, the heritage of Western civilization, written at the time when the Greeks were at the height of their culture and civilization, with only suggestions and sparse examples of the rough crudity of their primitive past. Remnants are found in the giants, centaurs, and myths such as those of the Minotaur or Europa, but these were largely vehicles for the deeds of a hero or involved explanatory deductions made concerning the world of nature.

The Greeks gave beauty and refinement to their deities, reality and reason to their myths and legends. This in no way weakened the power of the gods and the respect due them. The Greeks were comfortable with their gods, so familiar to them by reason of their appearance, actions, mode of life, character, and personality. The gods held no terror or fear for man. They mirrored human traits, but were exaggerated parallels to man, more handsome, stronger, more prone to courses of action not undertaken by mortals. Throughout Greek mythology there is evidence of a deep interest in character, and in the power of fate and the gods over man's destiny.

The Etruscans, living north of the Tiber River, had, upon contact with the Greeks, adopted many of the Greek deities, myths, and legends, and their own few deities, centering chiefly on natural phenomena such as thunder and lightning, had assumed a secondary position by the time the Romans arrived in Italy.

The Romans were practical people who lacked the imagination of the Greeks. Their mythology was largely copied and adopted from that of the Greeks and the Etruscans. Changes and originality were due to the differences in the Roman character. The Romans were fond of personification and gave it importance. Many qualities, such as faith, victory, and good fortune, although basically abstractions, were given the attributes of gods and goddesses and were regarded as such. Mars was raised in stature and importance over the position held by the Greek god Ares because of the Romans' interest in wars of conquest. Their aim was to glorify Rome and her past, as seen in the myths and legends of Aeneas, and Romulus and Remus, but they also enjoyed stories of love and entertainment, such as those of Ovid.

The Scandinavian and Teutonic peoples shared a common background of cultural and mythological heritage, but with distinctive branches and differences, since the Teutons to the south were closer to the Greek and Roman influences. Their myths and legends were, as far as we know, an exclusively oral tradition for many centuries. When these peoples were Christianized, the old religious ideas, cus-

xvi

toms, and myths were preserved mainly in Iceland, where the pagan Vikings settled, and were written down in the *Eddas.* The stories of the major heroes were recorded in the *Volsunga Saga* and the *Nibelungenlied,* parallel Scandinavian and Teutonic accounts, although often differing in detail and emphasis.

The harsh existence in the rugged world of Scandinavia led the people to admire courage and bravery, and the nobility of the warrior was emphasized by the glory of Valhalla. Their mythology does not lack variety, however, as shown by the wisdom of Odin, the might of Thor, the endearing qualities of Balder, and the mischief and tricks of Loki.

The Celts were centered in western Britain, Wales, Ireland, Scotland, and Brittany. Each area had its own distinctive myths and legends as well as many they shared in common. The Arthurian legends, tales of knighthood's chivalry, court life, high ideals, high-minded purpose, and self-sacrifice, belong mainly to Cornwall and Wales, while the Anglo-Saxon tale of *Beowulf,* written in Old English, was laid in Scandinavia.

Christianity was adopted only a few centuries after the Finns appeared as a distinct group of people. Their mythology is therefore relatively limited to a small number of nature deities and to the legends of the heroes of their fine national epic poem, the *Kalevala.*

The pagan myths and legends of the Slavs, stemming from their early history, were concerned mainly with agrarian life and survival. There were many minor deities and spirits, such as those of the hearth, storeroom, the woods, and the numerous matters concerning the farm and home. Some vestiges of these ancient beliefs and practices still exist among the peasants, but we have almost no firsthand records of Slavic mythology. Ilya-Muromyets was outstanding among the heroes.

As Hinduism spread from India to the east and north, it carried its mythology, and much of the mythology of India as a whole, with it. In China, the Hindu mythology was welcomed but was adapted to the indigenous beliefs and made to take its place beside the existing thought of Confucianism and Taoism, often undergoing changes accordingly, sometimes in character, sometimes in name.

Many gods of Chinese mythology achieved their divine rank through the process of deification. They were, on the whole, arranged in a hierarchy patterned after civilian bureaucracy. Their functions involved office and paper work for which they were held strictly accountable, since their future status depended on efficiency of performance and they could be promoted, demoted, or dispensed with.

The mythology of the Chinese is largely a cheerful, happy one, placed in settings surrounded by beauty.

Contact with the Asiatic mainland early in the Christian era brought the mythology of China to the Japanese. The native, regional myths and legends continued to exist but merged with the new to an extent that makes separation almost impossible, often impractical and undesirable. When strictly oral tradition was later joined by the written word, the texts, in Chinese characters or even the Chinese language, were doubtlessly colored by Chinese thought.

Quite naturally, the sea took precedence in the thinking of the peoples of Oceania, but, as is the case in most mythologies, the sun and moon and the creation of the world and man also loomed large in importance. There were often very few differences among the versions of the myths and legends of the various groups of Polynesians, even though the names and functions of the deities and heroes tended to change from island to island. Women had a prominent place in the mythology of Oceania, and there were a number of female deities. Maui became the great hero and demigod of most Polynesians.

The mythologies of the Americas range from the simple worship of a totem and beliefs centered on the necessities of survival, as found among primitive tribes, to the evolved pantheons of the highly developed cultures achieved by the Incas, Mayas, and Aztecs. The basic structure contains many elements shared by all mythologies—myths of creation, earthquake and flood, gods representing the forces of nature, minor deities and spirits, legends of heroes undergoing adventures and bringing culture to their tribes.

In North America the myths and legends, concerned with the omnipresent spirits and powers in all nature as represented by the orenda or manitou, contained many similarities. Three figures, Great Spirit, Earth Mother, and Coyote or Trickster, stand out in the mythologies of most tribes, even though their names differed according to each tribal language. The principle of dualism, often in the form of twin brothers, is also apparent in the myths of many tribes.

The Indian tribes of Central America and Mexico developed a colorful and imaginative mythology. The Aztecs, who assimilated gods of the Toltec and other tribes when they entered Mexico as conquerors, had a unique concept of the creation, in which each of four worlds ended in a natural disaster and each successive universe required a new sun.

Worship of the sun played a prominent role in the myths of the Aztecs and Mayas. The Incas, whose early mythology was based on animal worship, later shared this emphasis on the veneration of the sun.

The Olympian Gods

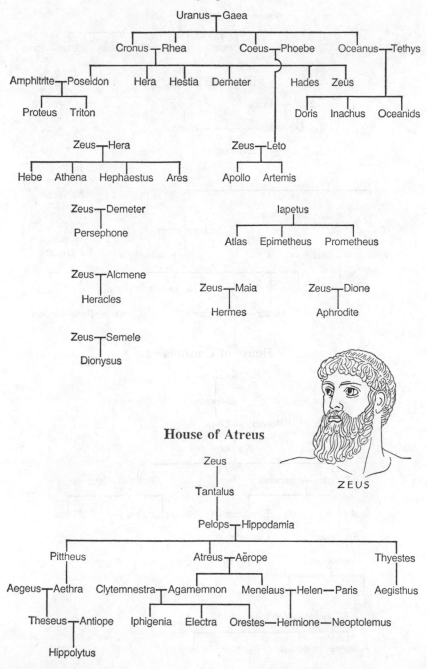

Uranus—Gaea

Cronus—Rhea   Coeus—Phoebe   Oceanus—Tethys

Amphitrite—Poseidon   Hera   Hestia   Demeter   Hades   Zeus

Proteus   Triton   Doris   Inachus   Oceanids

Zeus—Hera   Zeus—Leto

Hebe   Athena   Hephaestus   Ares   Apollo   Artemis

Zeus—Demeter   Iapetus

Persephone   Atlas   Epimetheus   Prometheus

Zeus—Alcmene   Zeus—Maia   Zeus—Dione

Heracles   Hermes   Aphrodite

Zeus—Semele

Dionysus

House of Atreus

Zeus

Tantalus

Pelops—Hippodamia

Pittheus   Atreus—Aërope   Thyestes

Aegeus—Aethra   Clytemnestra—Agamemnon   Menelaus—Helen—Paris   Aegisthus

Theseus—Antiope   Iphigenia   Electra   Orestes—Hermione—Neoptolemus

Hippolytus

ZEUS

The Family of Helen of Troy

Tyndareus —— Leda —— Zeus

Agamemnon — Clytemnestra   Castor   Pollux   Menelaus — Helen — Paris

House of Troy

Zeus — Electra   Teucer

Dardanus —————— Batea

Erichthonius

Tros

Assaracus   Ilus

Capys   Laomedon

Anchises — Aphrodite   Priam — Hecuba

Aeneas — Creusa   Cassandra   Deiphobus   Helenus   Troilus

Hector — Andromache   Oenone — Paris — Helen

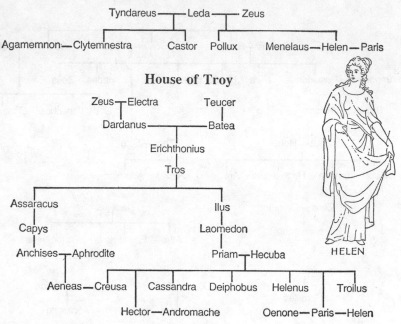

HELEN

House of Cadmus

Zeus — Io

Epaphus

Poseidon — Libya

Agenor

Cadmus — Harmonia   Europa — Zeus

Agave   Polydorus   Rhadamanthus   Minos

Pentheus   Labdacus

Menoeceus

Creon   Jocasta — Laius

Jocasta — Oedipus

Antigone   Eteocles   Polynices   Ismene

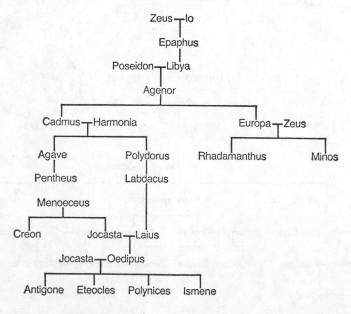

Egyptian Creation Deities

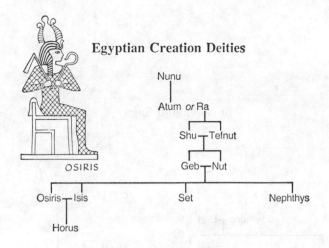

```
                    Nunu
                     |
                Atum or Ra
                     |
              ┌──────┴──────┐
            Shu ── Tefnut
                     |
            Geb ── Nut
    ┌────────────────┼────────────────┐
Osiris ── Isis      Set           Nephthys
    |
  Horus
```

OSIRIS

Assyro-Babylonian Creation Deities

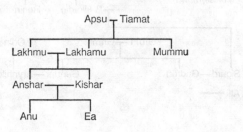

```
              Apsu ── Tiamat
     ┌───────────┬───────────┐
Lakhmu ── Lakhamu        Mummu
     |
Anshar ──── Kishar
     |
  Anu        Ea
```

The Volsunga Saga

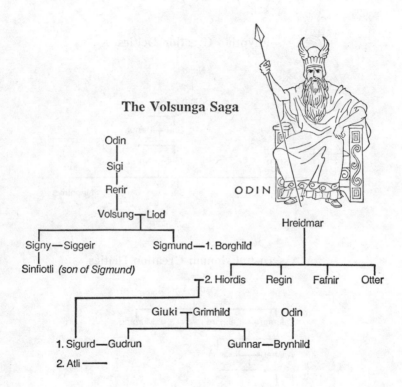

Odin

Sigi

Rerir

Volsung—Liod

Signy — Siggeir

Sinfiotli *(son of Sigmund)*

Sigmund—1. Borghild

2. Hiordis

Hreidmar

Regin   Fafnir   Otter

Giuki —Grimhild

Odin

1. Sigurd—Gudrun

2. Atli ——

Gunnar—Brynhild

ODIN

Aah (ah'-ah, ah), E, one of the names by which the god of the moon was known. He was also called THOTH and was represented wearing a crescent and a lunar disk on his head.

Abas (ah'-bus), G, 1. a son of King Celeus of Eleusis and Metanira who was changed into a lizard by DEMETER because he mocked her.

2. a king of Argos and father of ACRISIUS and PROETUS.

3. a companion of DIOMEDES who was transformed into a bird, because he tried to protect his friend from the vengeance of APHRODITE, incurred when he wounded her in the TROJAN WAR.

Absyrtus (ab-sur'-tus), G. *See* APSYRTUS.

Abu Simbel (u'-boo sim'-bel, -bul), E, a site south of Aswan where two temples were built by Rameses II in about the thirteenth century B.C. The larger was dedicated to AMON-RA, and the smaller was the sanctuary of the goddess HATHOR. Four colossal statues of Rameses II, over sixty-five feet high, were hewn from the rock to stand at the entrance of the Great Temple.

Abydos (u-bahy'-dos), E, 1. an ancient town on the Nile River near THEBES. Abydos is the site of several temple ruins and is the place where many pharaohs were buried. Outstanding among the temples is that of Seti I, which was dedicated to OSIRIS, AMON, and several other gods. UPUAUT was worshiped at Abydos as KHENTI AMENTI.

G, 2. an ancient town on the south side of the Hellespont that was favored by APHRODITE and was the home of LEANDER, who swam across the Hellespont each night to visit HERO in SESTOS.

Acestes (u-ses'-teez), G, king of Drepanum, a Trojan settlement in Sicily. An ally of PRIAM in the TROJAN WAR, Acestes played host to AENEAS during the latter's voyage to Italy and shared his country with those Trojans who wished to stay behind when Aeneas set sail again.

Achelous (ak-u-loh'-us), G, a revered river-god, oldest of the three thousand sons of the TITANS OCEANUS and TETHYS. In a wrestling contest with HERACLES for the love of Deianira, Achelous changed into a bull. One horn was torn off by Heracles, and the NYMPHS dedicated it to the goddess of Plenty. The horn was then called Cornucopia, the Horn of Plenty. According to another version, the Cornucopia was one of the horns of the goat AMALTHEA, who had nursed ZEUS as an infant.

Acheron (ak'-u-rahn), G, 1. the river of woe, one of the five rivers in HADES, across which the dead were ferried by CHARON.

2. a name used to refer to the entire underworld, Hades.

Achilles (u-kil'-eez), G, the son of PELEUS and the nymph THETIS (at whose wedding the Golden Apple was tossed, leading to the outbreak of the TROJAN WAR—the only instance in Greek mythology of a goddess having married a mortal). When Achilles was dipped into the river STYX by Thetis to make him invulnerable, he was held by the heel, which was left vulnerable. (Thus, the term "Achilles' heel," which refers to a vulnerable or weak spot.) Educated by PHOENIX and CHIRON, Achilles learned the arts of war and healing and led the MYRMIDONS in the Trojan War. The wrath of Achilles resulted in his withdrawal from the fighting, in the tenth year of the war. This came about when AGAMEMNON refused to end a plague against the Greeks by giving up the maiden CHRYSEIS until Achilles gave him BRISEIS, his captive in war, in her place. When PATROCLUS, clad in Achilles' armor, was killed by HECTOR, HEPHAESTUS forged new armor for Achilles, who re-entered the war to avenge his friend's death. He slew Hector in vengeance and dragged the body behind his chariot in the dust before the walls of Troy. Achilles died near the main gate of Troy when an arrow shot by PARIS, and guided by APOLLO, struck him in his vulnerable heel. Achilles and Hector were the two greatest heroes of the Trojan War, and with their deaths the prophecy that the war could not end so long as either lived was fulfilled.

Acrisius (u-kris'-ee-us), G, a king of Argos and the father of DANAË, the mother of PERSEUS. Acrisius was accidentally killed by Perseus' discus, thus fulfilling the prophecy that he would die at the hands of Danaë's son.

Acropolis (u-krahp'-u-lis), G, a hill or small plateau used as the citadel, sanctuary, or core settlement of the ancient Greek city. The name refers specifically to the Acropolis of Athens, the fortified site of the early settlement of the time of CECROPS and ERECHTHEUS. Foundations dating back into the second millennium B.C. have been unearthed. By the fifth century B.C. nearly all of the most famous buildings whose ruins are now seen on the Acropolis had been completed. These, some of the finest examples of Greek architecture, include the PARTHENON, the ERECHTHEUM, the Temple of Athena NIKE, and the Propylaea, the great gateway.

Actaeon (ak-tee'-un), G, son of ARISTAEUS and AUTONOË. While out hunting one day, he came upon ARTEMIS, bathing in a stream, whereupon the irate goddess changed Actaeon into a stag. His own dogs chased and devoured him.

Adad (ah'-dahd), A-B, the god of storms and floods who succeeded ENLIL in that role, when Enlil was elevated to his position as ruler of the earth. Adad's powers were used for both good and evil. Thus, he could bring gentle winds and nourishing rains as well as destructive storms.

The goddess SHALA was Adad's consort. Adad is generally depicted holding thunderbolts and carried on a bull. His symbol was lightning.

Adapa (ah'-dah-pah), A-B, a man created by EA to rule over the human race. He was king of ERIDU, and, in some later accounts, he was Ea's son.

Adapa angered ANU when he crippled the wind by breaking its wings after his boat overturned and cast him into the sea. The god intended to bring about Adapa's death, but, with the help of Ea, Adapa gained entrance to Anu's domain and won him over. Adapa, however, following the deceptive advice of Ea, lost the opportunity of immortality for man, because he feared the food Anu offered him, thinking it to be the food of death, whereas it was the food of lasting life.

Aditi (ad'-i-ti), I, the goddess of heaven, mother of the gods, the ADITYAS, and source of all things. Aditi was one of the attendants of INDRA. Her consort was said to be VISHNU.

Adityas, the (ah'-dit-yuz), I, the seven sons of the goddess ADITI, among whom were MITRA, SAVITRI, and VARUNA. At a later period there were twelve Adityas and they were guardians of the months of the year, representing the sun in its course.

Adliden (ud-lid'-un), NA. *See* ADLIVUN.

Adlivun (ud-liv'-un) or **Adliden** (-lid'-), NA, in Eskimo mythology, the realm of SEDNA at the depths of the ocean. The souls of those whose deaths were not violent went to Adlivun and received punishment according to their sins on earth. It could be reached only by an ANGAKOK or shaman.

Admete (ad-mee'-tee), G, the daughter of EURYSTHEUS, who assigned HERACLES his twelve labors. Because Admete wanted the girdle of HIPPOLYTE, queen of the AMAZONS, Heracles was sent to get it as one of his labors. Heracles was forced to kill Hippolyte in order to fulfill his task. *See also* LABORS OF HERACLES.

Admetus (ad-mee'-tus), G, a king of Thessaly who was told he would die unless he found someone to die in his stead. His devoted wife ALCESTIS sacrificed herself, but she was later brought back from HADES by HERACLES and reunited with her husband. Admetus was one of the ARGONAUTS.

Adonia (u-doh'-nee-u), G & R, the ceremonial festival held following the annual harvest in honor of ADONIS, mourning his death and celebrating his rebirth. The Adonia, observed in eastern Asia as well as throughout the Greek and Roman world, symbolized the vegeta-

3

tion cycle as represented by the seasonal death and resurrection of Adonis.

Adonis (u-dahn'-is, -doh'-nis), Ph & G, a Phoenician god of vegetation and fertility whom the Greeks assimilated and called Adonis. He was identified with and took the place of HEY-TAU and the deities ALEYIN and MOT.

Because Myrrha the mother of Adonis, conceived him by her own father, Cinyras, she underwent a metamorphosis and became a tree. PERSEPHONE, to whom APHRODITE gave the child for safekeeping, became entranced with his beauty as he grew to manhood and would not surrender him until ZEUS decided he could spend four months of the year with Persephone in the underworld; four months on earth with Aphrodite, who loved and favored him; and four wherever he himself chose to be.

Adonis was killed by a wild boar while he was hunting, and the anemone came into being from his blood.

Adonis was analogous to the gods TAMMUZ of Babylonia and OSIRIS of Egypt and his cult spread throughout the eastern Mediterranean world.

Adrastea (ad-ra-stee'-u), G, a NYMPH who, with IDA, cared for the infant ZEUS on Crete after he had been left there by his mother, RHEA, who feared that his father, CRONUS, would destroy him.

Adrastus (u-dras'-tus), G, king of Argos and a leader of the SEVEN AGAINST THEBES. Adrastus was the father-in-law of POLYNICES, on whose behalf the expedition was taken, and he was the only one of the leaders to survive the war.

Aeacus (ee'-u-kus), G, son of ZEUS and AEGINA and king of the island of Aegina. Aeacus was the ruler of the MYRMIDONS and the father of PELEUS and TELAMON. Because of his great integrity, Aeacus, following his death, was named by ZEUS to be one of the three judges of the UNDERWORLD.

Aeëtes (ee-ee'-teez), G, king of Colchis and the father of MEDEA and APSYRTUS. He was the guardian of the GOLDEN FLEECE sought by JASON and the ARGONAUTS.

Aegeus (ee'-jee-us, -joos), G, a king of Athens and the father of THESEUS by AETHRA. Aegeus was later married to MEDEA. When he saw his son's ship returning from Colchis, Aegeus, thinking the black sails signified that Theseus had been killed by the MINOTAUR, hurled himself from the promontory of Cape Sounion. Thus, the Aegean Sea was said to have received its name from Aegeus.

4

Aegina (i-jahy'-nu), G, a nymph, the daughter of Asopus and Metope, who gave birth to AEACUS, son of ZEUS, on an island in the gulf of the Aegean Sea. The island was then named for Aegina. It is the site of a Doric temple whose pediments depicted scenes from the TROJAN WAR.

Aegir (e'-jir), Sc, the god of the sea. Aegir was host at a banquet of the gods, when LOKI came uninvited, pushed his way in, and made himself unpleasant by humiliating each deity with accounts of weakness, misbehavior, and failure. As he left Aegir's feast under threat of THOR's hammer, Loki warned of the coming conflagration, RAGNAROK. Aegir's wife was Ran, who bore nine daughters.

Aegis (ee'-jis), G, the shield or breastplate of ZEUS and his daughter ATHENA. It had a GORGON's head in the center. The aegis is considered to be a symbol of power and protection.

Aegisthus (i-jis'-thus), G, son of THYESTES by his own daughter PELOPIA. Aegisthus was raised by ATREUS, his uncle, whom he murdered at the instigation of Thyestes in order to gain the rule of MYCENAE. Aegisthus became CLYTEMNESTRA's lover and helped her kill her husband AGAMEMNON on the latter's return from the TROJAN WAR. He was, in turn, slain by Clytemnestra's son ORESTES.

Aegle (eeg'-lee), G, 1. one of the HESPERIDES, who were the guardians of the GOLDEN APPLES.

2. a nymph who was sometimes said to have been the mother of the CHARITES.

3. one of the HELIADES, daughters of HELIOS and CLYMENE.

Aegyptus (ee-jip'-tus), G, son of the Egyptian king BELUS. Aegyptus gave his fifty sons in marriage to the fifty daughters (the DANAÏDS) of his twin brother DANAUS. All but one of the sons were murdered by their brides on their wedding night, as a result of which Aegyptus died of grief.

Aeneas (i-nee'-us), G & R, the hero of VERGIL's AENEID, who escaped from burning Troy following the TROJAN WAR with his father, ANCHISES, his son, ASCANIUS, and the Trojan household gods. Aeneas was destined to lead surviving Trojans to Italy and there establish the Roman nation. Although aided by his mother, APHRODITE, Aeneas and the Trojans were forced by the hatred of HERA, who had favored the Greeks in the war, to wander for seven years and undergo many dangers. After leaving Sicily, where Anchises died, the Trojans were blown by a storm to Carthage, on the north coast of Africa, where DIDO, queen of Carthage, fell in love with Aeneas. However, he eventually continued on to Italy. In a visit to the UNDERWORLD, the future of Rome was revealed to Aeneas by Anchises. Aeneas married LAVINIA, daughter of LATINUS, and founded Lavinium in Latium, in fulfillment of his destiny.

Aeneid, the (i-nee'-id), a Latin epic poem by Vergil in twelve books of quantitative dactylic hexameter verse. The subject is the last ninety days of the adventures of AENEAS. The whole seven years of Aeneas' wanderings are covered by flashback.

Books 1–6 contain accounts of the escape from Troy, visits to Thrace, DELOS, Crete, and Sicily, and a sojourn in Africa. The love affair between Aeneas and DIDO, the Carthaginian queen, and her suicide upon his departure are high points of romance and tragedy. The peak of religious and patriotic sentiment is reached when Aeneas descends into HADES, where the shade of ANCHISES foretells the future greatness and majesty of Rome. Books 7–12 are composed of stirring martial episodes in the struggle between the Trojans and their Latin allies against Rutulians, Etruscans, and Volscians. The climax occurs at the end of the poem, when Aeneas kills TURNUS, chief of the Rutulians, in single combat.

Observant, perceptive, and sensitive, Vergil creates moving scenes peopled with lifelike characters, e.g., the passionate Dido, the gallant prince PALLAS, the resentful Turnus, the valiant CAMILLA. If Aeneas seems to lack individuality, it is because his great mission takes precedence over everything—even his personality.

Aeolus (ee'-u-lus), G, 1. the king of the winds. Aeolus lived on the island of Aeolia, where he held the winds imprisoned in a cave, releasing or restraining them at will.

2. a king of Thessaly, son of HELLEN. Aeolus became the ancestor of the Aeolians, who, with the Dorians, Achaeans, and Ionians, formed one of the four divisions of the ancient Greeks.

Aërope (ay-er'-u-pee), G, the wife of ATREUS and the mother of AGAMEMNON, MENELAUS, and Anaxibia. After he learned Aërope had committed adultery with his brother THYESTES, Atreus killed Thyestes' three sons, boiled them, and served them to their father at a banquet. Thyestes then set a curse upon the House of Atreus, doomed to suffer tragedy and evil through each generation.

Aeschylus (es'-ku-lus), a Greek tragic poet and dramatist who lived from 525 to 456 B.C. and wrote about ninety plays. Aside from fragments, only seven of his works have been preserved. The extant plays furnish us with valuable insight into mythological topics dealing with such subjects as the SEVEN AGAINST THEBES, PROMETHEUS, AGAMEMNON, ORESTES, and other members of the House of ATREUS.

6

Aesculapius (es-kyu-lay′-pee-us), R, the god of medicine, who was identified by the Romans with the Greek god ASCLEPIUS.

Aesir, the (e′-sir), Sc, the pantheon of gods, whose leader was ODIN. The chief deities of the Aesir, who lived in palaces in ASGARD, were BALDER, HEIMDALL, Odin, THOR, and TYR. LOKI was later added to the Aesir. There was constant war between the Aesir and the VANIR until the Vanir gained admission to Asgard. In the final battle at RAGNAROK, the evil forces overcame and slew the Aesir, ending their dynasty.

Aeson (ee′-sun), G, a king of Thessaly and the father of JASON. He was restored to youth by MEDEA.

Aether (ee′-thur), G, the son or, in some versions, the brother of EREBUS and NYX. Aether was the personification of the upper reaches of the sky.

Aethra (ee′-thru), G, 1. the mother, by AEGEUS, king of Athens, of THESEUS.

2. one of the OCEANIDS and the mother of the HYADES by ATLAS.

Agamemnon (ag-u-mem′-nahn), G, king of MYCENAE and leader of the Greek forces in the TROJAN WAR. Agamemnon was the son of ATREUS and AËROPE and brother of MENELAUS. He was the husband of CLYTEMNESTRA and the father of ELECTRA, ORESTES, and IPHIGENIA. During the Trojan War a plague was sent upon the Greek warriors by APOLLO when Agamemnon refused to return the captive CHRYSEIS to her father, a priest of Apollo. Agamemnon agreed to give up Chryseis on the condition that he be given ACHILLES' captive, BRISEIS. The Greek chieftains acceded to his demands, which angered Achilles and caused him to withdraw temporarily from the war. When Agamemnon returned home, he was slain by Clytemnestra, who had turned against him for having sacrificed Iphigenia to ARTEMIS when the Greeks assembled at Aulis prior to sailing for Troy.

Aganju (ah-gahn′-joo), Af, in the belief of the Yoruba tribe of West Africa, the son of ODUDUA, the earth-goddess, and the brother of YEMAJA and also her husband. Their son was ORUNJAN, the sun-god.

Agave (u-gay′-vee), G, daughter of HARMONIA and CADMUS of THEBES and the mother of PENTHEUS. Having been driven mad by DIONYSUS, she murdered her son during a bacchanalian frenzy, under the misapprehension that he was a lion.

Agenor (u-jee′-nawr), G, 1. a son of ANTENOR and one of the heroes of the TROJAN WAR.

7

2. the son of POSEIDON. Agenor was king of Phoenicia and the father of EUROPA and CADMUS.

Ages of Mankind, the, G & R, a name for a concept first propounded by the Greek poet HESIOD in *Works and Days,* and later by other Greek scholars, and still later by the Romans, that mankind went through several periods or ages in mythological times, beginning with an age of perfection and ending in decline. The GOLDEN AGE, in the reign of CRONUS, was one of peace, prosperity, and happiness. During the SILVER AGE, people were weak and matured slowly. It was then that pride, foolishness, and sin appeared. Implements of metal along with physical strength and violence came in the BRONZE AGE. Mighty warriors held sway in the HEROIC AGE. The siege of Troy occurred at that time. The IRON AGE, the final period, brought labor and difficulties, dishonesty and injustice, and ultimate decadence.

Aglaia (u-glay'-u), G, 1. the youngest of the three CHARITES, daughters of EURYNOME and ZEUS. Aglaia represented splendor and brightness. Aglaia was said by HESIOD to be HEPHAESTUS' wife.

2. the wife of ABAS and mother of ACRISIUS and PROTEUS.

Aglauros (ay-glaw'-rahs), G, a variant of the name AGRAULOS.

Agni (ag'-nee), I, the Aryan god of fire, the youngest of the Vedic gods, who took the form of lightning and brought fertilizing rain to the earth. Agni was the fire at the heart of the sun, in lightning and at the hearth. As protector and friend of mankind, Agni brought prosperity and abundance.

Agraulos (u-graw'-lus), G, 1. the daughter of Actaeus and the wife of CECROPS, who became king of Athens upon the death of Actaeus.

2. one of the three daughters of Cecrops and Agraulos, representing dew and fertile crops.

Ahi (ah'-hee), E. *See* IHI.

Ahriman (ah'-ri-mun), Pe. *See* ANGRA MAINYU.

Ahsonnutli (ah-soh-noot'-lee), NA, a major deity of the Navaho Indians who was believed to have created heaven and earth and to have posted men at the four cardinal points to support the sky. He appears to have assumed many of the characteristics of ESTANATLEHI or to have taken her place in later Navaho myth, and is known as the Turquoise Hermaphrodite.

Ahura Mazda (ah'-huh-ru maz'-du) or **Ormazd** (awr'-muzd), Pe, originally the god of the Achaemenian dynasty of kings ruling in Persia from about 550 to 330 B.C., and elevated to a position of supremacy over the primitive deities, corresponding to that of the king over the earlier tribal rulers.

Ahura Mazda was the supreme god, lord of the skies and father of all. He was the god of the kings. The representation of light, truth, and good, and the steady, vigorous opponent of ANGRA MAINYU, he was the leader of the AMESHA SPENTAS. According to one source, the world was created in and from his body.

Ahura Mazda is depicted in bas-reliefs at Persepolis, the ancient capital of Persia, and on the BEHISTUN ROCK as a bearded man with a winged, plumed body.

Aino (ahy′-noh), F, the sister of JOUKAHAINEN, who promised her hand in marriage to VAINAMOINEN. In her efforts to escape the advances of the aged magician, Aino fell into the sea and was transformed into a water spirit.

Aizen-Myoo (ahy′-zen-myoo′), J, the god of love and sexual desire.

Ajax (ay′-jaks), G, the name of two heroes in the TROJAN WAR. 1. Ajax the Great was the son of TELAMON and was considered the greatest warrior after ACHILLES. He led the Greeks after Achilles withdrew temporarily from the War. When, following the death of Achilles, ODYSSEUS was awarded the hero's armor, Ajax became so enraged by jealousy he killed himself after he was maddened by ATHENA in punishment for his great pride.

2. Ajax the Lesser was the son of OILEUS. He led the Locrians in the war. Because he took CASSANDRA from the altar of Athena, Ajax was shipwrecked, due to Athena's anger, in the Aegean Sea on his way home from Troy, but was rescued by POSEIDON. When Ajax boasted of his escape, Poseidon struck the rocks with his TRIDENT and Ajax drowned.

Akitu (ah′-kee-too), A-B, a sanctuary near Babylon to which MARDUK's statue was carried in an annual ceremony with elaborate ritual honoring the king of the gods.

Alberich (ahl′-bur-iKh), T, a DWARF king, guardian of the treasure of the NIBELUNGS, and analogous to ANDVARI.

Alcestis (al-ses′-tis), G, daughter of PELIAS and wife of ADMETUS. When the FATES promised Admetus life if he could find someone to die in his place, Alcestis sacrificed herself. She was later restored to the upper world by Admetus' friend HERACLES.

Alcinous (al-sin′-oh-us), G, the husband of ARETE and father of NAUSICAÄ. Alcinous entertained ODYSSEUS and his companions when the Greeks stopped at Phaeacia en route home after the TROJAN WAR. At a banquet in the palace, Odysseus told Alcinous and his court the story of the ten years of wandering and adventure he and his companions had undergone.

9

Alcmene (alk-mee′-nee), G, the wife of AMPHITRYON and mother of HERACLES. Alcmene bore Heracles by ZEUS, who seduced her by assuming the guise of Amphitryon. She is said to have been the last mortal paramour of Zeus.

Alcyone (al-say′-u-nee) or **Halcyon** (hal′-see-un), G, a daughter of AEOLUS and wife of Ceyx. When Ceyx was drowned at sea, Alcyone and Ceyx were changed into kingfishers. Aeolus forbade the winds to blow during the week before and after the winter solstice so that their young could be born. Hence, "halcyon days" are days of calm.

Alcyoneus (al-sahy′-u-noos), G, 1. one of the GIANTS, sons of URANUS and GAEA. Because Alcyoneus was indestructible in his birthplace, HERACLES, who was on the side of the gods in their battle against the giants, dragged him away to another land to kill him.
2. a giant who stole the cattle of HELIOS and tried to block Heracles when he was crossing the Isthmus of Corinth with the cattle of GERYON. When Alcyoneus hurled a stone at him, Heracles struck it back with his club, killing him.

Alecto (u-lek′-toh), G, one of the three FURIES. HERA enlisted Alecto, as a goddess of vengeance and justice, to help her against AENEAS and his followers by tricking them into war against TURNUS and the Rutulians over the hand of LAVINIA.

Aleion (u-lay′-un), Ph. *See* ALEYIN.

Aleyin or **Aleion** (u-lay′-un), Ph, a water deity or spirit, the son of BAAL, who gave water to the crops and protected vegetation with moisture.

Alfheim (alv′-haym), Sc, the home of the ELVES, fairies, and friendly spirits.

Alignak (al-ig-nahk′) or **Aningan** (an-in-gahn′), NA, the name given to the moon by the Eskimos. After a brother and his sister committed incest, they became outcasts from the earth and were relegated to the heavens. Alignak became the moon; his sister, the sun. The spirit dwelling in Alignak is TARQUIUP INNUA.

Alpheus (al-fee′-us), G, a river-god of the Peloponnesus who fell in love with the NYMPH ARETHUSA. When he pursued Arethusa, ARTEMIS changed her into a fountain to aid her escape, but Alpheus followed her underground to Sicily, where their waters mingled.

Althaea (al-thee′-u), G, wife of OENEUS and mother of DEIANIRA, MELEAGER, and TYDEUS. When the FATES told Althaea that Meleager would die when a certain burning log was consumed, she pulled the log from the fire and hid it. After Meleager killed her two brothers in a struggle for the CALYDONIAN BOAR's skin, Althaea burned the rest of the log and Meleager died.

Ama (ah'-mah), J, the name of heaven, a beautiful spot reached by crossing a wide river.

Amalthea (am-ul-thee'-u), G, the mountain goat that nursed the infant ZEUS on Crete, or, in some versions, a NYMPH who fed him on goat's milk. One of her horns was said to have become the "Cornucopia," and Amalthea was honored by Zeus as the constellation Capricorn.

Amaterasu (ah'-mah-te-rah'-suh), J, the goddess of the sun and chief deity of the Japanese pantheon. She was born when IZANAGI, bathing in the sea after his visit to the kingdom of the dead, washed his left eye. Her father, Izanagi, gave her a necklace of jewels and made her ruler of the stretches of heaven. Amaterasu wove the garments of the gods.

When her brother SUSANOWO, overwhelmed with pride after he had created five gods, carried out acts of destruction, Amaterasu fled in terror to a cave, turning the world to darkness until the gods, assembled in countless numbers, lured her from her hiding place with a mirror and the sun's light was restored to the world.

Amaterasu personifies the sun and is regarded as the direct antecedent of the imperial family, who thus ruled by divine right. She represents the deities of Yamato province. Her chief sanctuary was established at ISE in the first century.

Amazons, the, G, a race of female warriors who lived in what is now the Black Sea region of southeastern Europe. The Amazons fought a number of heroes, among whom were BELLEROPHON, who drove them back from Lycia; HERACLES, whose task it was to get the girdle of their queen, HIPPOLYTE, for ADMETE; and THESEUS, when they invaded Attica. The Amazons fought on the side of the Trojans after the death of HECTOR, under the leadership of Queen PENTHESILEA. The Amazons cut off their right breasts in order to use their bows more easily in battle. They raised only their female young and only came into contact with men for purposes of breeding and as opponents in war.

Ambrosia (am-broh'-zhu) [from Greek "immortality"], G, the food or drink of the gods, which gave them immortality. The gods also used ambrosia to bestow immortality on certain selected humans and to preserve the bodies of some mortals.

Amen (ah'-mun), E. *See* AMON.

Amen-Ra (ah'-mun-rah), E. *See* AMON-RA.

Ament   (u-ment′), E. *See* AMENTI.

Amenti   (u-men′-tee) or **Iment** (i-ment′) or **Ament** (u-), E, a goddess who was depicted with an ostrich plume, and sometimes a hawk, on her head. She was at first a deity of a province west of Lower Egypt and later became a goddess of the entire west, especially in its reference to the dwelling place of the dead. The name was often used in this latter context. It was believed that the souls of the dead joined OSIRIS in his kingdom in the west, Amenti.

Amesha Spentas, the   (ah′-me-shu spen′-tuz), Pe, a group of six beneficent spirits of good, who were under the command of AHURA MAZDA and were his attendants, created by him. They were incarnations of noble qualities and goals, personifying those traits belonging to Ahura Mazda. The Amesha Spentas presided over the orderly pattern of the universe and of life on earth.

Amon or **Amen**   (ah′-mun), E, an early deity, personifying the air or breath of life, worshiped chiefly at THEBES. Amon was the husband of MUT and the father of KHONS. Together they formed the Theban triad of deities. Amon was a god of fertility and patron of agriculture.

Great sanctuaries at KARNAK and LUXOR were dedicated to Amon. The goose and ram were sacred to him, and he was sometimes depicted with a ram's head.

Amon-Ra or **Amen-Ra**   (ah′-mun-rah), E, the name given to AMON after he became identified in later times with the god RA. During the time of the power of THEBES, Amon-Ra was worshiped as the supreme deity and was known as the creator of the world and ruler of the gods. The pharaohs claimed descent from Amon-Ra.

Amor   (ay′-mawr), R, the god of love, corresponding to the Greek god EROS. He was the son of VENUS. Amor was also called CUPID by the Romans.

Amphion   (am-fahy′-un), G, the son of ZEUS and ANTIOPE and the husband of NIOBE. With his twin, ZETHUS, who was known for his physical prowess, Amphion built the walls of Thebes, his kingdom. An accomplished musician, he caused the stones to move into place with the music of his lyre. Amphion committed suicide when Niobe's pride destroyed his entire family.

Amphitrite   (am-fu-trahy′-tee), G, an ancient sea-goddess. Amphitrite was one of the NEREIDS, daughters of NEREUS and DORIS, in later mythology, and the wife of POSEIDON and mother of TRITON.

Amphitryon   (am-fit′-ree-un), G, the king of THEBES and the husband of ALCMENE, who became the mother of HERACLES by ZEUS after he seduced her in the guise of Amphitryon. He was the father, by Alcmene, of IPHICLES.

Amurru (u-muhr'-oo), Ph, a god who represented the west.

Amycus (am'-i-kus), G, a son of POSEIDON who made all strangers box with him. Those who refused were drowned; those who accepted were killed in the match. When the ARGONAUTS landed in Amycus' kingdom, he refused to give the visitors water and provisions unless their best boxer entered on a match with him. POLLUX, taking up the challenge, overcame and killed Amycus.

Amymone (am-u-moh'-nee), G, one of the DANAÏDS. She was the mother of NAUPLIUS by POSEIDON, who fell in love with her after rescuing her from a SATYR.

An (ahn), A-B, the sky-god of the Sumerians.

Anadyomene (an-u-dahy-om'-u-nee) [from Greek "rising from the sea"], G, another name for APHRODITE. The word refers to the manner in which, in some versions, the goddess was said to have been born.

Anahita (u-nah'-hee-tu), Pe, a river-goddess and a genius of water. She was one of the YAZATAS and was also worshiped in connection with the planet Venus.

Ananse (u-nan'-see), Af, in Ashanti legend, the spider who formed the material out of which NYAME brought the first human beings to life. Ananse is believed to have communicated man's complaints to Nyame and to have taken Nyame's daughter as his wife. He gave mankind grain and the tools of farming and was therefore looked upon as a culture hero.

Ananta (ah'-nun-tu), I. *See* SHESHA.

Anat (ah-naht'), Ph, a goddess of dew and the fertility it brings. She was the sister of BAAL. Anat brought about the sacrificial death of MOT at the time of the harvest. Ritual sacrifices were under her jurisdiction, and it was her task to see that they were properly carried out to ensure the immortality of the gods.

Anchises (an-kahy'-seez), G & R, the father of AENEAS by APHRODITE. Carried from burning Troy by Aeneas, Anchises died when the Trojans reached Sicily. When Aeneas visited him in the ELYSIAN FIELDS of the UNDERWORLD, Anchises foretold the founding of Rome.

Androgeus (an-drahj'-ee-us), G, the son of PASIPHAË and King MINOS of Crete. A great athlete, he won all events in the PANATHENAEA. When Androgeus was killed by the Bull of Marathon,

Minos blamed King AEGEUS of Athens and demanded human sacrifices for the MINOTAUR.

Andromache (an-drahm'-u-kee), G, the devoted wife of HECTOR and the mother of ASTYANAX. After Hector's death and the fall of Troy, Andromache became the concubine of NEOPTOLEMUS, the son of ACHILLES. She later married HELENUS, Hector's brother and the only son of King PRIAM to survive the TROJAN WAR.

Andromeda (an-drahm'-i-du), G, the daughter of CASSIOPEIA and CEPHEUS, king of Ethiopia. When Cassiopeia boasted she was more beautiful than the NEREIDS, POSEIDON sent a sea serpent to consume the Ethiopians. At the demand of the oracle of AMON, Cepheus chained Andromeda to a rock as a sacrifice to the sea monster. PERSEUS rescued Andromeda and took her to Argos as his bride. After her death, she was put into the heavens as a constellation by ATHENA.

Andvari (ahn'-dwah-ree), Sc, a DWARF who guarded the magic ring, DRAUPNIR, and the other treasures of the gods. When the god LOKI stole his ring and treasure to give to HREIDMAR as recompense for OTTER's death, Andvari put a curse on the ring and the gold, causing sorrow and violence to all who were to come in contact with it, until the deaths of GUDRUN and her children brought an end to the VOLSUNGS. In the NIBELUNGENLIED, Andvari is known as Alberich.

Angakok (ang'-gu-kahk), NA, in Eskimo belief, a sorcerer, both priest and medicine man, with the power to influence supernatural phenomena, heal the sick, affect the weather, and the like.

Angerboda or **Angurboda** (ahng'-gur-boh-du), Sc, a giantess who was the mother of HEL, FENRIR, and the MIDGARD SERPENT, offspring of LOKI.

Angra Mainyu (ang'-ru mahyn'-yoo) or **Ahriman** (ah'-ri-mun), Pe, a deity who was the representation of darkness, demons, and evil forces. He struggled in opposition to AHURA MAZDA in a war of nine thousand years, until Ahura Mazda vanquished his antagonist. Angra Mainyu's followers were the DEVAS.

Angurboda (ahng'-gur-boh-du), Sc. *See* ANGERBODA.

Angus (ang'-gus) or **Angus Og** (ohg), Ce, the son of DAGDA and BOANN and the god of love and a patron deity of young people.

Angus Og (ang'-gus ohg), Ce. *See* ANGUS.

Anhur (ahn'-hur) or **Onouris** (oh-noo'-ris), E, the god of war, symbolizing the god RA in that capacity. The Greeks identified him with ARES. He was often associated with SHU and called Anhur-Shu.

His wife was the lion-headed goddess MEHIT. Anhur was worshiped at ABYDOS as a solar deity.

Aningan (an-in-gahn'), NA. *See* ALIGNAK.

Anna (an'-u), R, the sister of Queen DIDO of Carthage. It was Anna who pleaded with AENEAS on Dido's behalf, but Aeneas carried out his plans to leave Carthage, thus bringing about Dido's suicide. Anna was said to have gone to Italy, where the jealousy of Aeneas' wife, LAVINIA, led her to drown herself.

Annfwn (ahn'-foon) or **Annwn** (ahn'-noon), Ce, the home of the dead, ruled by Arawn, generally described as a paradise island full of serenity and beauty. ARTHUR sailed with a large crew to raid Annfwn and carry off a magic cauldron.

Annwn (ahn'-noon), Ce. *See* ANNFWN.

Anshar (ahn'-shahr), A-B, the progenitor of the Babylonian pantheon and god of the sky and heavens. Anshar and his sister-wife KISHAR were the offspring of LAKHAMU and LAKHMU, and they, in turn, produced the gods ANU and EA.

Antaeus (an-tee'-us), G, the son of POSEIDON and GAEA who forced all strangers to wrestle with him. When HERACLES, on his way to the Garden of the HESPERIDES, encountered Antaeus and realized that he was invincible as long as he touched the earth, Heracles lifted the giant from the ground and strangled him.

Antenor (an-tee'-nawr), G, a counselor of PRIAM, who urged that HELEN be returned to the Greeks and the TROJAN WAR be ended. According to some sources, he suggested that the Greeks steal the PALLADIUM and build the Trojan Horse in order to end the war. He escaped after the fall of Troy and went on to found what is now Padua, in northern Italy.

Antigone (an-tig'-u-nee), G, the daughter of OEDIPUS and JOCASTA. After being with Oedipus when he died in exile at Colonus, Antigone returned to THEBES. When the edict of her uncle CREON, king of Thebes, forbade the burial of her brother POLYNICES because he had led the SEVEN AGAINST THEBES, Antigone went ahead and performed the rites and was put to death as a consequence. She was ordered to be buried alive, but according to some versions she killed herself before the sentence could be carried out. The tragedy was completed when Creon's son, Haemon, who loved Antigone, killed himself. The legend is the basis of a tragedy by SOPHOCLES.

Antinous (an-tin'-oh-us), G, the cruelest of the suitors of PENELOPE and the first to be killed by ODYSSEUS on his return from the TROJAN WAR.

Antiope (an-tahy'-u-pee), G, 1. the mother of AMPHION and ZETHUS by ZEUS.

2. an AMAZON queen, the sister of HIPPOLYTE. She was the captive of THESEUS, by whom she became the mother of HIPPOLYTUS.

Antum (ahn'-toom), A-B, a goddess who was the consort of ANU and mother of ENLIL.

Anu (ah'-noo) or **Anum** (-noom), A-B, the son of ANSHAR and KISHAR; the Akkadian sky-god, ruler of the upper heavens and lord of the other deities. Mankind and earthly problems were generally outside Anu's province, since his chief concern was for the gods, the regions of the sky, and the order of the universe. He took the part of arbiter of the disputes of the gods. His power and authority were wielded with the aid of his creation, the stars, acting as his troops, and whose place it was to punish the wicked.

At the request of ISHTAR, whose love for GILGAMESH had been rejected, Anu fashioned a bull to overpower the hero.

Anu, the counterpart of the god AN of the Sumerians, was worshiped especially at URUK. Other gods were later identified with him and took on the name Anu.

Anubis (u-noo'-bis), E, the dog- or jackal-headed deity of funerals and mummification. He was a deity of ABYDOS, considered to be the son of NEPHTHYS and OSIRIS, or of SET. Anubis conducted the dead to the underworld and presided over the scales that weighed the hearts of the dead when they stood trial before Osiris. He helped ISIS restore Osiris' body to life, after he was slain by Set.

Anuket (u-noo'-ket), E, the second wife of KHNUM. It was her task to control the narrow course of the upper Nile and the Cataracts. Anuket is depicted with a plumed crown. She was called Anukis by the Greeks.

Anum (ah'-noom), A-B. *See* ANU.

Anunnaki, the (ah-nuhn'-nah-kee), A-B, a name representing the deities of the Sumerian pantheon. They comprised the assembly over which AN and ENLIL presided. The Anunnaki were born of ANSHAR and KISHAR, but were also said to have been created by MARDUK. They were chiefly earth deities and gods of the underworld, and they decided the destiny of mankind in council.

Anzu (ahn'-zoo), A-B. *See* ZU.

Apepi (ah-pe'-pee), E. *See* APOPHIS.

Apet (ah'-pet), E. *See* TAUERET.

Aphrodite (af-ru-dahy'-tee), G, the goddess of love and beauty; one

16

of the twelve major deities who lived on Mt. OLYMPUS. The Romans identified Aphrodite with VENUS. According to HOMER, Aphrodite was the daughter of ZEUS and DIONE, the daughter of OCEANUS and TETHYS. In other versions, she was said to have been born from the foam of the sea (*aphros* means "foam") near the island of Cythera and carried by ZEPHYRUS to Cyprus. Aphrodite was also called CYTHEREA as well as ANADYOMENE and was worshiped by sailors and fishermen. She was described as golden, lovely, and fun-loving, and gods and humans, as well as animals and all nature, succumbed to her tricks and wiles. Aphrodite was the wife of HEPHAESTUS but was not faithful to him. She loved ADONIS and ARES and was the mother of HARMONIA and EROS by Ares. Also, she became the mother of AENEAS by ANCHISES. Among her other children were HERMAPHRODITUS and PRIAPUS. In the JUDGMENT OF PARIS, Aphrodite was awarded the golden apple, inscribed "For the Fairest," because she promised PARIS the most beautiful woman in the world (HELEN), and for that reason she aided the Trojans during the TROJAN WAR. Aphrodite's son Eros attended her constantly, and she was also accompanied by the CHARITES and HORAE. The girdle of Aphrodite was the cestus, which made its wearer irresistible. The rose and myrtle were sacred to Aphrodite as were the swan, dolphin, dove, and ram. The most famous of the statues of Aphrodite that have been preserved from ancient times is the "Aphrodite of Melos," or "Venus de Milo," now in the Louvre in Paris.

Apis (ay′-pis) or **Hapi** (hah′-pee), E, the sacred bull of MEMPHIS, believed to be the incarnation of OSIRIS or PTAH. Apis was worshiped as a god, and it was thought that his actions foretold the future. At the time of the Ptolemies, Apis was worshiped with Osiris in the form of SERAPIS, with his cult center at Alexandria.

Apo (ah′-paw), Pe, one of the YAZATAS, worshiped as the personification of water.

Apochquiahuayan (u-poch-kwee-u-wah′-yun), Az. *See* MICTLAN.

Apollo (u-pahl′-oh), G & R, the son of ZEUS and LETO and twin brother of ARTEMIS; one of the twelve principal deities. Apollo was born on the island of DELOS and was therefore sometimes called Delian Apollo. As god of the sun, the bringer of fertility and fruitfulness to the earth, and the deity of light, purity, and truth, Apollo was often designated as Phoebus, meaning "shining" or "bright." He was also the god of medicine, music, poetry, fine arts, and eloquence. Apollo killed the serpent of Mt. PARNASSUS, PYTHON, with his arrow. In honor of this achievement, the Pythian Games were established at DELPHI, and he was called Pythian Apollo. Apollo bestowed the gift of prophecy on certain mortals, such as CASSANDRA, and there were important oracles of Apollo at Delos and at Delphi in Greece and Cumae in Italy. Apollo was the protector of flocks and shepherds as well as of all colonists and those who established cities. As god of music, Apollo was associated with the MUSES. Apollo was the father of ASCLEPIUS by Coronis and was, thus, the god of healing. As a vengeful god, Apollo sent swift death with his bow and arrows. To avenge the death of Asclepius, Apollo put the CYCLOPES to death, because they had made Zeus's thunderbolt. Apollo was also the father of ARISTAEUS by CYRENE and of ORPHEUS by CALLIOPE. Apollo's attributes were the lyre and bow, and the laurel tree was sacred to him, because DAPHNE was changed into a laurel when she fled from his attentions. An unusually handsome young man is called an Apollo. The most famous of the ancient statues of Apollo that have come down to us in the marble "Apollo Belvedere" in the Vatican Museum in Rome.

Apollodorus (a-pahl-o-doh'-rus), an Athenian who wrote in the second century B.C. on the subjects of history, geography, mythology, and grammar. His surviving work, the *Bibliotheca,* is a rich source of mythological information relating to the gods and heroes.

Apollonius of Rhodes (ap-u-loh'-nee-us), an epic poet of Alexandria and Rhodes whose *Argonautica* relates the story of JASON and his fellow ARGONAUTS and their adventures in search of the GOLDEN FLEECE.

Apophis (u-poh'-fis) or **Apepi** (ah-pe'-pee), E, the huge serpent that lived in the other Nile that flowed through the vault of heaven. He attempted to thwart the god RA as he rode across the sky in his boat. Whenever Apophis was successful, an eclipse occurred. Apophis represented darkness and its struggle against the light of the sun. Because he was the sun's enemy, he was confused and identified with SET in later times.

Apsu (ahp'-soo), A-B, the personification of the sweet, primeval waters surrounding and supporting the earth. In early Akkadian mythology, Apsu was a feminine deity, but later, as a god, he was the husband of TIAMAT and father of the other gods.

Apsu was captured by EA, because he, believing the rest of the deities to be too noisy, planned to do away with them.

Apsyrtus (ap-sur'-tus), G, son of AEËTES, king of Colchis, and brother of MEDEA, who killed him in order to delay pursuit by her father while she fled with JASON and the GOLDEN FLEECE.

Apuleius, Lucius (ap-yu-lee'-us), a Roman philosopher and rhetorician of the second century A.D. He studied and traveled in Greece, where he was initiated into the MYSTERY religions. Apuleius was the author of the *Metamorphoses* or *Golden Ass,* a Latin novel relating the adventures of a man who was transformed into a donkey. The work includes a description of the details connected with the Mystery worship of ISIS and the episode of the story of CUPID and PSYCHE.

Apu-Punchau (ah'-poo-poon-chou'), SA. *See* INTI.

Aquilo (ak'-wi-loh), R, the north wind personified, the counterpart of the Greek BOREAS.

Arachne (u-rak'-nee), G, a Lydian girl who challenged ATHENA to a weaving contest. Athena depicted the power of the gods; Arachne represented the weaknesses and loves of the deities. When Athena destroyed Arachne's work, the maiden hanged herself in despair, whereupon the goddess transformed her into a spider and doomed her to hang and spin forever as punishment for her insolence. The scientific term for spider is *arachnid*.

Arallu (ah-rah'-loo), A-B, the underworld of Babylonian mythology, a kingdom ruled by ERESHKIGAL and her consort, NERGAL.

Arcadia (ahr-kay'-dee-ah), G, a district in the central Peloponnesus, surrounded by mountains, which cut off the region from neighboring areas. The inhabitants of Arcadia led an undisturbed and ideal pastoral life of rustic pleasures and habits. Arcadia was the home of PAN.

Arcas (ahr'-kus), G, the son of CALLISTO and ZEUS and the eponymous king of the Arcadians. Zeus raised Arcas to the heavens, where he became the star Arcturus, the guardian for his mother, changed by Zeus into the constellation Great BEAR.

Ares (ehr'-eez), G, the god of war, son of ZEUS and HERA; one of the twelve major Olympian deities. The Romans identified Ares with MARS, but theirs was a nobler and more popular deity. Because of his love of violence and his fondness for bloodshed and battle, Ares was disliked by mortals and hated even by his parents. Ares was accompanied in battle by his sister ERIS (Strife) and by his sons, Deimos (Fright) and Phobos (Fear) and also by Enyo, a goddess of battle. APHRODITE loved Ares and was the mother of EROS and HARMONIA by him. Ares and Aphrodite were caught up into a net by her angered husband HEPHAESTUS and held up for the gods to ridicule. Ares was twice wounded, once by DIOMEDES in the TROJAN WAR and again by HERACLES because of the death of CYCNUS. He was associated mainly with the rugged regions of Thrace, but the Areopagus, the Hill of Ares, where the court of Athens was held, was also sacred to him. The attributes of Ares were the burning torch and the spear, and the dog and the vulture were associated with him.

Arete (u-ree'-tee), G, 1. the wife of King ALCINOUS of PHAEACIA and mother of NAUSICAÄ.

2. the personification of manliness and courage.

Arethusa (ar-u-thoo'-zu), G, a NYMPH with whom ALPHEUS fell in love. ARTEMIS helped Arethusa to escape from the river-god, and Arethusa emerged in Sicily as a fountain on the island of Ortygia in the harbor of Syracuse.

Argo, the (ahr'-goh), G, JASON's fifty-oared ship, named for its builder, ARGUS. The *Argo* was built with the aid of ATHENA, who placed an oak beam, sacred to ZEUS and capable of speaking prophecies, in its prow. Jason dedicated the *Argo* to POSEIDON at the end of the voyage.

Argonauts, the (ahr'-gu-nawtz), G, the fifty mariners of the ship *Argo* under the command of JASON, who set out to bring the GOLDEN FLEECE back from Colchis to Thessaly. The story is of events antedating the TROJAN WAR. Included among the crew were ORPHEUS, HERACLES, PELEUS, CASTOR, and POLLUX. The Argonauts encountered many adventures in the course of their expedition. When they landed for water in Bithynia, Pollux met AMYCUS and slew him. At Lemnos, where the women had killed all the men of the island, HYPSIPYLE was said to have become Jason's wife and to have borne him twin sons. CYZICUS received the Argonauts kindly after they had sailed through the Hellespont and reached his island. Soon after they left Cyzicus, however, a storm drove the Argonauts back to the island, where they were mistaken for pirates and attacked. In the battle that followed, Cyzicus was killed by Jason.

The *Argo* sailed from Asia Minor without Heracles, who stayed behind to search for HYLAS. The Argonauts had rescued PHINEUS from the HARPIES in Thrace, and, with his helpful advice, they passed the SYMPLEGADES, the Clashing Rocks, safely. When the Argonauts reached Colchis, AEËTES told Jason he must yoke a pair of fire-breathing bulls and sow dragon's teeth. Armed men sprang up, but Jason, according to the instructions of MEDEA, who fell in love with him, threw a stone into their midst, causing them to fight and slay each other. Medea also gave Jason a charm, which brought sleep to the dragon that guarded the Golden Fleece, and she accompanied Jason when the Argonauts left Colchis with the coveted prize. When Aeëtes followed them, Medea delayed his pursuit by casting the limbs of her brother APSYRTUS over the sea, and they escaped. There are various stories about the return journey of the Argonauts. According to some accounts, they encountered CIRCE and the SIRENS, and also SCYLLA and CHARYBDIS, but Jason and the Argonauts did eventually reach Thessaly safely.

Argus (ahr'-gus), G, 1. the hundred-eyed monster sent by HERA to guard the goddess IO after the goddess changed the maiden, admired by ZEUS, into a heifer. When HERMES killed Argus after putting him to sleep by telling his stories, Hera put his eyes into the tail of the peacock, her favorite bird. A guard who keeps conscientious or zealous watch is called *Argus-eyed*.

2. the son of PHRIXUS and Chalcipe. He was the grandson of King AEËTES of Chochis.

3. the son of JASON and MEDEA.

4. the builder of the ARGO. Argus accompanied Jason on his voyage.

5. the faithful dog of ODYSSEUS. When his master returned to Ithaca, the dog recognized him and then died.

Ariadne (ar-ee-ad'-nee), G, the daughter of King MINOS and PASIPHAË of Crete. Ariadne fell in love with THESEUS and gave him a ball of thread with which to find his way out of the LABYRINTH. She then eloped with him, but he deserted her on the island of NAXOS. She was later rescued by DIONYSUS, who married her. Ariadne was made immortal and bore Dionysus many children.

Arianrhod (ahr-yahn'-rawd), Ce, a goddess, the sister of GWYDION and mother by him of LLEW LLAW GYFFES, whom she cursed.

Arikute (a-ri-koo'-tee), SA, the Tupi-Guarani god of the darkness and the night. He was the younger brother of TAWENDUARE.

Arion (u-rahy'-un), G, 1. a marvelous horse, the son of POSEIDON and DEMETER. Arion was owned at one time by HERACLES.

2. a son of Poseidon who was a noted musician. When he was returning to Corinth from a musical contest, the sailors tried to steal the riches he had won. Arion begged to play on his lyre once more and thus attracted the dolphins, which carried him to safety.

Aristaeus (ar-is-tee'-us), G, the son of APOLLO and CYRENE and husband of AUTONOË. Aristaeus, who is said to have been the inventor of beekeeping, fell in love with EURYDICE and was indirectly responsible for her death, since she stepped on a snake as she fled from his advances.

Aristophanes (ar-is-tahf'-u-neez), an Athenian poet, famous primarily for his comedies, who lived from the middle of the fifth century to the early fourth century B.C. Of his numerous plays, the eleven that have survived are filled with mythological references and material.

Arjuna (ahr'-ju-nu), I, the son of INDRA and KUNTI who became the boyhood friend of KRISHNA and fought with him in the war between the KURUS and their cousins the PANDAVAS. When Arjuna questioned the moral validity of war, Krishna answered him by pointing out his duty and explaining life and death. This dialogue is the theme of the BHAGAVAD-GITA; Arjuna, its principal hero.

Arnaknagsak (ahr-nuk-nahg'-sahk), NA. *See* SEDNA.

Artemis (ahr'-tu-mis), G, daughter of ZEUS and LETO and twin of APOLLO; one of the twelve major deities. Her Roman counterpart was DIANA. Artemis was called CYNTHIA, and also Delia, because of her birth near Mt. Cynthus on the island of DELOS. She had many characteristics in common with Apollo and was therefore sometimes known as PHOEBE or PYTHIA, corresponding with his names PHOEBUS and Pythian Apollo. Artemis was the chaste goddess of the moon and the hunt and all nature. She was the protectress of youth, especially girls and maidens, and brought favorable weather to travelers. Swift of foot, tall, and beautiful, Artemis brought healing to mortals but was also quick to punish with her bow and arrows. She helped Apollo to slay NIOBE's children, and it was she who demanded the sacrifice of IPHIGENIA at Aulis; also, she sent the CALYDONIAN BOAR against OENEUS because one of her sacred stags had been killed. Her attributes were the bow and quiver, and the cypress tree and all animals, the hind and the dog in particular, were sacred to her. In time, Artemis became identified with SELENE and HECATE because of her association with the moon and the night.

Arthur (ahr'-thur), Ce, a legendary hero and king of Britain, with possibly some link to historical fact, who performed great and heroic deeds and was served by the Knights of the Round Table. GUINEVERE was his wife. Arthur was the son of UTHER PENDRAGON and IGRAINE and became king at the age of fifteen after his father's death. He attacked and drove off the Saxon invaders and also defeated the Scots. He received mortal wounds in battle with MODRED and was carried to AVALON. There is a parallelism between the exploits of King Arthur and his knights and those of the Celtic deities and heroes.

Aruns (ar'-unz), R, an ally of AENEAS and the Trojans who killed CAMILLA, who fought on the side of TURNUS. DIANA brought about Aruns' death in vengeance.

Aruru (ah-roo'-roo), A-B, in early mythology, a goddess who helped MARDUK mold the first human and create mankind. In some accounts, it was her union with Marduk that gave birth to mankind. At the request of the gods, Aruru molded ENKIDU from mud to be the rival of GILGAMESH. Aruru was the personification of earth and the counterpart of the Sumerian goddess KI.

Ascanius (a-skay'-nee-us) G & R, the son of AENEAS and CREUSA. Ascanius founded Alba Longa, where he was destined to rule for thirty years. *See also* IULUS.

Aschere (us-chee'-ru), in the poem *Beowulf*, HROTHGAR's good friend and trusted adviser, who was slain in HEOROT HALL by GRENDEL's mother.

Asclepius (u-sklee'-pee-us), G, the son of APOLLO and Coronis. His Latin name was AESCULAPIUS. Asclepius was brought up by CHIRON, the CENTAUR, who taught him the art of healing. He became a skilled physician and was even able to restore the dead to life. ZEUS ended Asclepius' life with a thunderbolt, because the UNDERWORLD was being depleted. Asclepius then became the god of medicine, whose sacred symbol was the snake. His daughter was HYGEIA.

Asgard (ahs'-gahrd, as'-), Sc, a citadel in the sky, the dwelling place of the AESIR, which could be reached only by crossing the rainbow bridge BIFROST. The mansions and high seats of the gods and the home of the heroes killed in battle, VALHALLA, were in Asgard.

Asherah (u-sheer'-u), Ph, a fertility and mother goddess, called the creator and the mother of the gods. Her province was the sea, and she was credited with great wisdom. Asherah was the mother of BAAL, and the same name is given to Baal's wife, but it is not known whether the same goddess was given both roles. Asherah was identified at times with ASTARTE.

Ashipu (ah'-shee-poo), A-B, a sorcerer who practiced his art of wizardry to counteract evil spells. The name is sometimes construed as plural.

Ashtareth (ash'-tu-reth), Ph. *See* ASTARTE.

Ashtart (ash'-tahrt), Ph. *See* ASTARTE.

Ashtoreth (ash'-to-reth), Ph. *See* ASTARTE.

Ask (ahsk), Sc, the first man, made from an ash tree by ODIN and the other gods after the great flood. His wife EMBLA was created at the same time.

Assaracus (u-sar'-u-kus), G, a son of TROS and CALLIRRHOË and an ancestor of AENEAS.

Asshur (ash'-ur), A-B. *See* ASSUR.

Assur (as'-ur) or **Asshur** (ash'-), A-B, a tribal god who became the supreme god of the Assyrians, taking the place of MARDUK in their pantheon as lord and ruler of the gods and creator of all. Assur was a war-god, the patron god of battle and fighting men.

Assur came to be identified with ANSHAR, the Babylonian deity. His wife was generally considered to be NINLIL, although, in some versions, he had other consorts, ISHTAR among them. He was usually depicted as a winged disk, but sometimes was represented mounted on a bull.

Astarte (a-stahr'-tee) or **Ashtoreth** (ash'-to-reth) or **Ashtareth** (-tu-) or **Ashtart** (-tahrt), Ph, a goddess of Semitic origin who was worshiped by the Phoenicians as a fertility deity. She was worshiped at Tyre and Sidon as the chief goddess. Astarte represented the fertility of the female and of nature and the incarnation of the planet Venus. She was also considered to be a goddess of the moon and was depicted with a crescent or horns of the new moon.

Astarte is her Greek name. Her Semitic name was Ashtoreth, and Ashtart and Ashtareth are variants. In Babylonian mythology, she is the goddess ISHTAR. She was worshiped in the entire eastern Mediterranean world, although sometimes in differing forms. In Egypt, she took on the role of a war-goddess; in Greece, she was regarded as comparable to APHRODITE.

Asteria (u-steer'-ee-u), G, the daughter of the TITANS Coeus and PHOEBE and the mother of HECATE. To escape from the attentions of ZEUS, Asteria became a quail and jumped into the sea, becoming the island of Ortygia, later called DELOS or Asteria.

Astraea or **Astrea** (a-stree'-u), G, the daughter of ZEUS and THEMIS or, according to another version, of ASTRAEUS and EOS. Astraea, who represented justice and purity, abandoned the earth when violence appeared after the GOLDEN AGE and became the constellation Virgo, the Maiden.

Astraeus (a-stree'-us), G, the son of the TITAN Crius and Eurybia. Astraeus became the husband of EOS and father of the stars and winds.

Astrea (a-stree'-u), G. *See* ASTRAEA.

Astyanax (u-stahy'-u-naks), G, the son of HECTOR and ANDROMACHE. He was thrown from the walls of Troy by the Greeks after they had taken the city so that he could not avenge its destruction.

Asura (us'-oo-ru, -uh-ru), I, a demon or evil power who had magic skills and was hostile to the DEVAS.

Asushu-Namir (ah-soo'-shoo-nah'-meer), A-B, a being created by

EA to go to the underworld and free ISHTAR from the constraint put upon her by ERESHKIGAL.

Asvins, the (as'-vinz), I, handsome twin deities, sons of the sun-god SURYA and the cloud-goddess SARANYU. The Asvins were beneficent healers.

Atalanta (at-ulan'-tu), G, the swift and beautiful daughter of Schoeneus of Boeotia or of Iasus of ARCADIA. Abandoned in the mountains when a child because she was not a boy, she grew up to be a huntress and took part in the hunt for the CALYDONIAN BOAR. MELEAGER, who killed the boar, gave Atalanta the victor's prize, the boar's skin, because she had been the first to wound the animal. Atalanta lived in the woods because of an oracle's warning against marriage. Her suitors were challenged to race with her, and the losers met death. Atalanta was swifter than any man until APHRODITE gave HIPPOMENES three of the GOLDEN APPLES of the HESPERIDES, enabling him to outrun the maiden, who stopped to pick them up as he threw them to the ground one by one.

Ataokoloinona (at'-u-awk-oh-loi-noh'-nu), Af, in Madagascan legend, the son of NDRIANANAHARY who was sent to earth by his father to consider the advisability of creating mankind. Ataokoloinona, however, found the earth's surface too hot, and so he went down into the earth itself, but he did not reappear. His father then dispatched men from heaven to search for him and continued to do so, and these men became the human race.

Atar (at'-ahr), Pe, the god of fire, representing the personification of fire. Fire was of primary importance in the cult of AHURA MAZDA, whose son Atar was. Atar protected the world against evil, bringing mankind the best of life's gifts. He was one of the YAZATAS.

Atea (ah'-tee-u), O. *See* VATEA.

Aten (aht'-un), E. *See* ATON.

Athamas (ath'-u-mas), G, a king of Boeotia, the father of PHRIXUS and HELLE by his first wife, NEPHELE. Athamas later married INO and became the father of MELICERTES.

Athena (u-thee'-nu) or **Athene** (-nee), G, goddess of wisdom and purity; one of the twelve major deities of the Greek pantheon. Her Roman counterpart was MINERVA. According to most accounts, ZEUS swallowed his wife METIS because of a prophecy that she would bear a child stronger than he, and Athena sprang full-grown from the head of Zeus. She appeared in full armor at birth. The favorite of all the children of Zeus, she carried his AEGIS and thunderbolt. She was called *Parthenos*, "the Maiden," and her temple on the ACROPOLIS was therefore named the PARTHENON. Athena presided over the arts of peace as well as war and over the work of craftsmen and artisans of all kinds. She was also the patroness of the womanly arts of weaving and handiwork. Athena showed men how to yoke oxen and tame horses and was believed to be the inventor of the plow. In the contest with POSEIDON over the possession of Attica, Athena won by her offer of the olive tree, which she caused to spring from the rock of the Acropolis, and became the patron goddess of the city-state of Athens. Athena gave aid to many heroes, among them ODYSSEUS, HERACLES, JASON, and PERSEUS. As Athena NIKE she represented Victory and was generally depicted holding a winged victory in her hand. The oak and olive trees and the owl were sacred to her. Her attributes were a helmet, a spear, an aegis on her breastplate, and a shield with a GORGON's head.

Athene   (u-thee'-nee), G. *See* ATHENA.

Athor   (ath'-awr), E. *See* HATHOR.

Atlantis   (at-lan'-tis), G, a legendary island in the Atlantic Ocean beyond the Pillars of HERACLES. Atlantis is believed to have existed in the remote past of prehistory and to have sunk below the surface, probably after an earthquake.

Atlas   (at'-lus), G, the son of IAPETUS and CLYMENE and the brother of PROMETHEUS and EPIMETHEUS. Atlas was punished by ZEUS after the War of the Titans by having to stand at the western end of the earth and support the heavens on his shoulders. He was the father of CALYPSO and the PLEIADES, HYADES, and HESPERIDES.

Atli   (aht'-lee), Sc, the name of Attila, king of the Huns, in Scandinavian legend. His role in the VOLSUNGA SAGA is that of BRYNHILD's brother and GUDRUN's second husband. To acquire the treasure of the NIBELUNGS, he killed the brothers of Gudrun, who killed him in revenge. Atli's counterpart in the NIBELUNGENLIED is ETZEL.

Atmu   (aht'-moo), E. *See* ATUM.

Aton   (ah'-tun) or **Aten**   (aht'-un), E, a name given to the sun. Aton was worshiped in the time of Amenhotep IV as the one god. Amenhotep IV took the name Ikhnaton or Akhenaton, meaning "pleasing to Aton," declaring Egyptian religion to be monotheistic.

Atreus   (ay'-tree-us), G, son of PELOPS and HIPPODAMIA, king of MYCENAE, brother of THYESTES, and father of AGAMEMNON and MENELAUS. When Thyestes, who wanted the throne of Mycenae, fell in love with his wife, AËROPE, and planned to do away with him,

Atreus served Thyestes' young sons to him at a banquet. Thyestes, on discovering the crime, called down a curse on the House of Atreus that was not to be expiated until fate had wrought vengeance on two more generations. Of the thirty-three Greek tragedies that have survived, eight deal with members of this family.

Atropos (a'-tru-pahs), G, one of the three FATES. Atropos cut the thread of life with her shears.

Attis (at'-is) or **Atys** (ay'-tis), G & R, a Phrygian god of vegetation, the young lover of CYBELE. When he deserted the goddess for a NYMPH, Cybele brought madness to him out of jealousy, and he died after castrating himself.

Atum (ah'-tum) or **Atmu** (aht'-moo) or **Tum** (toom), E, a god who was originally a local god of HELIOPOLIS and was later identified with RA, especially in his form as the setting sun, and sometimes known as Atum-Ra. He is depicted with a human head, wearing the pschent, the double crown of the Egyptian pharaohs.

Atys (ay'-tis), G & R. *See* ATTIS.

Audhumbla (oud'-hoom-blah) or **Audhumla** (-hum-lah), Sc, a cow who nourished YMIR and was created, as was Ymir, from the mist of melting ice. BURI, the first god, was revealed when Audhumbla licked off the ice with which he was covered.

Audhumla (oud'-hoom-lah, -hum-), Sc. *See* AUDHUMBLA.

Augeas (aw-jee'-us), G, a king in Elis who had a stable of three thousand oxen. The sixth of the LABORS OF HERACLES was to clean the Augean stables in one day, which he did by routing the ALPHEUS and PENEUS rivers through them. Augeas was one of the ARGONAUTS.

Augur (aw'gur), R, an official who acted as a diviner or priest in the observation and interpretation of various signs and omens—e.g., the appearance of lightning, the movements of birds, or the condition of the internal organs of a sacrificial animal—in order to determine the attitude of the gods toward any public plan or project or governmental policy.

Aurora (aw-rohr'-u), R, the goddess of the dawn, the counterpart of the Greek goddess EOS.

Auster (aw'-stur), R, the south wind, the counterpart of the Greek NOTUS.

Autonoë (aw-tahn'-oh-ee), G, the daughter of CADMUS and HARMONIA, wife of ARISTAEUS, and mother of ACTAEON.

Avaiki (ah-vahy'-kee), O. *See* HAWAIKI.

Avalon (av′-u-lon), Ce, an idyllic island in the west, the home of heroes after death, conjectured to have been near Glastonbury by those linking myth with fact.

Avatar (av-u-tahr′), I, the appearance on earth of a deity in human form. The term was applied especially to the incarnations of VISHNU.

Avernus (u-vur′-nus), G & R, a lake about ten miles west of Naples, Italy, believed to be an entrance to the UNDERWORLD.

Avesta, the (u-vest′-tu), Pe, a collection of the sacred writings of Zoroastrianism. It took its present shape in about the sixth century B.C. Of the twenty-one original books, only one has survived, aside from scattered fragments of the others. Other than inscriptions, sculpture, and some literary evidence and records from other contemporary peoples, the *Avesta* is the sole source of our knowledge of the myths and cults of ancient Persia.

Avilayoq (u-vil-u-yawk′), NA, in Eskimo legend, the mother of the human race and of the animals by a dog, her husband. When Avilayoq was abducted by a sea bird, in the shape of a man, her father rescued her and carried her off in a boat. In the storm sent upon them by the sea bird, the father threw Avilayoq into the water in panic as a sacrifice to calm the waves. She clutched the gunwale, but he chopped off her fingers and put out one eye as she slipped down into the sea. Her fingers became the seals, whales, and other marine animals; she became the goddess SEDNA.

There are various versions of this legend in different areas, but the basic ideas remain the same.

Awonawilona (ah-woh-nu-wu-loh′-nah), NA, the GREAT SPIRIT of the Pueblo Indians. During the flood, men took refuge in caves until Awonawilona brought the earth and sky up out of the receding waters by causing the sun to shine over everything and renewing life for mankind.

Aya (ah′yah), A-B, the consort of SHAMASH and mother of MISHARU and KITTU.

Azhi Dahaka (ah′-zhi du-hah′-ku), Pe, a serpent with three heads. In early legendary accounts, he was the jealous opponent of YIMA, whom he forced from his position of power.

According to the Arabs, Azhi Dahaka was a king of Babylon and was the Persians' bitter enemy. In this human form, he was called ZOHAK.

Aztec Calendar Stone, the, Az, a monumental Aztec circular calendar, about twelve feet in diameter, three feet thick, and weighing about twenty tons, carved from a large block of basalt in about A.D. 1500 and discovered at Tenochtitlán. Apparently it originally stood on a monolithic platform atop one of the pyramid temples. The stone gives the names of the twenty days of the Aztec month; in the center is a representation of the sun-god TONATIUH.

Baal (bay'-ul, bayl), Ph, an ancient Semitic fertility and vegetation god whose enemy, MOT, constantly struggled against him. Baal appears to have been introduced by the Phoenicians when they migrated to the territory of the Semitic peoples. He was a storm-god and god of the winter rains, upon which the crops were so dependent. As a god of storms, Baal is represented as a warrior wearing a helmet, often with the horns of a bull, and carrying a spear. The yearly struggle between Baal and Mot symbolized the renewal of the seemingly dead vegetation of the autumn by the rains of winter.

Baal was subordinate only to EL in the Phoenician pantheon. In one poem, Baal's death was brought about by El, who sent monsters he had created to overcome him. Another account tells of the building of Baal's temple, which included the construction of windows, thus enabling Baal to control the rains and floods.

Since Baal is a general title meaning "lord," he was given various epithets to designate his more specific functions. Thus, as Baal Lebanon he was lord of that city; as Baal Tsaphon, lord of the northern districts. HADAD was the god who was referred to in the RAS SHAMRA tablets as Baal or Baal-Hadad, the Babylonian ADAD. The use of the title Baal corresponds to that of BEL in Babylonia and Assyria, and both the title and the name Baal were given to their local gods by the Semitic peoples. With time, each city came to have its Baal as the ruling lord and deity, or, in the case of a goddess, its BAALAT, the sovereign lady.

Baal was both the brother and the husband of ANAT. He was sometimes identified with the Greek god ZEUS.

Baalat (bay'-ul-at), Ph, a title meaning "Lady," applied especially to a goddess worshiped at BYBLOS from very early times. Baalat of Byblos was sometimes identified with the Egyptian goddess ISIS and with HATHOR, to whom she bore a resemblance. The chief deity of Byblos, ASTARTE, was called Baalat.

Baal-Hadad (bay'-ul-hay'-dad), Ph. *See* HADAD.

Baal-Hammon (bay'-ul-hay'-mun), Ph, a god of the sky and vegetation, the chief god of the Phoenician colony of Carthage. The ram was associated with Baal-Hammon, who was represented as an elderly bearded man.

Bacabs, the (bah'-kahbz), M, deities of agriculture, rain, and fertility. The Bacabs represented the four winds and the four cardinal points, and it was thought that they held up the four corners of the heavens.

Bacchanalia, the (bak-u-nay'-lee-u), R, a festival honoring BACCHUS, analogous to the Greek DIONYSIA. Beginning as religious rites celebrated by female BACCHANTES, they were, in time, opened to men and were held at frequent intervals during the year. The revelry of the rites developed into drunken orgies and were finally banned by the Roman Senate in the second century B.C.

Bacchanals (bah-ku-nahls'), R. *See* BACCHANTES.

Bacchantes (bu-kan'-teez) or **Bacchanals** (bah-ku-nahls'), R, 1. priests, priestesses, or followers of BACCHUS.
2. revelers who worshiped Bacchus in drunken orgies. *See also* MAENADS.

Bacchus (bak'-us), R, the god of wine, identified with the Greek DIONYSUS. Bacchus was also called LIBER by the Romans.

Balarama (bul-u-rah'-mu), I, the AVATAR or incarnation of VISHNU as KRISHNA's elder, or perhaps twin, brother.

Balder or **Baldr** or **Baldur** (bawl'-dur), Sc, the son of ODIN and FRIGG and the husband of NANNA, by whom he was the father of FORSETI. Balder was the sun-god and one of the AESIR. He was the brother, and possibly the twin, of HODER. Balder represented joy and goodness, wisdom and beauty, and was loved by all but LOKI. Frigg had all animals and nature swear not to harm Balder. When Loki learned that Frigg had overlooked the mistletoe, he guided Hoder's aim and Balder fell dead, slain by a piece of mistletoe. When HERMOD rode his father's swift horse SLEIPNER to HEL's kingdom to rescue his brother, Hel promised to restore Balder to life on earth if all nature wept, but Loki, in the guise of an aged giantess, did not weep, and Balder, therefore, remained in the underworld.

Baldr (bawl'-dur), Sc. *See* BALDER.

Baldur (bawl'-dur), Sc. *See* BALDER.

Bali (bul'-i), I, 1. a demon who became king of heaven and earth. VISHNU, incarnated in the form of a dwarf, VAMANA, appeared to Bali beside a sacred river and was offered the fulfillment of a wish. The dwarf requested as much land as he could pace out in three steps. His first two steps covered the universe, thus regaining it for the gods, and with his third step he pressed the demon Bali into PATALA.

(bah'-lee), Sc, 2. a son of ODIN and FRIGG and brother of HODER, whom he killed for having slain their brother BALDER.

Baltis (bal'-tis), Ph, the name by which the Greek goddess DIONE was known at BYBLOS.

Bast (bahst) or **Bastet** (bahs'-tut), E, an early local goddess of fertility who later became a national divinity. The Greeks identified her with ARTEMIS. Her sacred animal was the cat, and she was represented as a cat-headed woman holding in her right hand either a sistrum or an AEGIS. The worship of Bast was centered at Bubastis, the ancient capital of a Nile Delta province, where she was worshiped as the daughter of ISIS. HERODOTUS described her temple as one of the most impressive in all of Egypt, and he related that many thousands came to the fair held annually in her honor at Bubastis. Bast's other form was PAKHT.

Bastet (bahs'-tut), E. *See* BAST.

Ba-Tau (bah'-tou), E, the name by which the Egyptians called the Phoenician deity HEY-TAU.

Bau (bahw, bou), A-B, the daughter of ANU and wife of NINURTA. A yearly harvest festival was held in honor of Ninurta and Bau. The name Bau was sometimes given to the earth-goddess GA-TUM-DUG.

Baucis (baw'-sis), G, the wife of PHILEMON who received ZEUS and HERMES with hospitality.

Baugi (bou'-gee), Sc, a GIANT, the brother of SUTTUNG. When Baugi's helpers were haying, ODIN took on a disguise and caused them to argue over the fine whetstone he had, until they killed each other with their scythes. Baugi promised to pay Odin with a draft of the mead of inspiration for finishing the work of his men, then helped him to make a way into the mountain where Suttung kept the drink.

Bears, the Great and Little, G, two constellations which represent the transformations by ZEUS of CALLISTO and her son ARCAS respectively, also known as the Big Dipper and Little Dipper. OCEANUS, influenced by a jealous HERA, decreed that these constellations should never sink into the ocean.

Behdety (bed'-u-tee), E, the name given to HORUS in connection with his worship at Behdet, seat of a sanctuary in Upper Egypt which the Greeks held sacred to APOLLO and called Apollinopolis Magna, the "Great City of Apollo." Behdety led the forces of RA-HORAKTE against SET and was depicted as falcon-headed, with the winged disk of the sun.

Behistun Rock, the (bay-hi-stoon'), Pe, a cliff in Iran bearing on its

31

face bas-relief sculptures depicting the rebel leader Gaumata at the feet of Darius, recording the latter's victory at the end of the sixth century B.C. Above the scene hovers the winged figure of AHURA MAZDA. The trilingual inscription furnished the key to the decipherment of cuneiform in the mid-nineteenth century.

Bel (bayl, bel) and **Belit** (bay'-lit, bel'-it), A-B, names meaning "lord" or "king" and "lady" or "queen" respectively. The Babylonians gave the title Bel to MARDUK, calling him Bel-Marduk or simply Bel. When the deities of the Sumerians were integrated with their own, the god ENLIL became identified with Bel. Belit, the feminine form, was a title given to NINLIL.

Belili (be-lee'-lee), A-B, an early Sumerian goddess, sister and wife of TAMMUZ, and a deity of the underworld.

Belit (bay'-lit, bel'-it), A-B. *See* BEL and BELIT.

Belit-Ili (bay-lit-ee'-lee), A-B, a goddess of childbirth who protected the newborn infant. She was also called Nintud.

Belit-Seri (bay-lit-say'-ree), A-B, a deity of the underworld who acted as scribe.

Bellerophon (bu-ler'-u-fahn), G, a hero of Corinth, son of GLAUCUS. Bellerophon killed his brother by accident and fled to Argos. There, Antia, wife of King Proteus, fell in love with him, but he scorned her. Proteus sent Bellerophon to Antia's father, king of Lycia, with instructions to kill him. The king, in turn, sent Bellerophon against the invincible CHIMAERA and on other missions, but Bellerophon overcame all dangers with the aid of his winged horse, PEGASUS, and the king gave him his daughter in marriage and half his kingdom. When Bellerophon tried to fly to OLYMPUS, he was thrown by Pegasus and perished because of the anger of ZEUS.

Belus (bee'-lus), G, 1. the son of Libya and POSEIDON and the twin brother of AGENOR. He was king of CHEMMIS on the Nile and became the father of AEGYPTUS, CEPHEUS, and DANAUS.

R, 2. the father of DIDO and PYGMALION and king of Tyre.

Bendigeid Vran (ben-dig'-id vrahn'), Ce, the name by which BRAN the Blessed was known, especially in early mythology.

Bennu (ben'-oo), E, a legendary bird believed to be the reincarnation of the soul of OSIRIS and worshiped as such at MEMPHIS. Bennu was also sacred to HELIOPOLIS, where the bird was thought to be one of the forms assumed by the god RA. Bennu was believed to rise again from flame, as did the phoenix.

Benten (ben'-ten), J, a goddess of the sea, worshiped especially on the smaller islands, and of good luck, the only goddess among the deities of good fortune.

Beowulf (bay'-u-wuhlf), the hero of an Anglo-Saxon epic poem of about the eighth century who became king of the Geatas in Scandinavia. Beowulf went to the aid of the Danish king HROTHGAR to free his court of the monster GRENDEL. In a desperate struggle, he wrenched off Grendel's arm, and the creature went off to his lair to die. The rejoicing was short-lived, however, because his mother entered the palace the following night, killing ASCHERE. Beowulf pursued her to the depths of a lake and killed her in her cave. He severed Grendel's head from his dead body and took it back to Hrothgar.

The second part of the poem *Beowulf* takes place many years later, when Beowulf, now an old man after a successful reign of fifty years as king of the Geatas, with the help of WIGLAF killed a fiery dragon that was threatening his people, but he was mortally poisoned by the dragon. Beowulf was buried by the sea, his grave marked by a lighthouse.

Berecyntia (ber-i-sin'-tee-u), a name for the Phrygian goddess CYBELE, who was worshiped in the vicinity of Mt. Berecynthus.

Bes (bes), E, an ugly, hirsute DWARF, the joyful protector against evil omens and animals, and the god of marriage and birth as well as of music and the dance. Bes was known and worshiped throughout the eastern Mediterranean area.

Bhagavad-Gita, the (bug'-u-vud-gee'-tah), I, a section of the MAHABHARATA in the form of a dialogue between KRISHNA, an AVATAR of VISHNU, and ARJUNA, expounding philosophical theories on duty and death. The discourses took place when Arjuna was unwilling to do battle and questioned the remarks of Krishna, his charioteer, on the subject.

Bhagavata Purana, the (bug'-u-vu-tu puh-rah'-nu), I, a Sanskrit poem, of which the author and even the time are unknown. It records the myths of the hero-god KRISHNA and is perhaps the chief source from which these legends have found their way into later Indian poetry.

Bharata (bur'-u-tu), I, a son of Dasartha who acted as regent for his half brother RAMA during the latter's exile.

Bhishma (bish'-mah), I, a warrior who played a prominent role in the MAHABHARATA. Bishma, whose mother was the goddess GANGA, was loyal to the KAURAVAS. He was killed by ARJUNA at the battle of Kurukshetra.

Bielbog (beel'-bawg), Sl. *See* BYELBOG.

Bifrost (biv'-rost), Sc, a rainbow bridge, the only entrance to ASGARD, home of the gods, connecting it with MIDGARD, the world of mankind. HEIMDALL was the guardian of Bifrost.

Biral (bir'-ahl), O, the name given to the early hero of northern Australia who brought tribal culture and customs to his people. He corresponded to PUN-GEL in Victoria and NURRUNDERE in the region of the Murray River.

Bishamon (bee'-shah-mohn), J, the god of war and a deity of good luck. Bishamon is portrayed as an armed warrior. One of the SHI TENNO, he is guardian of the north. Bishamon is also called Tamon.

Biton (bahyt'-un), G, a son of Cydippe, a priestess of HERA, and the brother of CLEOBIS.

Boann (baw'-un), Ce, the goddess or priestess of the Boyne River in eastern Ireland, who, by her union with DAGDA, became the mother of ANGUS, BODB, BRIGIT, MIDER, and OGMA.

Bochica (boh-chee'-ku), SA, a sun-god, the chief deity of the Chibcha Indians. He was probably a culture hero who was deified after death. Bochica brought agriculture, social laws, crafts, and other skills of civilization to the people of the Chibcha and Muyscaya tribes of Colombia. His wife was CHIA.

Bodb (bohv), Ce, the son of DAGDA and BOANN who succeeded his father as ruler of the gods.

Bodhisattva (boh-di-sat'-wa), I, the name of the future BUDDHA, who entered MAYA's womb in the shape of a lovely white elephant. Bodhisattva had many incarnations.

Bona Dea (boh'-nu dee'-u), R, the goddess of fertility who was worshiped only by women. Bona Dea ("Good Goddess") was identified with FAUNA, MAIA, and OPS, as well as with RHEA.

Bonus Eventus (boh'-nus ee-ven'-tus), R, an ancient god of agriculture and good harvest. Later, Bonus Eventus, "Lucky Outcome," was looked upon as a god of success and good luck in general.

Book of the Dead, the, E, a collection of ancient mortuary texts—i.e., prayers, formulas, hymns, and incantations for the dead—which were written on papryus and, by the time of the New Kingdom, were customarily buried with the mummy. Most of the collection achieved its final form during the Twenty-sixth Dynasty, but parts of it have been found on temple walls and other objects dating from as far back as the Old Kingdom. Many of them contain formalized ritual confessions of sins, magical formulas or charms for ensuring admittance to the afterworld, and hymns of praise to RA and OSIRIS. The texts

34

also tell of the dead in a celestial kingdom, where they traveled with Ra in his course across the heavens or dwelt with the stars at the poles of the earth.

Boreas (boh'-ree-us), G, the north wind, one of the four sons of EOS and ASTRAEUS. Boreas was the husband of ORITHYIA. His Roman counterpart was AQUILO.

Borghild (bawrq'-hild), Sc, SIGMUND's first wife, who poisoned SINFIOTLI after he killed her brother.

Bouyan (bau'-yahn), Sl, an island of bliss, where a river flowed from under a magic, sacred stone, and its healing waters were a panacea for every ill. Below the river was the realm of the dead.

Bragi (brah'-gee), Sc, a son of ODIN and FRIGG. The god of wisdom and poetry, he sang of warrior heroes and welcomed those who entered VALHALLA. Bragi was one of the AESIR and a trusted adviser of Odin. He was the husband of IDUN.

Brahma (brah'-mu), I, the creator god, generally regarded as the first member of the TRIMURTI, or triad of deities, which also includes VISHNU and SHIVA. He was born from NARAYANA, the primeval egg.

Brahma is usually depicted as having four faces and four arms (representing the four VEDAS) and seated on a lotus throne.

Brahmanas, the (brah'-mu-nuz), I, a group of prose treatises dealing with the subject of Vedic sacrifice and ritual. The *Brahmanas* show the changes and development that took place from the early nature gods of the VEDAS to those gods more concerned with man.

Bran (bran), Ce, a brave giant, the brother of BRANWEN and MANAWYDDAN. He was the possessor of a cauldron with the power to bring the dead back to life, but without the restoration of the power of speech. Severely wounded in the battle against the Irish, Bran asked the other seven survivors to behead him. It was said that his head was buried in London with eyes toward France to ward off all invaders. Bran was sometimes called the Blessed and was also known as Bendigeid Vran.

Branwen (bran'-wen), Ce, the daughter of LLYR and sister of BRAN and MANAWYDDAN. Famous for her beauty, she attracted the king of Ireland, MATHOLWYCH. Their marriage temporarily united Britain and Ireland, until EVNISSYEN killed their son Gwern, bringing about war. Matholwych maltreated Branwen, resulting in Bran's attack on Ireland, in which he was killed.

Briareus (brahy-ehr'-ee-us), G, one of the three HECATONCHIRES. He was called Aegaeon by mortals.

Brigantia (bri-gan'-shi-u, -ti-), Ce, a goddess of northern England, the eponymous and protective goddess of the Brigantes, the largest tribe of Britain. She was a goddess of springs and streams and corresponds to the goddess BRIGIT of Ireland.

Brigit (brij'-it), Ce, the daughter of DAGDA and BOANN, goddess of civilization and culture. She was also the deity of the hearth and of fertility. Brigit has much in common with DANU and may be the same goddess or one who was confused with her. Brigit, an Irish goddess, was identified with the British goddess BRIGANTIA.

Briseis (brahy-see'-is), G, a maiden, wife of King Mynes of Lyrnessus, an ally of Troy, who was ACHILLES' prize of war. The wrath of Achilles against AGAMEMNON resulted when Agamemnon took Briseis after he had to give up his own captive, CHRYSEIS.

Brisingamen (bree'-sing-ah-men, bree-seen-gah'-), Sc, FREYA's splendid magic necklace, made by four DWARFS at the price of a night of sleeping with each of them. LOKI, tranformed into a flea, bit the sleeping goddess, then removed the necklace and took it to ODIN. Brisingamen was one of Freya's treasures and symbols.

Britomartis (brit-u-mahr'-tis), G, a Cretan goddess of fishermen and hunters. MINOS fell in love with Britomartis and pursued her for nine months, until she jumped into the sea. She was saved by falling into some fishing nets and became a goddess through the intervention of ARTEMIS, with whom she was identified.

Bronze Age, the, G, the third AGE OF MANKIND, the period when metals were introduced. The Bronze Age was an age of strength and warriors, when men destroyed each other by their might and violence.

Brunhild (broon'-hilt, -hild) or **Brunhilde** (broon-hil'-du), T, in the NIBELUNGENLIED, a queen of Iceland and the wife of GUNTHER who was won for him by SIEGFRIED through his prowess and strength. She got her revenge by ordering HAGEN to kill Siegfried. Brunhild is the counterpart of BRYNHILD in Scandinavian myths.

Brunhilde (broon-hil'-du), T. *See* BRUNHILD.

Brut or **Brute** (broot) or **Brutus** (broo'-tus), Ce, in Geoffrey of Monmouth's account of early history, a descendant of AENEAS who, after his conquest of Albion, became king of the island, then called Britain after his name.

Brute (broot), Ce. *See* BRUT.

Brutus (broo'-tus), Ce. *See* BRUT.

Brynhild (brin'-hild), Sc, one of the VALKYRIES. Brynhild became GUNNAR's wife after she was won for him by SIGURD, who awakened her from a spell of sleep cast over her. In jealous anger, Brynhild had Sigurd slain, then took her own life.

Buchis (byoo'-kis), E, a sacred bull that lived at Hermonthis in Upper Egypt. It was believed that MONT was often incarnated in Buchis.

Buddha (buhd'-u, boo'-du), I, the ninth AVATAR or incarnation of VISHNU, indicating an assimilation of the new religion into the Vedic as his teachings and the dogma of Buddhism became imbued with popular mythology. Thus, Buddhism had its beginning in Hinduism, with BRAHMA, Vishnu, and SHIVA forming the triad of major gods, the TRIMURTI, but regarded as ordinary men and simply mortal beings.

Bumba (buhm'-bu), Af, a major god of the Bantus, who set forth laws and government for men and who brought forth the planets and stars, then created several animal species, the origin of all others. Bumba taught KERIKERI the secret of making fire.

Bunene (buh-nay'-nay), A-B, the coachman of the sun-god SHAMASH.

Bun-Jil (bun'-jil), O, the one who molded the first two men from clay. His brother, or son, was believed to have found the first two women at the bottom of a lake. Bun-Jil was a sky hero who established tribal rituals and customs and taught the skills of farming and hunting to the people of Australia. He was known as Biral in northern Australia, Nurrundere in the vicinity of the Murray River, and Pun-Gel in the region of Victoria.

Bur (buhr), Sc. *See* BURI.

Buri (buhr'-ee) or **Bur** (buhr), Sc, the primeval god, grandfather of ODIN. AUDHUMBLA, YMIR's cow, exposed Buri by licking off the salty ice that covered him when he came into being.

Busiris (byoo-sahy'-ris), G, 1. a son of POSEIDON. As king of Egypt, Busiris sacrificed a stranger yearly to rid his country of famine. When he tried to make HERACLES, who was on his way to the Garden of the HESPERIDES, a victim, he was slain by the hero.

E, 2. the site of a religious sanctuary in the Nile Delta of Lower Egypt where the DJED was kept.

Butes (byoo'-teez), G, 1. a son of PANDION or POSEIDON and the brother of ERECHTHEUS, PROCNE, and PHILOMENA. Butes was a priest of ATHENA and of Poseidon.

2. one of the ARGONAUTS who jumped into the sea on hearing the SIRENS' song. APHRODITE rescued him and took him to western Sicily, where he became the father by her of ERYX.

37

3. a son of BOREAS who ravished the Lapith Coronis (*see* LAPITHAE). DIONYSUS punished him with madness.

Buto (byoo'-to), E, a town and marshy area in the Nile Delta and also the name of its patron goddess, who represented the area of Lower Egypt and the north. Buto was often depicted wearing a red crown on her head. She was sometimes shown as a snake, often a cobra, or as a woman with her head surmounted by a vulture and crown.

Byblos (bib'-lus), Ph, the Greek name for the Phoenician seaport city Gubla. Byblos was the seat of the cult of ASTARTE, who was known there by her title BAALAT, and was the earliest center of the cult of ADONIS.

Byelbog or **Bielbog** (beel'-bawg), Sl, a god of light, the day, and good fortune. He brought prosperity to his followers and watched over those who traveled in the woods. Byelbog was the "white god," whose opposite was CHERNOBOG.

Cacus (kay'-kus), R, a half-human three-headed GIANT who was the son of VULCAN. Cacus was slain by HERACLES after stealing some of the cattle of GERYON.

Cadmus (kad'-mus), G, a son of AGENOR and TELEPHASSA and the man credited with introducing the alphabet into Greece. While he was searching for his sister EUROPA, whom ZEUS had kidnaped, he was told by the Delphic oracle to follow a cow until she stopped to rest and then establish a city there. Cadmus was led to Boeotia, where he prepared to sacrifice the cow to ATHENA, but his comrades were slain by a dragon at the sacred well. Cadmus killed the dragon and sowed the teeth, according to Athena's advice. Armed men sprang up and struggled until all but five were killed. The surviving warriors helped Cadmus build Cadmea, later called THEBES, and became the ancestors of the noblest families of Thebes. Cadmus married HARMONIA and was the father of AGAVE, AUTONOË, INO, SEMELE, and POLYDORUS. When tragedy and misfortune later fell on their children, Cadmus and Harmonia fled to Illyria, where they were turned into serpents by Zeus and carried to ELYSIUM.

Cagn (kah'-gun), Af, the supreme deity of the Bushmen, creator of all living creatures, whose dwelling place was known only to the antelopes and who was kept informed by his messengers, the birds. Cagn was quite probably a hero, perhaps a tribal chief, around whom a cult was built up. He is identified and also confused with KAGGEN.

Calchas (kal'-kus), G, the soothsayer and prophet of the Greeks in the TROJAN WAR. Calchas prophesied that the Greeks could not sail from Aulis until IPHIGENIA was sacrificed, that the plague on the Greek army would last until CHRYSEIS was returned to her father, and that Troy would not fall until after a ten-year siege. Calchas died of grief when, as he himself had prophesied, he met a man (Mopsus) who was more skilled in soothsaying.

Calliope (ku-lahy'-u-pee), G, the MUSE of epic poetry and mother of ORPHEUS. Calliope is depicted holding a parchment roll or a tablet and stylus. The musical instrument is named for her.

Callirrhoë (ku-leer'-oh-ee), G, 1. the wife cf TROS and mother of GANYMEDE.

2. a daughter of ACHELOUS and wife of Alcmaeon. When she prayed her two small sons would grow to be men in one day to avenge their father's death, ZEUS granted her wish.

3. a young girl whose lover sacrificed himself in her place to end a plague brought upon Calydon by DIONYSUS. She then took her own life.

Callisto (ku-lis'-toh), G, the mother of ARCAS by ZEUS, who transformed her into the constellation Great Bear to protect her from HERA's anger.

Calydonian Boar, the (kal-i-doh'-nee-un), G, a wild boar sent by ARTEMIS to lay waste to the countryside when OENEUS, king of Calydon, neglected to sacrifice to her. Many Greek heroes, including THESEUS, JASON, CASTOR AND POLLUX, and PELEUS, joined in a hunt for the boar, and many met death. Finally, ATALANTA wounded the boar, and MELEAGER, son of Oeneus, killed it and gave the hide and head to Atalanta. Meleager slew his mother's brothers when they tried to rob Atalanta of the prize of victory.

Calypso (ku-lip'-soh), G, an island NYMPH, the daughter of OCEANUS or ATLAS. Calypso held ODYSSEUS on the island of OGYGIA and offered him immortality if he would marry her, but, in spite of comforts and luxury, Odysseus longed for his wife and home. HERMES, sent by ZEUS, persuaded Calypso to set Odysseus free, with a raft and supplies.

Camelot (kam'-u-lot), Ce, the name of King ARTHUR's capital and court. Numerous sites have been named as the location of Camelot, among them Exeter and Cadbury Castle near Glastonbury, where Arthur is said to have been buried.

Camilla (ku-mil'-u), R, the virgin warrior who had been dedicated to DIANA as an infant and brought up in the woods by shepherds. Camilla fought with her followers on the side of TURNUS against AENEAS until she was killed in battle by the Etruscan ARUNS.

Capys (kay'pis, kap'-is), G, 1. the father of ANCHISES and grand-father of AENEAS.

2. The Trojan who warned of the dangers the Trojan Horse would bring to the city. After the fall of Troy, Capys became the founder of Capua in Italy.

Cassandra (ku-san'-dru), G, the beautiful daughter of PRIAM and HECUBA. APOLLO gave Cassandra the gift of true prophecy, but when she rejected him, he provided that her utterances would never be believed. When Troy fell, AGAMEMNON rescued Cassandra, after AJAX the Lesser had dragged her from the asylum of ATHENA's altar and took her home to MYCENAE, where they both met death at the hands of AEGISTHUS and CLYTEMNESTRA. Among her predictions—none of which were heeded—were that PARIS would cause the fall of Troy; that the TROJAN WAR would end in disaster; that the Trojan Horse was a Greek trap; that Agamemnon would be murdered, and ORESTES would avenge his death.

Cassiopeia (kas-ee-u-pee'-u), G, the wife of CEPHEUS and mother of ANDROMEDA. When Cassiopeia claimed that the NEREIDS were less beautiful than she, POSEIDON sent a sea serpent to destroy her country, Ethiopia.

Castalia (kas-tay'-lee-u), G, a NYMPH, the daughter of ACHELOUS. Castalia was pursued by APOLLO, until she threw herself into a fountain on Mt. PARANASSUS. The spring was henceforth sacred to Apollo and to the MUSES.

Castor (kas'-tur) **and Pollux** (pahl'-uks), G & R, the twin sons of LEDA. In most accounts, Castor was the son of TYNDAREUS, father also of CLYTEMNESTRA, and thus mortal, while POLLUX and his sister HELEN were the children of ZEUS and immortal. Castor was known by the same name in both Greek and Roman mythology, but his twin was called Polydeuces by the Greeks and Pollux by the Romans. Together, they were called Dioscuri, "Sons of Zeus."

Castor and Pollux sailed with the ARGONAUTS. On that expedition, Pollux, a skillful boxer, met and killed AMYCUS in a boxing bout. They also took part in the CALYDONIAN BOAR hunt. In their struggle against IDAS and LYNCEUS, in which Idas killed Castor, Pollux slew Lynceus. Zeus then enabled Pollux to join his twin in death in spite of his immortality, and they became the constellation Gemini. According to another version, the twin brothers spent alternate days in the UNDERWORLD and on earth.

Castor and Pollux, Temple of, R, a Corinthian temple erected near the middle of the Roman Forum early in the fifth century B.C. be-

40

cause of the belief that CASTOR AND POLLUX aided the Romans in the Battle of Lake Regillus and watered their horses at the nearby spring after they brought the news of the Etruscan defeat to Rome. Three of the columns and a section of the entablature are still in place.

Catequil (kah-tee'-kwil), SA, the Incan god of lightning and thunder who was propitiated by the sacrifice of children.

Cecrops (see'-krops), G, a being, half man and half dragon, who was the earliest king of Attica. Cecrops established Athens, also called Cecropia, and brought civilization, laws, and religious worship to Attica. It was he who decided the contest between ATHENA and POSEIDON for the possession of Attica. Cecrops was the husband of AGRAULOS and the father of three daughters, Agraulos, HERSE, and PANDROSOS.

Cenote (say-noh'-tay), M, a deep, natural limestone well found in many parts of the Yucatán Peninsula and Central America. The cenotes formed receptacles for sacrificial offerings of objects made of gold, jade, copper, and other precious materials.

Centaurs, the (sen'-tawrz), G, fierce creatures, half man and half horse, who lived in Thessaly and were followers of DIONYSUS. The most famous Centaur was CHIRON, the teacher of ACHILLES and other heroes. When the Centaurs tried to carry off HIPPODAMIA, bride of PIRITHOUS, king of the LAPITHAE, a great contest developed, in which the Centaurs were defeated.

Centimani, the (sen-tu-may'-nahy), R, the counterparts of the HECATONCHIRES.

Cephalus (sef'-u-lus), G, the son of HERMES and HERSE, husband of PROCRIS. He was forced to flee from Attica when he killed Procris in the mistaken belief that she was a wild animal.

Cepheus (see'-fee-us), G, the king of Ethiopia who chained his daughter ANDROMEDA to a rock in order to rid his country of a sea monster that was devastating the land.

Cerberus (sur'-bur-us), G, the three-headed dog who guarded the entrance to HADES to keep the living from entering. AENEAS, ORPHEUS, and ODYSSEUS succeeded in getting past him when they visited there. Cerberus was overcome by HERACLES as his final labor and carried to MYCENAE, but he was later returned to the UNDERWORLD.

Ceres (seer'-eez), R, the goddess of agriculture and grain and the mother of PROSERPINA. She was the Roman counterpart of DEMETER.

The Romans held an annual harvest festival in honor of Ceres. The word "cereal" is derived from her name.

Chac (chahk), M, the god of rain, analogous to the Aztec god TLALOC. The Mayas sacrificed to Chac, propitiating him in the hope of obtaining the rain that was so essential to their crops. Chac is widely depicted in the Mayan temples, often wearing a mask.

Chalchihuitlicue (chahl-chee-wee′-tleek), Az, the goddess of the streams and springs, wife or sister of TLALOC. She ruled the sun of the fourth universe, which the flood destroyed, and was called upon as the protectress of marriage and infants.

Chang-o (jahng′-oh) or **Heng-o** (hung′-), Ch, the goddess who dwells in the moon. She had been the wife of the Excellent Archer, named Yi, who possessed the drink of immortality. So angered was he at discovering she had taken the drug in his absence that she took refuge in the moon. This is an ancient legend, still part of traditional belief.

Chaos (kay′-ahs), G, 1. a dark and limitless void, which was all that existed before the creation of the universe.
2. the deity representing the personification of the infinite space and shapeless matter that preceded the creation. Chaos was the husband of NYX and father of EREBUS.

Charites, the (kar′-i-teez), G, the goddesses of grace and beauty, who were companions of the MUSES and represented song, dance, and happiness. The Charites are more commonly known by their Roman name, Gratiae, GRACES. The Charites were daughters of ZEUS and EURYNOME, who lived on Mt. OLYMPUS. They were AGLAIA, goddess of brilliance and splendor, EUPHROSYNE, goddess of joy and mirth, and THALIA, goddess of bloom and good cheer. They always attended APHRODITE, who, according to some sources, was their mother by DIONYSUS.

Charon (kehr′-un), G, the son of EREBUS and NYX who ferried the souls of the dead across the STYX River into the UNDERWORLD, provided they had received proper burial in the upper world and had passage money in their mouths, put there at the time of burial. Those who had not met these conditions were forced to wander on the river shores one hundred years before being allowed to enter Charon's boat. Among those who managed to circumvent Charon were HERACLES, who frightened him, AENEAS, who bribed him, and ORPHEUS, who charmed him with his songs.

Charybdis (ku-rib′-dis), G, a monster who became a whirlpool at what is now the Strait of Messina on the coast of Sicily that, three

42

times daily, sucked in and poured forth water. Charybdis stood opposite SCYLLA, endangering all ships that passed near. It was said that ZEUS had turned Charybdis, who was a daughter of POSEIDON and GAEA, into a whirlpool because she stole HERACLES' oxen.

Chasca (chahs'-kah), SA, a goddess who brought forth flowers and protected maidens. Chasca was identified with the planet Venus and was worshiped as an attendant of the sun, INTI, by the Incas.

Chemmis (kem'-is), E, the place, sometimes referred to as a floating island, to which his mother, ISIS, took the infant HORUS to protect him against the anger of SET. It was there that the goddess BUTO found him when she came to the defense of the baby in aid of Isis.

Chernobog (cher'-noh-bawg) or **Czarnobog** (zahr'-), Sl, a god of darkness, the night, and evil, who brought bad luck and affliction. He was the "black god," in contrast to BYELBOG.

Ch'i (chy), Ch, the ether. In the beginning there was Ch'i, "ether," a single cell. This divided into YIN AND YANG as a result of the vibrations set in motion by TAO, a force, and thus creation began with the appearance of two opposite ethers, able to produce the elements, which went on to combine and form everything in the universe.

Chia (chee'-ah), SA, the lovely wife of BOCHICA. Partly in jealousy over Bochica's accomplishments and partly as a mischievous prank, Chia used her powers of magic to flood the land, a disaster that had few survivors. Bochica punished Chia by banishing her to a permanent home in the sky, where she was transformed into the moon.

Chichén Itzá (chee-chen' eet-sah', eet'-sah), M, the ruins of an ancient Mayan city on the Yucatán Peninsula established in about the sixth century. The extensive remains furnish a picture of Mayan civilization of the period from about A.D. 500 to 1100. Among the notable ruins are pyramid temples, heavily ornamented shrines, and sanctuaries adorned with relief sculpture. Outstanding are the Temple of the Warriors and the great pyramid with broad stairways rising on all four sides. The CENOTE, or sacred well, has yielded a valuable archaeological store of statuettes, carvings, and other artifacts of jade, gold, bone, and rubber.

Chicomecoatl (chee-koh-may-kaw-ah't'l), Az, the goddess of grain and agricultural abundance, whom the Aztecs associated with COATLICUE, because of her powers of fertility.

Chih-nii (chee'-nyee'), Ch, the Heavenly Spinster, a goddess, believed to be a daughter of TUNG WANG KUNG, the Jade Emperor, who wove fine garments for her father. This so pleased him that he gave her in marriage to the Heavenly Cowherd, a star in the constellation Aquila. Then, because the goddess had too little time for his robes, the Jade Emperor put the Milky Way between his daughter, the goddess of a star in the Lyre, and her husband. It was believed that, once a year, crossing by a bridge made by magpies, the couple was reunited.

Children of Don, the   (dawn), Ce, deities of Wales and Britain, similar to the Irish TUATHA DE DANANN. The two most important of the Children of Don were GWYDION, an all-powerful god, who was a beneficent teacher and controlled war and peace, and his sister-wife ARIANRHOD.

Children of Llyr, the   (hloorr), Ce, a generation of Welsh and British deities who followed the CHILDREN OF DON. LLYR became the father of MANAWYDDAN by DON's daughter Penardun and of BRAN and BRANWEN by Iweridd.

Chimaera (ki-meer'-u), G, a fire-breathing monster, part lion, part goat, and part serpent, slain by BELLEROPHON.

Chiminigagua (chi-mi-ni-gah'-gwu), SA, in Chibcha myth, the creator of all. When the world began, all was in darkness, because the light was closed up in him. He set the light free, creating blackbirds to carry it over the earth.

Chiron (kahy'-rahn), G, the most famous and greatest of the CENTAURS. The son of CRONUS and the NYMPH Philyra, he was famous for his knowledge of medicine and archery and was the teacher of ACHILLES, HERACLES, ASCLEPIUS, and JASON, among others. When Heracles wounded him unintentionally, Chiron gave up his immortality to PROMETHEUS and was made the constellation Sagittarius by ZEUS.

Chryseis (krahy-see'-is), G, the beautiful captive awarded to AGAMEMNON as a prize during the TROJAN WAR. When Agamemnon refused to return her to her father, Chryses, who was a priest of APOLLO, the god sent a pestilence that killed many in the Greek camp. It ended only when Agamemnon sent her back.

Chrysippus (krahy-sip'-us), G, the illegitimate son of PELOPS who was killed by his jealous stepmother, HIPPODAMIA, and her sons, ATREUS and THYESTES.

Cihuatcoatl (see-waht-kaw-ah't'l), Az, a mother deity, the goddess of childbirth. MIXCOATL was her son.

Cilix (sil'-iks), G, one of the sons of AGENOR and TELEPHASSA. After EUROPA was carried off by ZEUS, her brothers searched for her,

44

but without success. Cilix settled in southern Asia Minor, becoming the eponymous ancestor of the Cilicians.

Cinteotl (seen-tay-oh't'l), Az, the god of grain, the son of TLAZOLTEUTL. In ancient myth, Cinteotl was sometimes represented as a goddess, but had the same attributes.

Circe (sur'-see), G, an enchantress, daughter of HELIOS and PERSA. Circe lived on the island of Aeaea and transformed men into animals by sorcery. Because of her love for GLAUCUS, Circe poisoned SCYLLA and turned her into a monster. Circe turned ODYSSEUS' companions into swine, but Odysseus escaped with the aid of HERMES, and his men were restored by Circe, who became a mistress to Odysseus, by whom she had a son.

Clashing Rocks, the, G. *See* SYMPLEGADES.

Cleobis (klee'-u-bis), G, son of Cydippe, one of HERA's priestesses. Having no horses or oxen, Cleobis and his brother BITON yoked themselves to a chariot to take their mother to Argos to see the gold and ivory statue of Hera which had been fashioned by the great Polyclitus. When Cydippe prayed to Hera for a gift for her devoted sons, they sank smiling into death amid lightning and thunder.

Clio (klahy'-oh), G, the MUSE of history, generally depicted with a scroll.

Clotho (kloh'-thoh), G, one of the three MOERAE, or FATES. Clotho spun the thread of life and destiny.

Clymene (klim'-u-nee), G, 1. an OCEANID who became the mother of PHAËTHON and the HELIADES by HELIOS.

2. an ocean NYMPH who, in some accounts, was the mother of PROMETHEUS by IAPETUS.

3. a daughter of King Catreus of Crete and the sister of AËROPE. Clymene was sold to NAUPLIUS when her father accused her of plotting against him.

4. a daughter of King Minyas of Thessaly whose daughter Alcimede was, in some versions, JASON's mother.

Clytemnestra (klahy-tum-nes'-tru), G, the daughter of LEDA and TYNDAREUS of Sparta, wife of AGAMEMNON, sister of HELEN, CASTOR, and POLLUX, and mother of IPHIGENIA, ORESTES, and ELECTRA. With her lover, AEGISTHUS, she murdered Agamemnon and CASSANDRA, his captive, on his return from the TROJAN WAR. She was then murdered by Orestes in revenge for his father's death.

Clytië (klahy'-tee-ee), G, a NYMPH who was loved, and deserted, by APOLLO, and who sat staring at the sun pining for him until she turned into a heliotrope (from *helios,* a flower "turned toward the sun").

Cnossus or **Knossos** (nos'-us), G, the site of the palace of King MINOS, on the north coast of Crete near modern Heraklion, excavated in the early twentieth century by Sir Arthur Evans. It was built originally in about 2000 B.C. or earlier, although numerous changes and additions were made until the palace was finally destroyed in about 1400 B.C.

The palace was built on a low uneven hill and therefore had various levels and stairways. It covered five to six acres and accommodated about one thousand persons, while a city of fifty thousand grew up around it. A number of courtyards separated the various sections of the palace into areas concerned with the administration of the court, household matters, domestic quarters, or storage. Countless rooms were reached by connecting corridors and passages, stairways, and terraces.

From his excavation of the palace of Minos, Evans was able to recreate the culture and civilization of the Minoan Age. The fresco paintings, especially those found in the royal apartments and the throne room, are of exceptionally fine quality and are colorful as well as informative.

Coatlicue (koh-ah'-tleek), Az, the goddess of the earth, celebrated in spring grain festivals. Coatlicue was the mother of HUITZILOPOCHTLI, who was conceived when a crown of feathers fell upon her from the heavens. She was represented wearing a skirt of serpents.

Cocytus (koh-sahy'-tus), G, the dark river of wailing and lamentation in HADES, a branch of the STYX flowing into the ACHERON.

Concordia (kahn-kawr'-dee-u), R, the goddess of harmony and concord. She represented plenty, prosperity, and peace. A temple to this deity was erected in Rome, at the foot of the Capitoline Hill, in the fourth century B.C., and later reconstructed in marble. Only the foundations and a few fragments remain of the temple, which also commemorated the end of civil strife in Rome.

Consus (kahn'-sus), R, the god of grain and crops and a deity of the earth and harvest. The Consualia was a festival celebrated in honor of Consus each year after the sowing and again after the harvest.

Cora (kohr'-u) or **Core** or **Kore** (-ee), G, a name, meaning "Maiden," used to refer to PERSEPHONE.

Core (kohr'-ee), G. *See* CORA.

Corybantes, the (kawr-u-ban'-teez), G, 1. attendants and followers of CYBELE who accompanied her through the mountains with wild dances and loud music.

2. priests of the Phrygian Great Mother goddess, Cybele.

Coyote (kahy-oh'-tee, kahy'-oht), NA, the trickster, a demiurge found in the myths of a number of Indian tribes. Coyote, who had a multiplicity of names, ranging from Old Man to Wisagatcak, was a supernatural figure, a legendary trickster, but he was basically a culture hero and a creator. Although Coyote's creations were often the offhand result of his mischievous activities and pranks, or accidental in origin, they were natural phenomena and inventions that were beneficial or helpful to mankind.

Creon (kree'-ahn), G, 1. the brother of JOCASTA and king of THEBES, who sent OEDIPUS into exile. After Oedipus' sons, POLYNICES and ETEOCLES, killed each other in the expedition of the SEVEN AGAINST THEBES, Creon threw ANTIGONE into prison because she buried her brother Polynices against his royal command.

2. a king of Corinth and father of CREUSA. He was killed with his daughter, also known as GLAUCE, trying to save her from the poisoned robe sent her by MEDEA.

Creusa (kree-oo'-su), G, 1. the daughter of ERECHTHEUS and sister of ORITHYIA and PROCRIS. Creusa became the mother of ION by APOLLO and was later married to Xuthus.

2. the daughter of PRIAM and HECUBA. Creusa was the wife of AENEAS and mother of ASCANIUS. She was lost during the escape from burning Troy.

3. another name for GLAUCE.

Cronos (kroh'-nahs), Ph. *See* CRONUS.

Cronus (kroh'-nus) or **Cronos** or **Kronos** (-nahs), Ph, 1. in Damascius' version (fifth century A.D.) of the creation legend of the Phoenicians, Cronos, the representation of time, existed before anything came into being. The Greeks, attempting to explain the mythology of the Semitic peoples according to their own, gave Greek names to many of the deities of the Middle East.

2. G, a TITAN, the son of URANUS and GAEA. The Romans identified Cronus with SATURN. Cronus deposed Uranus and became the ruler of the world, married his own sister RHEA, and was the father of the Olympian deities DEMETER, HADES, HERA, HESTIA, POSEIDON, and ZEUS. Cronus swallowed each of his children at birth because of a prophecy that he would be deposed by one of them. Rhea substituted a stone for the infant Zeus and thus saved him. Later, Zeus gave

Cronus a potion and recovered the other five children. Zeus and the Olympians overthrew Cronus and the other Titans and gained supremacy of the world.

Cuchulainn or **Cu Chulainn** (koo-kul'-in, koo'-khoo-lin), Ce, a skilled and brave hero, the defender of Ulster. Cuchulainn won a contest against a monster and became the champion of Erin. The conditions were that the hero who cut off the monster's head would next lose his own. Cuchulainn, the only warrior to accept the challenge, killed the monster, which came back to life, but purposely missed when he came to cut off Cuchulainn's head. After many noble accomplishments, Cuchulainn met death according to a prophecy of a short life, and his wife Emer died of grief. According to one account, Cuchulainn was the son of LUG.

Cumaean Sibyl, the (kyoo-mee'-un sib'-il), R, a SIBYL who dwelt in a cave near the sacred grove of ARTEMIS and APOLLO at Cumae and was generally called the Cumaean Sibyl. She had the power of foretelling the future and wrote her prophecies on leaves. She had once had nine books of prophecy which she offered to Tarquin the Proud, king of Rome. When he refused them, she burned three of the books and offered him the remaining six at the same price. Again he refused, and again she burned three. Tarquin then bought the three that were left. These books, known as the Sibylline Books, were consulted by the Roman Senate. It was the Cumaean Sibyl who accompanied AENEAS to the UNDERWORLD on his visit to his father, ANCHISES.

Cupid (kyoo'-pid), R, the god of love, the son of VENUS and MERCURY or MARS, the counterpart of the Greek god EROS. He is depicted as a winged boy with bow and arrows. Cupid was the lover of PSYCHE, whose story was told by APULEIUS.

Cupra (koo'-pru), goddess of fertility, one of the earliest of the deities of the Etruscan pantheon. She hurled the thunderbolt as her weapon.

Curetes, the (kyoo-ree'-teez), G, demigods of Crete and priests of RHEA who, by the clash of their armor, drowned the cries of the infant ZEUS to protect him from CRONUS.

Cuycha (kwee'-chah), SA, the Incan deity of the rainbow.

Cuzco (koos'-koh), SA, 1. the center of the earth, sought by the legendary family migrating from the east in prehistoric times.

2. the name given to the part of the mountain town where MANCO CAPAC and his sister, MAMA OCCLO, settled and ruled. In time, a sacred city developed on the site and became the capital of the Inca Empire.

Cuzco, dating from about the eleventh century, and located in southern Peru at an elevation of over eleven thousand feet in the Andes, fell to Pizarro and his conquistadors in 1533. The extensive ruins of palaces and temples, including the great Temple of the Sun, are remarkable for their construction, all built of huge, closely fitting stone blocks.

Cybele (sib'-u-lee), a goddess of Phrygia and Lydia who was an earth- and nature-goddess, associated with mountains and wild animals. The CORYBANTES were her priests. Cybele was identified with RHEA by the Greeks and with OPS by the Romans. The worship of Cybele spread to Greece and later to Rome and her empire, but never gained strong popularity in that part of the ancient world. She was also called BERECYNTIA and the GREAT IDAEAN MOTHER.

Cyclopes, the (sahy-kloh'-peez), sing. Cyclops, (sahy'-klops), G, one-eyed giants, the children of URANUS and GAEA. The Cyclopes, each of whom had one eye in the middle of the forehead, lived in Sicily and helped HEPHAESTUS forge ZEUS's thunderbolts and the arms of the heroes beneath Mount Aetna. The most famous Cyclops was POLYPHEMUS, who was blinded by ODYSSEUS after eating some of his men. APOLLO slew the Cyclopes in anger, because his son ASCLEPIUS had been struck down with a thunderbolt of Zeus.

Cycnus (sik'-nus), G, the name (which means "the swan") of four different men: 1. the son of APOLLO and Hyrie. Cycnus hurled himself into Lake Canopus, when his companion of the hunt deserted him, and was then changed into a swan by Apollo.

2. the son of POSEIDON and Calyce, Cycnus was the king of Colonae, near Troy, and fought against the Greeks in the TROJAN WAR. When Cycnus was killed by ACHILLES, Poseidon changed him into a swan.

3. the son of ARES and PELOPIA or of Pyrene. Cycnus attacked strangers in the Vale of TEMPE and became a swan after he was slain by HERACLES.

4. the friend of PHAËTHON whom Apollo changed into a swan and placed among the stars after Phaëthon's death.

Cynthia (sin'-thee-u), G, another name for ARTEMIS, so called because she was born on Mt. Cynthus on the island of DELOS.

Cyrene (sahy-ree'-nee), G, a NYMPH of Thessaly and mother of ARISTAEUS by APOLLO.

Cytherea (sith-u-ree'-u), G, another name for APHRODITE, so called because she was said to have been born from the sea near the island of Cythera.

Cyzicus (siz'-i-kus), G, the king of the island of the same name who received the ARGONAUTS hospitably. When the Argonauts were blown back to the island and mistaken for pirates, Cyzicus was killed in the attack.

Czarnobog (zahr'-noh-bawg), Sl. *See* CHERNOBOG.

Dabog (dah'-bawg), Sl. *See* DAZHBOG.

Daedalus (ded'-u-lus), G, a skilled artisan who fled from Athens to Crete after killing his nephew TALOS because he threatened to surpass Daedalus in building and other arts. Daedalus was the architect of the Palace of MINOS and of the LABYRINTH, in which the MINOTAUR was restrained. He gave ARIADNE the clue to guide THESEUS from the Labyrinth by a thread. Imprisoned by Minos because of his advice to Ariadne, Daedalus fashioned wings of feathers and wax for himself and his son ICARUS and escaped to Sicily, although Icarus was lost in flight.

Dagan (dah'-gahn), A-B, a god of the earth and agriculture, analogous to the Phoenician god DAGON.

Daganoweda (dah-gah-noh-wee'-dah), NA, the name given to HIAWATHA by the Iroquois. He was revered as a hero of divine nature and given the stature of a demigod.

Dagda (dahg'-du, dahg'-thu), Ce, the good god of earth and fertility, who controlled life and death with his great club. He was the chief of the Irish deities, the husband of BOANN, and father of ANGUS, BODB, BRIGIT, MIDER, and OGMA. Dagda was the victorious leader in the battle with the Fomorians, the dynasty of ancient Ireland that preceded the TUATHA DE DANANN. His cauldron had magic power, and his versatile skills made him an able craftsman as well as a staunch warrior.

Dagon (day'-gahn), Ph, an earth-god and deity of agriculture. He had the title BAAL and was called the father of HADAD. Dagon was also considered to be a god of the sea in later mythology.

Daikoku (dahy'-koh-kuh), J, the god of wealth and one of the gods of luck. He was the father of the god of labor, EBISU. Daikoku is often depicted with a magic hammer or mallet that brings man good fortune and happiness.

Daksha (duk'-shu), I, the son of BRAHMA, whose thumb gave birth to him. Daksha was an early Vedic god who was later one of the ADITYAS. He was the father of SATI, an aspect of SHIVA's wife. After a long feud, Daksha was killed by the god in anger.

Damkina (dahm-kee'-nu), A-B. *See* NINKI.

50

Dana (thah′-nu, dah′-nu), Ce. *See* DANU.

Danaë (dan′-u-ee), G, the daughter of ACRISIUS, king of Argos, and mother of PERSEUS. When Acrisius imprisoned Danaë to avert the prophecy that her son would kill him, ZEUS came to her as a shower of gold, and she gave birth to Perseus by the ruler of the gods. Acrisius cast Danaë and her child into the sea in a chest, but they were carried to the island of Seriphus, where they were rescued by DICTYS. Perseus later rescued Danaë from King POLYDECTES, and they returned to Greece. The prophecy was then fulfilled when Perseus killed Acrisius by accident. "Danaë and the Shower of Gold" is a famous painting by Titian.

Danaïdes (du-nay′-u-deez), G. *See* DANAÏDS.

Danaïds, the (du-nay′-idz), or **Danaïdes** (-u-deez), G, the fifty daughters of DANAUS who were worshiped in Argos as NYMPHS of springs and rivers. When they were forced to marry the fifty sons of AEGYPTUS, all but one, HYPERMNESTRA, slew their husbands on the wedding night and were condemned to carry water in leaking jars eternally in the UNDERWORLD.

Danaus (dan′-ee-us), G, the son of BELUS, twin of AEGYPTUS, and father of the DANAÏDS. After fleeing Egypt he settled in Argos. The people of Argos were called Danaans or Danai, and by the time of the TROJAN WAR the name Danai referred to all the Greeks.

Danu (thah′-noo) or **Dana** (-nu, dah′-nu), Ce, the mother of the TUATHA DE DANANN, the People of Danu, the deities of the Irish pantheon. Danu represented the earth, mother of all. The Welsh identified her with DON.

Daphne (daf′-nee), G, a NYMPH, the virgin daughter of PENEUS, a river-god of Thessaly. When Daphne begged to escape APOLLO's love, she was transformed by her father into a laurel tree, which then became sacred to Apollo.

Daphnis (daf′-nis), G, the son of HERMES by a NYMPH. Raised and educated by PAN as a shepherd in Sicily, he was credited with the invention of pastoral poetry. An avid hunter, he starved himself to death after his favorite dogs were killed.

Dardanus (dahr′-du-nus), G, the son of the PLEIAD ELECTRA and ZEUS. Dardanus, who went to Phrygia from his native ARCADIA, established the city of Dardania on Mount IDA and became the founder of the Trojan race.

Dazhbog (dahzh′-bawg) or **Dabog** (dah′-), Sl, a god of fire, deity of the hearth and, thus, of the home, who held an important place in pagan Russian worship. The son of the sky-god SVAROG, Dazhbog was the sun-god, who traversed the vault of heaven in a gleaming chariot drawn by fiery steeds. Just as he dispersed the cold and gloom of winter and brought the pleasures and delights of summer, so he took vengeance on the evildoers, while he gave recompense to the deserving. He was also called Svarozhich, although there is not enough evidence to say with certainty that this was not the name of a different individual god. A statue to Dazhbog was erected in Kiev.

Deianira (dee-yu-nahy'-ru), G, the daughter of OENEUS of Calydon and ALTHAEA. Deianira became the second wife of HERACLES, whom she unintentionally killed by giving him a cloak soaked with the blood of NESSUS.

Deïphobus (dee-if'-u-bus), G, one of the fifty sons of PRIAM and HECUBA and a hero of the TROJAN WAR. Deïphobus wed HELEN after the death of PARIS and was killed by MENELAUS at the end of the war.

Delos (dee'-lahs), G, a tiny island in the Aegean Sea where LETO gave birth to APOLLO and ARTEMIS. On Delos there was a sanctuary of Apollo, who was often referred to as Delian Apollo.

Delphi (del'-fahy), G, the most important shrine of the Greek world. Delphi, situated high on the slopes of Mt. PARNASSUS, was considered by the Greeks to be the center of the earth, marked by the marble OMPHALOS. Delphi became sacred to APOLLO after his victory over PYTHON, the serpent that lived in the mountain caves of that area. It was the seat of the famous Delphic oracle, consulted by Greeks and foreigners alike, who came to hear the god Apollo speak his prophecies through the priestess PYTHIA.

Worshipers purified themselves at the Castalian Spring, a spring sacred to Apollo and the MUSES, before entering the hallowed precinct. On the lower slope were the Palaestra, Gymnasium, and Bath, all connected with the training of the athletes. On the upper slope was the Sacred Way, bordered by statues, monuments, numerous votive offerings, and Treasuries. The Sacred Way led up to the Doric Temple of Apollo. Above the temple were the theater, where dramatic contests were held, and the stadium, which seated seven thousand. At the end of the nineteenth century, the town that had grown up on the site was moved to a new location about a mile away, and extensive excavation followed.

Demeter (di-mee'-tur), G, the daughter of CRONUS and RHEA and goddess of the grain, agriculture, and fertility. Her Roman counterpart was CERES. Demeter searched for nine days until she learned

52

from HELIOS that her daughter PERSEPHONE had been carried off by HADES. Demeter then descended from OLYMPUS to earth and wandered in the guise of an old woman to Eleusis, where she cared for Demophoön, the infant son of the king. Demeter's identity was revealed to the child's mother, who saw Demeter placing Demophoön in the fire to make him immortal. As a result, a temple was erected to Demeter at Eleusis. Demeter, in her grief for Persephone, caused all vegetation to cease. At length, Hades promised Persephone she could spends two thirds of each year on earth with her mother, who bestowed the blessings of abundant grain upon the world in her gratitude.

Dendera (den'-dur-u), E, a town in Upper Egypt ruled over by the goddess HATHOR and sacred to her. A large temple was built at Dendera in the time of the Ptolemies as a sanctuary of Hathor.

Deucalion (doo-kay'-lee-un), G, the son of PROMETHEUS, who built a wooden chest and, with his wife PYRRHA, was carried after nine days to Mt. PARNASSUS, the only spot left dry by the Deluge. When the oracle told them to veil their heads and cast the bones of their mother in back of them, Deucalion and Pyrrha interpreted this to mean the stones of Mother Earth. The stones they threw brought forth a new and sturdy race. Those that Deucalion threw became men; those of Pyrrha, women. Deucalion was the father of HELLEN.

Devaki (day'-vu-kee), I, the mother of KRISHNA.

Devas, the (day'-vuz), Pe, 1. in the AVESTA, malevolent spirits, genii of evil, created as counterparts of the AMESHA SPENTAS by ANGRA MAINYU, who ruled over them.

I, 2. in the VEDAS, deities who were divine spirits of good.

Devi (day'-vee), I, 1. a name for PARVATI, consort of SHIVA.

2. a mother goddess, the representation of different aspects of Shiva's wife under various names according to her forms, among them DURGA, KALI, and SATI.

Diana (dahy-an'-u), R, an ancient Italian deity, goddess of the moon and the hunt, identified with the Greek goddess ARTEMIS.

Dicte (dik'-tee), G, a grotto in the mountains of eastern Crete where ZEUS was said to have been born.

Dictynna (dik-tin'-u), G, an ancient goddess of sailors and hunters who was identified with BRITOMARTIS and with ARTEMIS.

Dictys (dik'-tis), G, a fisherman, the brother of POLYDECTES. Dictys found DANAË and her son PERSEUS, when they were carried on the sea to the island of Seriphus, where Polydectes was king.

53

Dido (dahy'-doh), R, the daughter of the Phoenician king BELUS. Dido fled from Tyre when her brother PYGMALION slew her husband SYCHAEUS, and became the founder and queen of Carthage. She committed suicide on a funeral pyre when AENEAS, whom she loved, sailed away.

Dike (dahy'-kee), G, one of the three HORAE, daughters of ZEUS and THEMIS. Dike personified justice and law.

Diodorus Siculus (dahy-oh-dohr'-us sik'-yu-lus), a Greek historian of the late first century B.C. who wrote a history of the known world in forty books. His work contains accounts of legends, myths, and religious beliefs, including a description of the Egyptians' beliefs regarding OSIRIS, and explanatory material.

Diomedes (dahy-u-mee'-deez), G, 1. the son of ARES and the nymph CYRENE. Diomedes was the king of the Bistones, who fed his horses on strangers. It was one of the LABORS OF HERACLES to take Diomedes' mares from Thrace to Mycenae, which he did by overcoming Diomedes and feeding him to the mares.

2. the son of TYDEUS and Deipyle and husband of Aegiale. Diomedes took part in the sack of Thebes and was one of the outstanding Greek warriors in the TROJAN WAR. Diomedes wounded not only AENEAS but APHRODITE and Ares as well and helped ODYSSEUS steal the PALLADIUM. Because Aphrodite, in revenge, made Aegiale unfaithful, Diomedes went to live in Italy, where he married the daughter of King Daunus.

Dione (dahy-oh'-nee), G, the consort of ZEUS in early mythology before she was replaced by HERA. Dione was a TITANESS, daughter of OCEANUS and TETHYS, and was sometimes, as in the ILIAD, said to be the mother of APHRODITE.

Dionysia, the (dahy-u-nish'-ee-u), G, festivals held in honor of DIONYSUS. They were celebrated with revelry, orgies, and dramatic performances. The most famous in the series, the Greater Dionysia observed at Athens in the spring, was a festival marked by the works of the best of the Greek dramatic poets and musicians.

Dionysus (dahy-u-nahy'-sus), G, the son of ZEUS and SEMELE. As a god of vegetation, fertility, and wine, Dionysus was widely worshiped, often with frenzied and ecstatic ceremonies. He was originally worshiped in Thrace, and, according to legend, was born near Thebes and brought up in Thrace by INO and the NYMPHS, who later became the HYADES. His teacher and mentor was SILENUS. Dionysus brought civilization and the cultivation of the vine to many countries, and the MAENADS were his followers. While bound for the island of NAXOS, he was mistaken for a wealthy prince and held for ransom. His bonds fell away, and vines and ivy appeared everywhere on the ship, whereupon the frightened sailors jumped into the sea and became dolphins. He found ARIADNE on Naxos, where THESEUS had abandoned her, and married her. He then descended to the UNDERWORLD to find Semele and placed her on OLYMPUS with the gods. The DIONYSIA were festivals celebrated in honor of Dionysus.

Dioscuri, the (dahy-u-skyuhr'-ahy), G. *See* CASTOR AND POLLUX.

Dirae (dahy'-ree), R. *See* FURIES.

Dis (dis), R, 1. a deity of the UNDERWORLD, identified with the Greek god PLUTO and with ORCUS.
   2. a name of the underworld.

Discordia (dis-kawr'-dee-u), R, the goddess of discord or strife, who preceded the chariot of MARS. She was the Roman counterpart of ERIS.

Djed, the (jed), E, a shape in which OSIRIS sometimes appeared, especially as a warrior leader. The Djed, a sacred object or fetish, was at first the trunk of an evergreen tree and was later stylized in the form of a column topped by four capitals.

Djehuti (je-hoo'-tee) or **Zehuti** (ze-), E, a name by which the god THOTH was known in early times. The name derives from Djehut, a former province of Lower Egypt.

Dodona (du-doh'-nu), G, the oldest of the principal sanctuaries and oracles of ZEUS, located in Epirus, in northwestern Greece. The oracle uttered prophecies through the sound of rustling oak leaves.

Domovoi (daw-mu-voi'), Sl. *See* DOMOVOY.

Domovoy or **Domovoi** (daw-mu-voi'), Sl, generally, an apelike creature, with many human characteristics and feelings, who watched over the home and guarded its inhabitants by warning them against threatened misfortunes or trouble. In return for being a protective spirit or genius of the house, he demanded propitiation and kind treatment, or the household would lose his favor until he received proper redress.

   Sometimes Domovoy took the shape of an animal, or an everyday farm object familiar to the peasant's life, or of a human being.

Don (dawn), Ce, the goddess of fertility, who was associated in Wales and Britain with the Irish earth mother DANU. Don was the mother of GWYDION and ARIANRHOD and the other CHILDREN OF DON, as related in the fourth branch of the MABINOGION.

55

Donar (doh'-nahr), T, the thunder-god of the Teutonic peoples, corresponding to the Scandinavian god THOR. The German *Donnerstag*, Thursday, gets its name from Donar.

Doris (dohr'-is), G, one of the OCEANIDS, wife of NEREUS, and mother of the fifty NEREIDS.

Dorus (dohr'-us), G, the son of HELLEN. He was said to be the ancestor of the Dorians, who settled in southern Greece and Asia Minor.

Dragons, the, Ch, creatures said to represent the yang force (see YIN AND YANG). They were associated with the waters of lakes, rivers, and the sea. Four brothers were lords of the seas surrounding the earth. Each had his palace, court, and attendants. A dragon called Enlightener of the Darkness had control over light and darkness by the opening and closing of his eyes. His breath brought wind and rain, cold and fire.

Draupnir (droup'-nir), Sc, a magic ring made by the DWARFS for ODIN and guarded by ANDVARI. When BALDER died, Odin placed his ring on the funeral pyre.

Druids, the (droo'-idz), Ce, the priests and teachers who were responsible for the religious ceremonies and ritual of the Celts. The Druids venerated nature, used magic and the study of the stars in their teaching, and often held their religious rites in oak groves.

Dryades, the (drahy'-u-deez), or **Dryads** (-uds), G, the NYMPHS of the woods and trees. A dryad often took the shape of a huntress or shepherdess. The oak trees were sacred to the dryades, who were also called HAMADRYADS.

Dryads (drahy'-uds), G. *See* DRYADES.

Dumuzi (doo'-muh-zee), A-B, a Sumerian god of crops and shepherds, later identified with TAMMUZ.

Dup Shimati, the (doop shi-mah'-tee), A-B, the name of the TABLETS OF FATE.

Durga (duhr'-gah), I, a name of PARVATI, the wife of SHIVA, representing the shape she assumed to battle a monstrous demon that threatened the gods. In a fierce struggle and with a weapon in each of her ten arms, she overpowered and killed the demon. Hence, Durga is a manifestation of Parvati as an often malevolent goddess of destruction.

Dwarfs, the, Sc & T, small bearded men who lived in the hills and below the earth. They were skilled artisans and worked mainly with metals and jewels. It was they who made ODIN's magic sword, FREYA's necklace, FREY's ship, and numerous other treasures of the gods.

Dyaus (dyous) or **Dyaus-pitar** (-pit'-ur), I, the early Aryan sky-god who, by the time of the VEDAS, had taken a position of less importance. Dyaus was the husband of the earth-goddess PRITHIVI and the father of INDRA.

Dyaus-pitar (dyous-pit'-ur), I. *See* DYAUS.

Ea (ay'-ah), A-B, the Akkadian god of rivers, springs, and all water. Ea, the son of ANSHAR and KISHAR, was called ENKI by the Sumerians. He was the patron deity of smiths and carpenters. As god of wisdom, which sprang from APSU, Ea had powers of prophecy and oracular divination.

Ea captured Apsu when the latter formed a plan to eliminate the deities whom he and TIAMAT had created and their offspring. When ISHTAR was held prisoner in the underworld, it was Ea's power of magic that brought her release through the intervention of ASUSHU-NAMIR.

Ea's consort was called NINKI or Damkina. The city of ERIDU, his earthly dwelling place, was sacred to him. Ea was often represented holding a vase, or with waves on his shoulders. He was sometimes depicted with the body of a goat and the tail of a fish.

Eabani (ay-ah-bah'-nee), A-B. *See* ENKIDU.

Eanna (ee-ahn'-nah), A-B, the dwelling place of ANU on earth.

Easter Island, O, the site of numerous remains of a prehistoric Polynesian culture. The ruins include massive stone walls, similar to those of MYCENAE, and over six hundred stone statues of huge size. These statues, the largest about thirty-five feet tall, were carved from a single block of rock, generally basalt or tuff. The early myths of the island speak of the rivalry between the "small Ears" and the "Big Ears." The latter, depicted in the colossal images of the island, are as yet unexplained, since the petroglyphics found on the island have not been deciphered. The Polynesian name of the island is Rapa Nui.

Ebisu (e'-be-suh), J, the son of DAIKOKU. He is the god of labor and one of the gods of luck and is often depicted with a fish and rod.

Echidna (i-kid'-nu), G, the half-woman and half-serpent daughter of TARTARUS and GAEA, and mother of CERBERUS, the HYDRA of Lerna, and the NEMEAN LION. She was slain by the hundred-eyed monster ARGUS.

Echo (ek'-oh), G, a daughter of GAEA, whom HERA made mute except for the repetition of sounds, because she had occupied Hera with talk to cover up ZEUS's affairs with the NYMPHS. Echo fell in love with NARCISSUS, but he spurned her, and she hid in the woods and dissolved with grief, leaving only her voice.

Eddas, the (ed'-us), Sc, two Icelandic accounts of Scandinavian and Teutonic mythology, one in poetry and the other in prose, both dating from the Middle Ages. 1. The *Elder,* or *Poetic, Edda* consists of a group of poems on topics relating to religion and myth, compiled in Iceland in the late eleventh or early twelfth century in a work of unknown authorship.

2. the *Younger,* or *Prose, Edda* is a fine prose account written largely by Snorri Sturluson, an Icelandic historian, in the early thirteenth century. It is a collection of the known myths and legends of his time and material on other subjects, such as poetry, and is our main source of Scandinavian mythology.

Edfu (ed'-foo), E, the location of a temple in Upper Egypt, sacred to the god HORUS as well as to the goddess HATHOR. The temple contains bas-reliefs showing Horus as the falcon-headed diety BEHDETY going into battle with the troops of RA-HORAKTE against SET.

Edimmu, the (ay'-du-moo), A-B, the evil genii. These UTUKKU were the souls of unburied dead or those dead who had not received proper burial and funeral rites. They were a ceaseless thorn of revenge on the living, difficult to appease.

Eileithyia (ahy-lahy-thahy'-yu), G. *See* ILITHYIA.

Ekchuah (ek-choo'-ah), M, the god of travelers and of planters.

El (el, ayl), Ph, the chief god in the hierarchy of the Phoenician pantheon. He was a deity of the rivers and streams and their gift of fertility, and his dwelling place was at the source of the rivers. The name El means god in the sense of the supreme deity. El, the father of gods and men, is depicted in the RAS SHAMRA tablets as an old bearded man and is characterized as kindly but strong, powerful, and wise.

Elaine (i-layn'), Ce, the name of several characters in Arthurian literature. The most important are 1. the daughter of King Pelles and mother of GALAHAD.

2. Elaine, called the Fair, the Lily Maid of Astolat, who loved LANCELOT, but he remained true to his love for GUINEVERE.

Electra (i-lek'-tru), G, 1. the daughter of AGAMEMNON and CLYTEMNESTRA. To avenge the death of their father, Electra and her brother ORESTES slew Clytemnestra and her lover AEGISTHUS, Agamemnon's murderers. The term "Electra Complex" connotes a

58

daughter's unconscious attachment toward her father and hostility toward her mother.

2. one of the PLEIADES and the mother of DARDANUS by ZEUS. Electra was said to have withdrawn from the other Pleiades so that she could not see the destruction of Troy, which Dardanus had founded, and she was therefore not readily visible in the sky.

3. the mother of IRIS and the HARPIES.

Eleusinia, the (el-yuh-sin'-ee-u), G. *See* ELEUSINIAN MYSTERIES.

Eleusinian Mysteries, the (el-yuh-sin'-ee-un), or **Eleusinia, the** (-u), G, religious ceremonies and festivals established at Eleusis in Attica in honor of DEMETER and her gifts to mankind. The Eleusinian Mysteries came to be the most outstanding of their kind and included initiates from the entire Greek world and later from the Roman. They were shrouded in secrecy, but the rites dealt, in general, with the death and rebirth of nature as told by the story of Demeter and PERSEPHONE and its symbolic connection with the birth, death, and afterlife of man. They continued to be celebrated until Emperor Theodosius abolished them in the late fourth century.

Elfheim (elf'-haym), Sc. *See* ALFHEIM.

Elves, the, Sc, the supernatural, small creatures of ponds and woods, who, according to the EDDAS, lived in ALFHEIM. The white elves, or elves of light, were lovely, beneficent beings who loved music and dancing. The black elves were ugly and maleficent. They were skilled artisans, but lived underground, coming out only at night to carry on their mischief in order to avoid the sun, which turned them to stone.

Elysian Fields (i-lizh'-un), G. See ELYSIUM.

Elysium (i-lizh'-ee-um) or **Elysian Fields** (-un), G, the place where the good people, especially heroes, lived an eternal life after their life on earth in beautiful and blissful fields on the ISLES OF THE BLESSED, located on the shores of OCEANUS at the western end of the earth. Later accounts placed Elysium in the UNDERWORLD.

Embla (em'-blah), Sc, the first woman, created by the gods from a vine of elm tree. Embla was the mother of the race of humans, and her dwelling place was MIDGARD.

Emma-O (em'-u-oh'), J, a Buddhist god, the ruler of YOMI and judge of the dead. The deeds of each sinner are weighed before judgment is handed down, condemning him to an appropriate section of hell. Emma-O is depicted with a menacing expression and dressed in the robes of a judge.

Enceladus (en-sel'-u-dus), G, a GIANT with one hundred arms, son of TARTARUS and GAEA. ATHENA buried Enceladus beneath Mt. Aetna

59

because of his part in the war of the giants against the gods. When Enceladus stirred, Sicily was rocked by tremors; thus, the myth was used by the ancients to explain earthquakes and volcanic eruptions.

Endymion (en-dim'-ee-un), G, a king of Elis to whom SELENE bore fifty daughters, representing the fifty lunar cycles between the Olympic Games. According to another version, Endymion was a handsome shepherd, loved by Selene, who visited him nightly as he lay in eternal sleep on Mt. Latmus. The myth forms the basis of "Endymion," the allegorical poem by Keats.

Enigohatgea (ee-ni-gaw-aht'-gee-u), NA. *See* ENIGORIO AND ENIGOHATGEA.

Enigorio (ee-ni-gawr'-ee-oh) **and Enigohatgea** (-gaw-aht'-gee-u), NA, twin brothers who represented the principle of dualism among the Iroquois. Enigorio was kindly, constructive, and a creator who gave mankind those things necessary to sustain life; Enigohatgea, the opposing force, was evil and destructive. They correspond to the twin brothers IOSKEHA AND TAWISCARA in the myths of the Hurons.

Enki (en'-kee), A-B, the Sumerian counterpart of the Akkadian god EA. The attribute of Enki, a name meaning "Lord of the earth," was wisdom. Enki instructed men in husbandry and related skills.

Enkidu (en'-kee-doo), A-B, one who, according to the GILGAMESH EPIC, was shaped from mud by ARURU, in the likeness of the god ANU, to be superior to GILGAMESH and thus overcome him. He lived a wild life with the animals and befriended them, until the people were afraid to go near them. Enkidu was alienated from his animal friends by his passion for a courtesan, who utterly captivated him and took him to URUK, where Gilgamesh was king. After encountering each other in a wrestling match, Enkidu and Gilgamesh became good friends.

Enlil (en'-lil), A-B, the Sumerian god of the air and the power of natural forces. He was the son of ANU. In early mythology, Enlil was a primitive deity of wind and storm and was worshiped as such at Nippur, the sacred city of Sumer. Later, he became king and lord of the earth, with control over the destiny of mankind. Human kings received their power from Enlil.

Enlil's consort was NINLIL, and he was the father of SIN and NINURTA. When Enlil was adopted by the Babylonians, they called him BEL.

Ennead, the (en'-ee-ahd), E, the deities of HELIOPOLIS, consisting of RA and the eight gods and goddesses descended from him, namely, SHU and TEFNUT, GEB and NUT, OSIRIS, ISIS, SET, and NEPHTHYS. Other deities, including HORUS and KHENTI AMENTI, were sometimes considered to be among the company of gods of the divine Ennead.

Enuma Elish (ee-noo'-mah ee'-lish), A-B, the Babylonian creation legend, named for its opening words, "When on high." One version dates from about 2000 B.C., but the principal version is recorded in a cuneiform text of the seventh century B.C. This consists of seven tablets, describing APSU and TIAMET, the primordial cosmic forces, and the birth of the deities, and recounting the story of the creation of the universe from the primeval waters of chaos.

Eos (ee'-ahs), G, the goddess of dawn, daughter of HYPERION and THEIA. She was the mother of the stars and the WINDS and bore MEMNON to TITHONUS and PHAËTHON to CEPHALUS. The Roman goddess AURORA was identified with Eos.

Epaphus (ep'-u-fus), G, a son of ZEUS and IO who was born on the Nile and became king of Egypt.

Epimetheus (ep-u-mee'-thee-us), G, the son of IAPETUS and CLYMENE, brother of ATLAS and PROMETHEUS, and husband of PANDORA. Epimetheus was impulsive, and his chief characteristic is symbolized by the meaning of his name, "afterthought." When he and Prometheus were entrusted with the creation of man and other animals, he endowed the wild animals with such qualities that man would not have been superior except for Prometheus' assistance. Although Prometheus warned him never to accept a gift from ZEUS, he married Pandora. Their daughter was PYRRHA.

Erato (er'-u-toh), G, the MUSE of love poetry, often depicted holding a small lyre.

Erebus (er'-u-bus), G, 1. the darkness, born of CHAOS, and brother of NYX, by whom he was the father of HEMERA.

2. the part of the UNDERWORLD first reached by the souls of the dead.

Erech (ee'-rek, er'-ek), A-B, the biblical name of URUK.

Erechtheum, the (i-rek'-thee-um), G, a temple on the north side of the ACROPOLIS, which gets its name from ERECHTHEUS, the legendary early king of Athens, who was later worshiped there with ATHENA and POSEIDON. The present temple was built in the fifth century B.C. after the partial destruction of Athens during the Persian Wars. The south porch is the famed Porch of the Maidens with its architrave supported by six marble caryatids, one of which is now in the British Museum, replaced by a cast copy of the original.

Erechtheus (i-rek'-thee-us), G, a son of PANDION, the twin brother of BUTES and brother also of PHILOMELA and PROCNE. Erechtheus was a legendary king of Athens and the father of PROCRIS.

Ereshkigal (ay-resh'-kee-gahl), A-B, the goddess and queen of the underworld, over which she ruled alone until NERGAL entered her domain and she became his wife. When ISHTAR went to Ereshkigal's kingdom in search of TAMMUZ, she was held prisoner at the order of her sister, until EA gained her release through the intervention of ASUSHU-NAMIR, whom he had created for the task.

Erichthonius (er-ik-thoh'-nee-us), G, 1. the son of HEPHAESTUS and GAEA, who was cared for as an infant by ATHENA. Erichthonius was the legendary king of Athens and instituted the worship of Athena there. Erichthonius was identified and confused with ERECHTHEUS.

2. a son of DARDANUS and father of TROS.

Eridu (ay'-ri-doo), A-B, the sacred city of the Babylonians, located in the south near the Euphrates River, that was the center of the cult of EA.

Erinyes, the (i-rin'-ee-eez), G, the goddesses of vengeance and justice, who meted out fair punishments for trespasses against the social order in order to benefit society. They were sometimes called EUMENIDES. The Erinyes were adopted by the Romans, who called them FURIES. The Erinyes were born of the blood of URANUS and were three in number, according to most accounts: ALECTO, Megaera, and TISIPHONE. They attended PERSEPHONE and were indestructible as long as sin remained on earth.

Eris (er'-is), G, goddess of discord and strife. Because she was the only deity excluded from the marriage of PELEUS and THETIS, Eris threw a golden apple, marked "For the Fairest," into the wedding banquet and brought about the JUDGMENT OF PARIS, which led to the TROJAN WAR. The apple is known as the Apple of Discord.

Eros (er'-ahs), G, the god of love. The Roman counterpart of Eros was CUPID. According to HESIOD, Eros was born with Heaven and Earth out of CHAOS, but later accounts made him the son and constant companion of APHRODITE. Eros was represented as a boy or youth who created love in the hearts of men and gods with his bow and arrow. He was the husband of PSYCHE.

Erymanthus, Mt. (er-i-man'-thus), G, a mountain in ARCADIA, the haunt of the wild boar which HERACLES had to capture and take to EURYSTHEUS as one of his labors. *See also* LABORS OF HERACLES.

Erysichthon (er-i-sik'-thahn), G, a man who lived in Thessaly and was plagued with endless hunger after he had cut down an oak tree sacred to DEMETER. In the end, Erysichthon consumed his own body.

Erytheïs (er-u-thee'-is), G, one of the HESPERIDES. When the ARGONAUTS came, she transformed herself into an elm tree.

Eryx (er'-iks), G, a son of APHRODITE and BUTES or POSEIDON. King of Eryx in Sicily, he was a powerful boxer, who challenged all strangers, killing those he defeated. He was killed in a match with HERACLES.

Esagil (ee'-su-gil), A-B, the sanctuary of MARDUK in Babylon.

Eshmun (esh'-mun, esh-moon'), Ph, a deity of health and healing who was worshiped especially at Sidon, where he was the patron deity. The Greeks compared Eshmun to ASCLEPIUS.

Estanatlehi (es-tan-aht'-lu-hee), NA, a highly revered deity of the Navahos, the creator of the first human couple. An earth mother, Estanatlehi was renewed and refreshed each spring as a young girl. She brought knowledge and tribal lore and rites to her people and bore twin sons, NAGENATZANI AND THOBADESTCHIN.

Etana (ay-tah'-nah), A-B, the one who was chosen by the gods to be the first ruler of mankind on earth and who was later deified. Carried by an eagle to ANU's kingdom in the sky, in answer to his prayers to SHAMASH for a son and heir, Etana became dizzy when the eagle continued to fly on after he had humbled himself at the feet of the gods, and they fell to earth.

Eteocles (i-tee'-u-kleez), G, the son of OEDIPUS and JOCASTA, brother of ANTIGONE and POLYNICES. The two brothers were to rule THEBES alternately, but at the end of his year of rule Eteocles refused to surrender the throne. Polynices then organized the expedition of the SEVEN AGAINST THEBES, in which he and his brother killed each other.

Eterah (e-teer'-u), Ph, a moon-god who led his forces against the Phoenicians and was resisted by KERET.

Etzel (et'-sul), T, the name given to Attila in Germanic legend. Etzel became the husband of KRIEMHILD after SIEGFRIED's death. Etzel is the counterpart of the Scandinavian ATLI.

Eumenides, the (yoo-men'-i-deez), G, a name for the ERINYES who, when they were benign and gracious, were called the Eumenides, which means "the kind ones." The name was often used as a euphemism.

Euphrosyne (yoo-frahs′-u-nee), G, one of the three CHARITES. Euphrosyne represented joy.

Euripides (yuh-rip′-i-deez), an Athenian tragic poet of the fifth century B.C. who wrote over seventy-five plays, nineteen of which are extant. Fragments of most of the others have survived. Since his dramas were presented at religious festivals, they dealt with legendary heroes and myths, a requirement for entry. The titles include ANDROMACHE, HECUBA, IPHIGENIA *in Aulis,* MEDEA, ORESTES, and *The Trojan Women,* and all his works give us insight into the characters portrayed through his intellectual approach and psychoanalytic treatment.

Europa (yuh-roh′-pu), G, the daughter of AGENOR and TELEPHASSA of Phoenicia and sister of CADMUS. She became the mother of MINOS, SARPEDON, and RHADAMANTHUS by ZEUS, who seduced her in the shape of a bull and carried her on his back to Crete.

Eurus (yuhr′-us), G, the east wind personified.

Euryclea (yuhr-u-klee′-u), G, the old nurse of TELEMACHUS. She recognized ODYSSEUS by a scar as she bathed his feet, when he returned from the TROJAN WAR after twenty years, disguised as a beggar.

Eurydice (yuh-rid′-i-see), G, 1. a NYMPH, the wife of ORPHEUS. When Eurydice fled from the advances of ARISTAEUS, she stepped on a snake and died. Eurydice was released from the UNDERWORLD on the condition that Orpheus would not look back at her on the journey out. Orpheus could not resist a glimpse of her, however, and Eurydice had to return to the underworld forever.

2. the mother of ALCMENE, in some versions.

3. the wife of NESTOR, according to HOMER.

Eurynome (yoo-rin′-oh-mee), G, one of the OCEANIDS and mother by ZEUS of the three CHARITES.

Eurystheus (yuh-ris′-thee-us), G, the king of MYCENAE who imposed the twelve LABORS OF HERACLES upon his cousin. He was later killed by Heracles' son Hyllus.

Euterpe (yoo-tur′-pee), G, the MUSE of lyric poetry and music. Her symbol was the flute, of which she was said to have been the inventor.

Evadne (i-vad′-nee), G, the devoted wife of Capaneus of Argos. When Capaneus was struck down by a thunderbolt of ZEUS for attempting to scale the walls of THEBES during the expedition of the SEVEN AGAINST THEBES, Evadne threw herself on his funeral pyre.

Evander (i-van′-dur), R, the son of HERMES, who founded a town on the Tiber River that eventually became Rome. He called the settlement Pallanteum after his birthplace in Arcadia. Evander aided AENEAS in the war against the Rutulians. He is said to have introduced the Greek alphabet and Greek deity worship into Italy. His daughter was ROMA.

Evnissyen (ev'-nis-yen), Ce, the stepbrother of BRAN, BRANWEN, and MANAWYDDAN. Evnissyen caused a battle between Ireland and Britain when he killed Gwern, the son of MATHOLWYCH and Branwen, by casting him into the fire on the hearth.

Excalibur (ek-skal'-u-bur), Ce, the name of King ARTHUR's magic sword.

Ezuab (ay'-zoo-ahb, e'-), A-B, the home of EA, located in the sacred city of ERIDU.

Fafnir (fahv'-nir, fawv'-), Sc & T, the son of HREIDMAR and brother of OTTER and REGIN. Fafnir, in the shape of a dragon, killed his father to acquire the treasure LOKI had stolen from ANDVARI for him. Fafnir was then killed by SIGURD, urged on by Regin. Sigurd, roasting Fafnir's heart, tasted the dragon's blood and thus learned the language of the birds.

Fama (fay'-mu), R, a swift-footed goddess, the personification of rumor.

Fates, the, G & R, the three daughters of ZEUS and THEMIS, who determined the future of all mortals, comparable to the NORNS of Scandinavian mythology. CLOTHO spun the thread of life, LACHESIS allotted to each one his destiny and the length of his life, and ATROPOS cut the thread of life. The Greek name for the Fates was MOERAE, and the Latin was PARCAE.

Fauna (faw'-nu), R, the goddess of the earth and fields, the female counterpart of FAUNUS, regarded as his daughter or wife. Fauna was identified with BONA DEA.

Faunus (faw'nus), R, a deity of the countryside and grandson of SATURN. Faunus, who was associated with PAN, watched over the woods, fields, and shepherds and had the power of prophecy.

Favonius (fu-voh'-nee-us), R, the personification of the west wind, identified with the Greek ZEPHYRUS.

Feng-tu (fung'-tuh'), Ch, the principal city of Hell. The gate is approached by three bridges, one of gold, one of silver, and one without railings, perilous to cross. These bridges are for the gods and for the souls of the good and of those deserving punishment. Within the gate are the palaces of the YAMA-KINGS and the dwellings of the numerous officials and assistants and of all those who carry out the functions of the world of the dead.

Fenrir (fen'-rir) or **Fenris Wolf, the** (-ris), Sc, a wolf, the monster son of LOKI and the giantess ANGERBODA. Fenrir was an enemy of the gods, who finally restrained him by binding him with the chain GLEIPNIR. Set free when RAGNAROK came, Fenrir was slain by VIDAR after he consumed ODIN.

Fenris Wolf, the (fen'-ris), Sc. *See* FENRIR.

Feridun (fay'-ri-doon), Pe, a noble hero. Because, at the time of his birth, ZOHAK had ordered all children to be killed, his mother entrusted her son to the care of an old man in India. Grown to manhood and sworn to vengeance, Feridun overpowered Zohak with his mighty club and threw him into chains. Feridun's reign of five hundred years did away with the forces of evil, restoring good and justice to the kingdom.

Fides (fahy'-deez), R, the goddess of faith, fidelity, and honor.

Fingal (fing'-gul), Ce. *See* FINN.

Finn (fin) or **Fingal** (fing'-gul), Ce, a famed Irish hero, said to have lived for over two hundred years. He was the leader of the Fenians, who were hunters, protectors of men, and helpers of the gods.

Flora (flohr'-u), R, the goddess of flowers and the spring. She was honored each spring by a festival called the Floralia. Flora was identified with the Greek goddess Chloris, wife of ZEPHYRUS.

Forseti (fawr'-se-tee), Sc, one of the AESIR, a son of BALDER and NANNA, and god of justice and peace.

Fortuna (fawr-too'-nu), R, the goddess of good fortune, welfare, and happiness. Her Greek counterpart was TYCHE.

Fravak (fru-vahk') **and Fravakain** (-vah'-kayn), Pe, the couple from whom, in the early mythical history of ancient Persia, the fifteen human races descended.

Fravakain (fru-vah'-kayn), Pe. *See* FRAVAK AND FRAVAKAIN.

Fravashis, the (fru-vah'-sheez), Pe, guardian genii who were spirits of good in the battle against evil. They defended all living creatures.

Frey (fray) or **Freyr** (frayr), Sc, the son of the VANIR NIORD and the giantess SKADI and the brother of FREYA. Frey was the god of fertility and the fruitfulness of the earth and controlled the sun and rain. He was a leader of the Vanir. Frey was admitted to ASGARD as a peace compromise following a bitter struggle between the AESIR and the Vanir. He had three noteworthy possessions: SKIDBLADNIR, a large ship that carried the gods; Bloodyhoof, an earth-shaking horse; and an infallible sword of victory, which he gave to his servant SKIRNIR to court GERDA for him. As a result, he married Gerda, but he did not regain his sword, and when RAGNAROK came, quickly fell in face of his adversary, SURT.

Freya (fray'-u, -ah) or **Freyja** (-yah), Sc, the goddess of fertility, love, and marriage and sister of FREY. The DWARFS made a fine necklace, called BRISINGAMEN, for Freya, which was stolen by LOKI, causing his fight with HEIMDALL. When THRYM stole THOR's hammer and demanded Freya's hand in marriage in return for it, Loki and Thor rescued her from the GIANT.

The word "Friday" is derived from her name ("Freya's day"). In Germany, Freya was often confused with FRIGG.

Freyja (fray'-yah), Sc. *See* FREYA.

Freyr (frayr), Sc. *See* FREY.

Frigg (frig) or **Frigga** (frig'-u) or **Frija** (free'-yah), Sc & T, the queen of the gods and goddess of the home and nature. Frigg was often identified with FREYA. The two goddesses shared many characteristics and may have had a common origin. Frigg appears at an early date as an earth- and fertility-goddess, but later her role was a material and domestic one.

Frigga (frig'-u), Sc & T. *See* FRIGG.

Frija (free'-yah), Sc & T. *See* FRIGG.

Fuchi (foo-chee'), J, a fire-goddess who gave her name to Mt. Fuji.

Fu-hsi (foo'-shee'), Ch, a legendary sage who instructed men in the skills of hunting and fishing and in the art of cooking.

Fu-hsing (foo'-shing'), Ch, the god of happiness. Once a mortal, he became a deity after death. His symbol was the bat, and he is often represented in company with the god of long life and the god of salaries.

Fukurokuju (foo'-kuh-roh'-kuh-joo), J, the god of wisdom and long life, one of the gods of luck. He is depicted with a narrow, elongated head and often has a tortoise or crane with him.

Furiae (fyuhr'-ee-ee), R. *See* FURIES.

Furies, the, or **Furiae** (fyuhr'-ee-ee), R, deities similar to the ERINYES. In the upper world, the Furies motivated men to sin, but they generally inflicted punishment on those in the UNDERWORLD rather than on those on earth. The Furies were also called DIRAE.

Gaea (jee'-u) or **Ge** (jee), G, the primeval earth-goddess, created after CHAOS. Her Roman counterpart was TELLUS. Gaea was the mother and wife of URANUS and gave birth to the TITANS, CYCLOPES, HECATONCHIRES, and other huge monsters. When Uranus mistreated his children, Gaea stirred CRONUS to revolt against his father. Gaea personified Mother Earth and was worshiped as the beneficent mother of all.

Gaga (gah'-gah), A-B, the messenger of ANSHAR.

Galahad (gal'-u-had), Ce, the son of LANCELOT by ELAINE, daughter of King Pelles. Galahad came to the Round Table led by an old man. He easily removed the sword, on which it was written that no one but the best knight could do so, from the stone where it was planted. He was the purest of the Round Table knights, and none of the other knights could equal him. Galahad searched with Bors and PERCIVAL and found the GRAIL.

Galatea (gal-u-tee'-u), G, a NYMPH of the sea, daughter of NEREUS and DORIS. When the GIANT POLYPHEMUS slew Acis in jealousy, Galatea turned her beloved into the Acis River of Sicily.

Gandharvas, the (gun-dahr'-vuz), I, a class of beings who were genii of music. They were attendants of INDRA and choristers of his heaven, SWARGA.

Ganesha (gu-nay'-shu), I, the son of PARVATI, who created him from dust mixed with her body's mist. In one version, he was the guardian deity of Parvati's gate, and when his head was cut off after he stopped SHIVA from entering, he was given the head of an elephant. Ganesha was the patron deity of literature and god of wisdom and prosperity. He was very fat, jolly, and well liked because he bestowed good fortune. He is depicted with four arms, and his mount was a rat.

Ganga (gung'-gah), I, the daughter of the Himalayas and consort of the gods. She was the goddess of the Ganges, the most sacred river of India, sent down to earth by the gods. Her weight was supported by SHIVA, until he separated her into seven parts, and the waters flowed from his head onto the mountains and valleys amid great rejoicing.

Ganymede (gan'-u-meed) or **Ganymedes** (gan-u-meed'-eez), G, the handsome son of TROS and CALLIRRHOË who was borne away to OLYMPUS by an eagle of ZEUS (some versions say by Zeus in the guise of an eagle) to become the cupbearer of the gods.

Ganymedes (gan-u-meed'-eez), G. *See* GANYMEDE.

Gaoh (gah-oh'), NA, chief of the winds among the Iroquois, who pictured him as a giant, holding the winds under his command.

Garm (gahrm) or **Garmr** (gahr'-mur), Sc, the watchdog of NIFLHEIM, the home of the dead. As RAGNAROK approached, his howls summoned all the underworld to battle. Garm was slain at Ragnarok by TYR, who met his death by Garm's claws.

Garmr (gahr'-mur), Sc. *See* GARM.

Ga-Tum-Dug (gah-toom'-duhg), A-B, the name of the earth-goddess as she was worshiped at Lagash, where a temple was erected to her. She corresponds to the goddess BAU.

Gawain (gah'-win, gaw'-), Ce, a courageous, daring soldier and an exemplary hero and knight of the Round Table who set off to search for the GRAIL. Gawain was ARTHUR's nephew, the son of MORGAN LE FAY. He supported Arthur against MODRED and died of wounds received in the fighting.

Gayomart (gah-yoh'-mahrt), Pe, the first man and father of MASHYA AND MASHYOI, the first human couple, who were born of his seed after it lay in the earth for forty years. He was created by AHURA MAZDA after GOSH, the pristine bull, the giver of food. Gayomart was slain by ANGRA MAINYU.

Ge (jee), G. *See* GAEA.

Geb (geb) or **Keb** (keb) or **Seb** (seb), E, the son of SHU and TEFNUT. Geb was the god of the earth and was similar to the Greek god CRONUS. He was the husband of NUT and father of OSIRIS, SET, ISIS, and NEPHTHYS and was depicted with a goose head. Geb was forcefully separated from his sister Nut by Shu. Geb followed Shu as ruler of the earth and was succeeded, in turn, by his son Osiris. Geb was one of the company of gods comprising the ENNEAD and was, according to the PYRAMID TEXTS, one of the oldest of the deities.

Gefion (gev'-yun), Sc, a giantess whose sons, transformed by her into huge oxen, created the island of Zealand by plowing it away from the Swedish peninsula and moving it off to Denmark.

Geirrod (gayr'-rud), Sc, a GIANT who forced LOKI to lure THOR to him without the defense of his belt and his hammer. Thor, however, was armed by a giantess with a staff, gloves of iron, and a belt, all of which enabled him to meet the trials set before him and escape from Geirrod's kingdom unscathed.

Gemini (jem'-u-nahy), G & R. *See* CASTOR AND POLLUX.

Genea (jen-ay'-u), Ph. *See* GENOS AND GENEA.

Genius (jee'-ni-us), R, one of the Genii, the deities who guarded the spirits of all beings and places. A Genius was said to be present at the birth of each man and to guard him throughout his life.

Genos (jen'-us) **and Genea** (jen-ay'-u), Ph, the first to inhabit the land that was called Phoenicia and to honor the sun with worship.

Geraint (ji-raynt'), Ce, one of King ARTHUR's knights of the Round Table. Geraint was the husband of the faithful Enid.

Gerd (gurd, gehrd), Sc. *See* GERDA.

Gerda (gur'-du, gehr'-du) or **Gerd** (gurd, gehrd), Sc, the consort of FREY, who sent SKIRNIR to plead his suit for him. Gerda was a GI-ANT's daughter and very beautiful, won only by the threat of being turned into an old woman.

Geryon (jeer'-ee-un), G, a three-headed (in some versions three-bodied) monster, who lived on the island of Erythia and who was slain by HERACLES when he carried off Geryon's cattle as one of his labors. *See also* LABORS OF HERACLES.

Ghanan (gah'-nahn), M. *See* YUM CAAX.

Giants, the, G, 1. a race of monsters with the bodies of serpents and heads of men that sprang from the blood of URANUS after he was mutilated by CRONUS. The giants attacked OLYMPUS and made war on the gods, using rocks and tree trunks for weapons. Since a prophecy said the gods could not win without the help of a mortal, HERACLES was called to their aid, and the giants were defeated.
Sc, 2. large and often evil people whose realm was JOTUNHEIM. The giants opposed the gods and brought about their deaths and the total destruction of the universe at RAGNAROK.

Gibil (gib'-il), A-B, a fire-god and giver of light and the symbol of the sacrificial flame. He was the patron of those who worked with metal and also acted as an arbiter of law and order. Gibil was said to be the son of ANU.

Gigantes (ji-gan'-teez), G. *See* GIANTS.

Gilgamesh (gil'-gu-mesh), A-B, the legendary ruler of the city of URUK. When their king became too powerful and arbitrary in his actions and seized any girl or woman he fancied, the people of Uruk begged the gods to create a rival to overcome Gilgamesh. ARURU fashioned ENKIDU, but, although they engaged in combat, Gilgamesh and Enkidu became friends. One of their more outstanding adventures together was a journey to a distant cedar forest, where they slew the monster KHUMBABA. When Gilgamesh spurned the love of

ISHTAR, the goddess caused a bull to be made by ANU. Gilgamesh was almost overpowered by the bull, but Enkidu saved his friend by destroying the animal. Ishtar then caused Enkidu to fall mortally ill and he died in the arms of Gilgamesh.

Gilgamesh, hoping to regain Enkidu and fearing death for himself, left his kingdom to seek UTA-NAPISHTIM and learn the secrets of life and immortality. After Uta-Napishtim had related to Gilgamesh the story of the Deluge, he told him to pick the thorny plant of life and eternal youth from the bottom of the sea. Gilgamesh succeeded, but on his return, he lost the plant to a serpent, which thus obtained the secret of regaining youth by shedding its skin. The spirit of Enkidu appeared to Gilgamesh, telling him of death and the rewards that courage and heroism could bring.

Gilgamesh Epic, the (gil'-gu-mesh), A-B, a poem relating the exploits of the hero GILGAMESH, who was quite likely a historical Sumerian king of URUK who became a legendary figure. The epic was written in cuneiform on twelve tablets. The most complete account is from the library of King Ashurbanipal, king of Assyria in the seventh century B.C. This text was taken from an earlier Babylonian account of about 2000 B.C., based, in turn, on a much older Sumerian text. Fragments found at a number of excavation sites help to fill in the lacunae.

Girru (gir'-oo), A-B, the god of the fires of heaven and earth and of the sacrificial fires.

Gitche Manitou (gich'-ee man'-i-too), NA. *See* KITCHE MANITOU.

Giuki (gyoo'-kee), Sc, king of the NIBELUNGS, husband of GRIMHILD, and father of GUNNAR and GUDRUN.

Gizeh (gee'-zu), E, a site near Cairo where the great SPHINX and the Fourth Dynasty pyramids of Cheops, Khafre, and Menkaure, as well as many shaft tombs, are located. The pyramid of Cheops, who was also called KHUFU, is the largest, about 450 feet in height.

Glauce (glaw'-see), G, another name for CREUSA, the daughter of CREON. When JASON spurned MEDEA and intended to marry Glauce, Medea killed her with a poisoned robe sent as a wedding gift.

Glaucus (glaw'-kus), G, 1. the son of SISYPHUS and MEROPE and father of BELLEROPHON. He was destroyed by his horses because he incurred the anger of the gods by feeding his horses on the flesh of humans.

2. a grandson of Bellerophon and a leader of the Lycians in the TROJAN WAR. He was later killed by AJAX THE GREAT.

3. a fisherman who ate of some grass by the sea and was compelled to rush into the water. He became a god of the sea and fell in love with SCYLLA, who fled from him. Glaucus sought aid from CIRCE, who lost her heart to him and turned Scylla into a monster out of jealousy.

4. a son of PASIPHAË and MINOS, who was killed by being smothered in a casket of honey and was restored to life by a magic herb.

Gleipnir (glayp'-nir), Sc, the magic chain, made by the DWARFS out of the sound of a cat's step, roots of stones, the breath of fish, and other like items, to bind the monster FENRIR.

Gluskap (glus'-kap) **and Maslum** (mahs'-lum), NA, twin brothers in Algonquin myth, who were opposing, dualistic forces, representing good and evil, creation and destruction. After their mother's death, Gluskap created mankind from her body and bestowed many benefits on the human race, always counteracting Maslum's harmful deeds and ultimately defeating his brother.

Gog (gahg) **and Magog** (may'-gahg), Ce, giants said to have been the sole survivors after BRUT succeeded in destroying the giants of Britain. Brut installed them as porters at the palace gates of London.

Goldbristles, Sc, a golden boar, one of the treasures of FREY. The boar, fashioned by the DWARFS, gleamed brilliantly and had the power to protect warriors.

Golden Age, the, G, the first of the AGES OF MANKIND. The Golden Age began during the reign of CRONUS, after the creation of men and before women were created. It was an age of peace, goodness, prosperity, fertility, and happiness.

Golden Apples, the, G, a wedding gift to HERA from GAEA. The Golden Apples were guarded by the HESPERIDES, daughters of ATLAS, in a garden on the edge of OCEANUS. It was one of the LABORS OF HERACLES to take the Golden Apples to EURYSTHEUS. Heracles held the heavens on his shoulders, while Atlas went to get the apples for him.

Golden Bough, the, R, a branch of mistletoe which was said to yield its bough to those whom fate favored and to sprout a new one immediately. When AENEAS wanted to descend to the UNDERWORLD, the CUMAEAN SIBYL told him he must first pick a golden bough, which was sacred to PROSERPINA. Aeneas was guided to it by two doves.

Golden Fleece, the, G, the fleece of a ram sent by HERMES (in some versions ZEUS) to rescue PHRIXUS from being sacrificed and which carried him on its back to Colchis on the Black Sea. At Colchis, Phrixus sacrificed the ram to Zeus and gave the Golden Fleece to King AEËTES, who kept a sleepless dragon to guard it. Many attempts to obtain the Golden Fleece failed, until JASON and the ARGONAUTS took it with MEDEA's help.

Gordian Knot, the (gawr'-dee-un) G, a knot tied by Gordius, king of Phrygia, which, according to a prophecy, could be untied only by a future ruler of Asia. Legend has it that Alexander the Great cut the Gordian Knot with his sword and conquered Asia. Gordius was the father of MIDAS by CYBELE. The term "Gordian knot" refers to a great problem or difficulty.

Gorgons, the (gawr'-gunz), G, the three daughters of PHORCYS and his sister Ceto. The Gorgons were winged monsters with hair of snakes, who turned men to stone by their gaze, and lived near the HESPERIDES. Euryale and Stheno were immortal, but MEDUSA was mortal. According to AESCHYLUS, the Gorgons shared one eye and one tooth, and PERSEUS cut off Medusa's head while they were exchanging the eye. However, most versions give those attributes to the GRAEAE.

Gosh (gohsh), Pe, the primordial bull, the source, with GAYOMART, of all creatures.

Götterdämmerung (guht-ur-dem'-u-ruhng), T, the Twilight of the Gods, the time of their destruction by the forces of evil, corresponding to RAGNAROK in Scandinavian mythology.

Gou (gau), Af, in Dahoman myth, the moon, son of LISSA and the brother of MAOU, the sun.

Graces, the, G & R, the daughters of ZEUS and EURYNOME, goddesses of beauty, worshiped by the Greeks as the CHARITES and by the Romans as the GRATIAE.

Graeae, the (gree'-ee), or **Graiae** (gray'-ee), G, three daughters of PHORCYS and Ceto, sisters and protectors of the GORGONS. The Graeae, the gray-haired women, had but one eye and one tooth, which they shared between them. Their names were Dino, Enyo, and Pemphredo.

Graiae (gray'-ee) G. *See* GRAEAE.

Grail, the (grayl), Ce, a vessel, quite possibly a cup, in the keeping of the Fisher King, who was crippled but could be made whole if a hero sought and found the Grail and then asked the proper question. In addition, fertility and plenty would, according to some accounts, come once again to the devastated land of the Fisher King. The

73

search for the Grail became the goal of PERCIVAL, GALAHAD, and other knights of King ARTHUR's court.

In medieval times, Christian legends surrounding the Holy Grail, said to have been carried to Britain by Joseph of Arimathea and placed in a chapel erected at AVALON, were associated with the Celtic Arthurian legends of the Grail. These beliefs were strengthened as Glastonbury, site of a great abbey, was identified with Avalon, the burial place of King Arthur and Queen GUINEVERE.

Gratiae, the (gray'-shee-ee), R, the Roman name for the GRACES, known to the Greeks as CHARITES.

Great Idaean Mother, the (ahy-dee'-un), a name for CYBELE, to whom Mt. IDA in Phrygia was sacred.

Great Spirit, NA, the principal deity of many Indian tribes of North America, whose name varied according to the language of each tribe. He represented a great father or power, often showing himself to man in the form of the sun.

Grendel (gren'-dul), in the epic *Beowulf,* a man-eating monster who finally met his death after his arm was torn off by BEOWULF.

Gri Gri (gree' gree), Af, a fetish, charm, or amulet, regarded as a protection against evil spirits.

Grimhild (grim'-hild), Sc, the wife of GIUKI and mother of GUNNAR and GUDRUN. Grimhild used her powers of sorcery to make SIGURD forget BRYNHILD and marry Gudrun.

Gucumatz (goo-koo-mahts'), M, a sky-god. He was also a god of farming and domestic life and was able to assume the shapes of many different animals. Gucumatz resembled QUETZALCOATL in many respects, and, like the Aztec god, he was represented as a feathered serpent. He was primarily a Guatemalan deity.

Gudrun (guhd'-roon), Sc, the daughter of GIUKI and GRIMHILD and sister of GUNNAR. Gudrun's first husband was SIGURD. After his death, she married ATLI, whom she killed to avenge the murders of her brothers, slain by Atli to gain the NIBELUNG gold. After Gudrun joined Sigurd in the land of the dead and her children had met their violent deaths, the curse of the ring of ANDVARI had run its course. Gudrun corresponds to KRIEMHILD in the NIBELUNGENLIED.

Guhkin-Banda (guh'-kin-bahn'-du), A-B, the god and patron of goldsmiths.

Guinevere (gwin'-u-veer), Ce, the wife of King ARTHUR. She betrayed him by becoming LANCELOT's mistress.

74

Gula (goo'-lah), A-B, a goddess who brought both illness and good health. She was believed, with NIN-KARRAK, to be the daughter of ANU. In some localities, Gula was said to be the wife of NINURTA. A dog was her symbol.

Gungnir (guhng'-ner), Sc, ODIN's huge spear, made for him at the forges of the DWARFS. The spear could not be turned from its target, and it had the power to determine the outcome of battle when it was cast.

Gunnar (guhn'-nahr, -ur), Sc, GUDRUN's brother, son of GIUKI and GRIMHILD. SIGURD won BRYNHILD for Gunnar and she became his wife. Later, in anger over his deceit, Brynhild brought about Sigurd's death. Gunnar corresponds to GUNTHER in the NIBELUNGENLIED.

Gunther (guhn'-tur), T, the brother of KRIEMHILD and husband of BRUNHILD. To avenge SIEGFRIED's murder, Kriemhild killed Gunther, who was king of the Burgundians.

Gwawl (gwahl), Ce, a suitor of RHIANNON who was unsuccessful against his rival, PWYLL.

Gwydion (guhd'-yon), Ce, a mythical hero of Wales, considered a benevolent protector and teacher of mankind. Gwydion became the father of LLEW LLAW GYFFES by his sister ARIANRHOD and subsequently tricked her three times into doing what she had sworn she would not do. First, she gave her son his name after he hit a bird on a ship Gwydion created with his magic. She gave Llew armor when she saw a fleet of ships, also the result of Gwydion's sorcery, approaching. Lastly, she refused Llew a wife of the earthly race, but Gwydion and MATH created a woman from flowers.

Gwynn (gwin), Ce, one of the early Celtic gods of the underworld and ruler of the souls of slain warriors. He was the son of LLUDD.

Hadad (hay'-dad), Ph, a god of clouds and storms and of the sky. It was he who sent rain and hurled the thunderbolt. Hadad is called the son of DAGON. His mother and his wife both have the name ASHERAH. There is insufficient evidence to distinguish between the two.

Hadad was the Phoenician counterpart of the Babylonian god ADAD. He was often referred to as BAAL-Hadad, considered to be lord and sovereign, and was sometimes represented with a bull, a symbol of strength and power.

Hades (hay'-deez), G, 1. the brother of ZEUS and god of the UNDERWORLD, in which the spirits of the dead resided. Son of CRONUS and RHEA, Hades kidnaped PERSEPHONE and made her his queen. He was called PLUTO by the Romans and was identified with DIS.

2. the kingdom over which Hades ruled; the underworld, land of the dead.

Hagen (hah'-gun), T, SIEGFRIED's killer, who was slain by his victim's wife, KRIEMHILD.

Hakea (hah'-kee-u), O, the goddess of the land of the dead in Hawaiian myth.

Halcyon (hal'-see-un), G. *See* ALCYONE.

Hamadryad (ham-u-drahy'-ud), G, another name for a wood NYMPH or DRYAD, referring especially to the deity dwelling in and presiding over a specific tree.

Hanuman (hah'-nuh-mahn), I, a monkey chief who plays a prominent role in the RAMAYANA. Hanuman was the son of the wind-god VAYU and was general of the army of the monkey king, Sugriva, who attacked LANKA.

Haoma (hou'-mu), Pe, 1. the name of a sacred, sacrificial plant and of the drink of immortality that was produced from it.

2. a deity, the personification of the ambrosia haoma.

Hapi (hah'-pee), E, 1. the god of the Nile River who was worshiped by the Egyptians as the protector of all the many gifts of that river, especially the inundation that was so important to their crops. Hapi was depicted with his head crowned with papyrus or lotus, both plants growing along the Nile.

2. a variant of the name APIS.

Harakhtes (hahr-ahk'-teez), E, the Greek name of HORUS as god of the horizons of the sun's path, called Harakhte by the Egyptians. In time, Harakhtes became so closely associated with RA that their characteristics and powers were inseparable, and Ra was known as Ra-Harakhte or RA-HORAKTE.

Harendotes (hahr-en-doh'-teez), E, a Greek name of HORUS which was applied to him after he avenged his father, OSIRIS, by taking up arms against SET.

Harmakhis (hahr-mah'-kis), E, the Greek name of the SPHINX of GIZEH, called Hor-m-akhet by the Egyptians. In the fifteenth century B.C., a stela was placed between the sphinx's front legs, telling how Thutmose, asleep nearby, dreamed that the colossal sculpture begged him to clear the sand that covered it. As a reward for doing this, Harmakhis made him a pharaoh and granted him many blessings.

Harmonia (hahr-moh'-nee-u), G, the daughter of ARES and APHRODITE and wife of CADMUS. Harmonia's necklace, made for her by HEPHAESTUS as a wedding present, inspired in her children a lust

76

for wickedness, which led to much fighting and bloodshed. Harmonia was the mother of AGAVE, AUTONOË, INO, SEMELE, and POLYDORUS.

Haroeris (hahr-oh-ee′-ris), E, a name by which HORUS was called, the Greek form of Har Wer, an Egyptian name meaning "Horus the Elder" or "the Great."

Harpiae (hahr′-pi-ee), G. *See* HARPIES.

Harpies, the (hahr′-peez), or **Harpiae** (-pi-ee), G, foul winged creatures with the bodies of birds and the heads of women, who were originally personifications of the damaging storm winds. The daughters of THAUMAS and the OCEANID ELECTRA, they contaminated the food of their victims, in addition to bearing away the souls of the dead. They were also often used to mete out divine punishment.

Harpokrates (hahr-pahk′-ru-teez), E, a name given to the child HORUS by the Greeks, who looked upon him as the god of silence, since he was depicted with his finger to his mouth.

Harsaphes (hahr′-su-feez), E, a god who was portrayed as ram-headed and was identified with HERACLES by the Greeks. The chief center of his worship was at Heracleopolis Magna (the "Great City of Heracles").

Harsiesis (hahr-si-ee′-sis), E, a Greek epithet of HORUS, called Horsa-iset by the Egyptians, meaning "Horus, son of ISIS," the infant who avenged his father, OSIRIS.

Hartomes (hahr′-toh-meez), E, an epithet of HORUS, meaning the "Lancer." He was depicted in bas-reliefs in the sanctuary at EDFU using his lance against his enemies, the armies of SET.

Hastsehogan (hahst-see-hoh′-gawn, -gun), NA, among the Navaho Indians, the god of the dwelling or home.

Hathor (hath′-awr) or **Athor** (ath′-awr), E, the goddess of joy and love and of the sun, who was also worshiped as a mother goddess and cosmic deity. Hathor was sometimes identified with ISIS and was similar in many ways to APHRODITE. The sistrum, thought to drive away spirits of evil, was a musical rattle or instrument sacred to Hathor and was her fetish.

The seat of the worship of Hathor was at DENDERA, where her sanctuary was located. OMBOS and EDFU were also sacred to her. Hathor was represented as a cow or with the head or horns of a cow.

Hathors, the (hath′-awrz), E, a group of young women, usually seven in number, who were able to predict the future of a newborn child and who covered infants with their protection.

Hawaiki (hah-wahy'-kee), O, 1. according to eastern Polynesian mythological tradition, the original home of the peoples of the Pacific islands. It also called AVAIKI and is sometimes identified with Samoa.

2. a land of spirits to which the souls of the dead went. It was situated variously somewhere in the sky, or below the sea, or on an island generally thought to be in the west.

Hebe (hee'-bee), G, the daughter of ZEUS and HERA and goddess of youth. Hebe was the handmaiden and cupbearer of the Olympian gods until GANYMEDE replaced her. She was wed to HERACLES after his deification. Hebe, who was also known as Ganymeda, is generally represented carrying, or pouring from, a pitcher.

Hecate (hek'-u-tee), G, the daughter of the TITANS Perses and ASTERIA. Hecate was invoked as a powerful goddess for good or evil in heaven and on earth. She was later associated with PERSEPHONE as a goddess of the UNDERWORLD and of magic, and with ARTEMIS as goddess of moonless nights and crossways.

Hecatonchires, the (hek-u-tahn-kahy'-reez), G, the hundred-handed sons of URANUS and GAEA, named BRIAREUS, Cottus, and Gyes or Gyges. Uranus threw his monster sons into TARTARUS, but the gods called on them to aid in the war against the TITANS. After the victory of the gods, the Hecatonchires guarded the Titans in Tartarus. They were called CENTIMANI by the Romans.

Hector (hek'-tur), G, the eldest son of PRIAM and HECUBA, husband of ANDROMACHE, and father of ASTYANAX. He was the noblest and bravest of the Trojan heroes and was commander in chief of his father's army in the TROJAN WAR. ACHILLES slew Hector in anger to avenge the death of PATROCLUS, who had fallen at Hector's hand, and dragged his body behind his chariot. Achilles then surrendered Hector's corpse to Priam for proper funeral rites.

Hecuba (hek'-yuh-bu), G, wife of PRIAM and queen of Troy. Hecuba was the mother of nineteen sons and several daughters, including HECTOR, PARIS, and CASSANDRA. Most of her children died during the TROJAN WAR. After the fall of Troy, Hecuba was taken as a captive to Greece and was later transformed into a mad dog that bayed constantly at the moon, lamenting the loss of her children.

Heh (hee), E. See NEHEH.

Heimdall (haym'-dahl), Sc, the guardian of the rainbow bridge BIFROST, the entrance to ASGARD. Heimdall could hear grass grow and could see far into the night and day. He was therefore well able to protect the gods against sudden attack by their enemies. Heimdall's trumpet, kept hidden under the sacred ash tree, YGGDRASIL, sounded the battle call of RAGNAROK. When LOKI stole FREYA's necklace, Heimdall fought Loki to regain it. Heimdall was successful, but in their struggle at Ragnarok they both fell at each other's hands.

Heket (hek'-et), E, an early goddess of the Egyptian pantheon who was a deity of childbirth and was an attendant of RA as he was born again each morning.

Hel (hel) or **Hela** (hel'-ah), Sc, 1. the daughter of LOKI and the giantess ANGERBODA. Hel was goddess of death and queen of the realm of the dead. She lived beneath the roots of YGGDRASIL, the sacred ash tree.

2. the abode of the dead, also called NIFLHEIM.

Hela (hel'-ah), Sc. *See* HEL.

Helen (hel'-un), G, the beautiful daughter of ZEUS and LEDA, sister of CASTOR AND POLLUX and of CLYTEMNESTRA. She was the wife of MENELAUS of Sparta and mother of HERMIONE. Helen was given to PARIS by APHRODITE, causing the TROJAN WAR. After Paris' death, Helen married DEÏPHOBUS, whom she betrayed to the Greeks, and after the fall of Troy she was reunited with Menelaus.

Helenus (hel'-u-nus), G, a son of PRIAM and HECUBA who, like his twin, CASSANDRA, had the power of prophecy. After PARIS' death, he lost to DEÏPHOBUS in the contest for the hand of HELEN. It was Helenus who told the Greeks they must steal the PALLADIUM. Following the TROJAN WAR, Helenus settled in Epirus, and ANDROMACHE became his wife upon the death of NEOPTOLEMUS. When AENEAS stopped in Epirus, Helenus gave him good advice regarding the remainder of his journey.

Heliades, the (hi-lahy'-u-deez), G, the daughters of HELIOS and the nymph CLYMENE who grieved bitterly over the death of PHAËTHON, their brother. They were transformed by the gods into poplar trees, ever weeping amber tears.

Heliopolis (hee'-lee-op-u-lis), E, an ancient city on the Nile Delta, site of a religious sanctuary. Heliopolis was sacred especially to the god RA, and also to the company of the gods of the ENNEAD.

Helios (hee'-lee-ahs) or **Helius** (-us), G, son of HYPERION and THEIA, brother of EOS and SELENE, and god of the sun. Helios crossed the heavens daily in his gold chariot drawn by four white horses. He was the father of AEËTES, CIRCE, PHAËTHON, and PASIPHAË, among others. The Colossus of Rhodes, the colossal bronze statue that stood at the entrance to the harbor of Rhodes, was a representation of Helios. His Roman counterpart was SOL.

Helle (hel'-ee), G, the daughter of ATHAMAS and NEPHELE. While being carried with her brother PHRIXUS on the back of the ram with the GOLDEN FLEECE, she fell into the sea, thus giving her name to the Hellespont, the Sea of Helle.

Hellen (hel'-un), G, a king of Thessaly, the son of DEUCALION and PYRRHA. He was considered to be ancestor of the Greek people, who were therefore called Hellenes.

Hemera (hem'-ur-u), G, the Day, daughter of EREBUS and NYX, identified with the goddess EOS.

Heng-o (hung'-oh), Ch. *See* CHANG-O.

Heno (hee'-noh), NA. *See* HINO.

Heorot Hall (hee'-ur-ut), in *Beowulf*, HROTHGAR's palace, and extensive hall that was plagued by the monster GRENDEL.

Hephaestus (hi-fes'-tus), G, the son of ZEUS and HERA and god of fire; his Roman counterpart was VULCAN. Because he was ugly and lame, Hera threw him into the ocean, where EURYNOME and THETIS hid and cared for him for nine years. In revenge on his mother for what she had done, he made a golden throne, which bound his mother with invisible chains. ARES failed to bring Hephaestus back to OLYMPUS to release Hera, but DIONYSUS made him drunk and succeeded. Hephaestus was again thrown from Olympus, this time by Zeus, when he took Hera's part in a quarrel, and he fell on the Aegean island of Lemnos. Hephaestus had three wives, Charis, AGLAIA, and APHRODITE, according to different versions, all beautiful, and fathered a number of children, including ERICHTHONIUS. At his forges beneath Mt. Aetna, he fashioned many artistic pieces, such as the necklace of HARMONIA, the shield of HERACLES, ACHILLES' armor, and the chariot of HELIOS.

Hera (heer'-u), G, sister and wife of ZEUS and queen of the gods. Her Roman counterpart was JUNO. Hera, daughter of CRONUS and RHEA, was born on the island of Samos and brought up by OCEANUS and TETHYS. Zeus wooed her in the form of a cuckoo, and they were wed. The GOLDEN APPLES were a wedding gift to Hera from GAEA. Hera bore ARES, HEBE, HEPHAESTUS, and ILITHYIA to Zeus and was jealous of his other children, especially DIONYSUS and HERACLES. In anger after the birth of ATHENA, Hera bore TYPHON unaided. One quarrel with Zeus resulted in the casting of Hephaestus from OLYMPUS by Zeus. In another punishment, Zeus caused Hera to be hung from the sky by golden bracelets on her arms and anvils on her ankles. At another time, Hera left Zeus after he was unfaithful, but she was brought back when Zeus pretended to take a new bride, which turned out to be but a veiled wooden statue. Hera was on the side of the Greeks in the TROJAN WAR because she had lost in the JUDGMENT OF PARIS. With Zeus, Hera had power over storms and lightning. She was worshiped as the goddess of marriage and women and the protectress of womanhood. The HORAE and IRIS were the handmaidens of Hera, and the pomegranate and peacock were sacred to her.

Heracles (her'-u-kleez) or **Hercules** (hur'-kyu-leez), G & R, most renowned of the mythological heroes, famed for his courage and strength. He was the son of the mortal ALCMENE by ZEUS, who appeared to her in the form of her husband, AMPHITRYON. The jealousy and hatred of Zeus's wife HERA led her to send two serpents to destroy the infant Heracles, but he strangled them. He was taught charioteering by Amphitryon, the use of weapons by CASTOR, boxing by POLLUX, the sciences by CHIRON, virtue and wisdom by RHADAMANTHUS, and music by Linus, whom he subsequently killed with his lute when he was reprimanded. Because of this, Amphitryon sent Heracles to tend his flocks on Mt. Cithaeron. While he was there, two lovely women, Pleasure and Virtue, appeared and forced upon him the "choice of Heracles." He chose Virtue and a life of glory through toil. He slew the lion of Cithaeron, which had been attacking Amphitryon's cattle, and thereafter wore the lion's skin. He returned to THEBES and freed the city from the tribute of one hundred oxen demanded annually by Erginus of Orchomenus by overcoming Erginus' men when they came to collect the oxen. King CREON of Thebes gave Heracles his daughter MEGARA in marriage and other gifts came from the gods: a bow and arrow from APOLLO, a sword from HERMES, armor and a club from HEPHAESTUS, and an embroidered cloak from ATHENA. In a fit of madness sent by the still jealous Hera, Heracles murdered his children, whereupon he was told by the Delphic Oracle to go into the service of King EURYSTHEUS as penance, which resulted in his performing the twelve labors (LABORS OF HERACLES). On completion of the labors, Heracles rescued ALCESTIS from HADES. After three years in the service of OMPHALE, he went to Troy, where he killed LAOMEDON and many of his sons because Laomedon had not given him the reward he had promised for the rescue of his daughter HESIONE. Heracles fought on the side of the gods in the war against the GIANTS and helped bring about their victory. He died when DEIANIRA gave him a poisoned cloak. After his death, he was deified and became the husband of HEBE. Hercules is the Latin form of his name.

Hercules (hur'-kyu-leez), R, the Latin form of the name HERACLES.

Hermanubis (hur-mu-noo'-bis), E, a name given to the god ANUBIS

81

in connection with his role as conductor of the souls of the dead, a function he shared in common with the Greek god HERMES.

Hermaphroditus (hur-maf-ru-dahy'-tus), G, the child born to APHRODITE by HERMES. Hermaphroditus united the male and female beauty of his parents as well as their names. When Hermaphroditus was bathing in the pool of the NYMPH Salmacis, who was in love with him, they became united in one body of their combined sexes as she clung to him.

Hermes (hur'-meez), G, the son of ZEUS and the PLEIAD MAIA and one of the twelve major deities. His Roman counterpart was MERCURY. As messenger of the gods, Hermes was also god of eloquence. As god of highways and travelers, he brought good fortune in commerce and good luck to thieves. Images, called Hermae, were set up to mark boundaries, which he watched over as a protecting deity. Hermes conducted the souls of the dead to HADES. He was associated with ARCADIA and a pastoral life, since he brought fertility to the countryside. Hermes shared many characteristics with APOLLO, such as the gifts of music and prophecy, but he was also full of tricks and cunning. He was believed to be the inventor of the lyre, mathematics, and gymnastics. His attributes were the caduceus, the petasus (a winged cap or hat), winged sandals, and the herald's staff.

Hermes Trismegistus (hur'-meez tris-mi-jis'-tus), E, the Greek name for the god THOTH, meaning "Thrice Greatest," attributed to him because he was believed to have control over the gods and the elements by token of his magic powers. Thoth was identified with HERMES by the Greeks.

Hermione (hur-mahy'-u-nee), G, the daughter of MENELAUS and HELEN. Hermione became the wife of PYRRHUS, also called NEOPTOLEMUS, and, later, of ORESTES.

Hermod (her'-mood, -muhd), Sc, the swift son of ODIN who rode for nine days to HEL to rescue his brother, BALDER. Hermod was told that Balder could be free if all the world wept for him, but LOKI, disguised as a giantess, refused to weep. Hermod was able to bring DRAUPNIR back from the realm of Hel.

Hermopolis (hur-mop'-u-lis), E, a site on the west side of the Nile, almost opposite TELL EL AMARNA, that became the chief center of the worship of THOTH. The view was held that it was at Hermopolis that Thoth's voice brought about the creation of the early deities from NUNU.

Hero (heer'-oh), G, a priestess of APHRODITE loved by LEANDER, who swam the Hellespont nightly from ABYDOS to SESTOS to visit her.

82

When Leander was drowned, Hero threw herself into the sea. The literary source of their love story is the poem "Hero and Leander," composed by the Greek grammarian Musaeus in the fifth century A.D.

Herodotus (hi-rahd'-u-tus), a Greek historian of the fifth century B.C., known as the "Father of History." Herodotus traveled widely in Egypt, Phoenicia, Assyria, Babylonia, and Persia, recording his observations, research, and the information he gathered in a history of the civilizations and conflicts of the Persians and Greeks, written in nine books. Interspersed in his history are the myths and legends of the areas he visited as well as those of Greece, including the stories of IO, MEDEA, and HELEN.

Heroic Age, the, G, the AGE OF MANKIND that followed the BRONZE AGE and was superior to it. It was the time of the TROJAN WAR and the expedition of the ARGONAUTS. The heroes, often of divine or semidivine origin, were great warriors, such as CADMUS, ODYSSEUS, AENEAS, PROMETHEUS, HERACLES, and CASTOR AND POLLUX, who took part in expeditions, wars, and adventures. The Heroic Age was a period of concerted action for good and of individual deeds and the establishment of cities, with the civilizing influence they brought.

Herse (hur'-see), G, one of the three daughters of AGRAULOS and CECROPS. Herse was a priestess of ATHENA and the mother of CEPHALUS by HERMES.

Hesiod (hee'-see-ud), a Greek poet whose two important didactic poems, *Works and Days* and the *Theogony,* were written in about the eighth century B.C. The *Theogony,* one of the chief sources of Greek mythology, was an early attempt to bring unity and some degree of consistency to the numerous myths surrounding the deities of the Greeks and to their genealogies and characteristics.

Hesione (hi-sahy'-u-nee), G, the daughter of LAOMEDON and Leucippe and sister of PRIAM. When POSEIDON sent a sea monster to plague Troy, Laomedon was forced to offer up Hesione. HERACLES rescued Hesione, and she was wed to TELAMON, to whom she bore TEUCER. Angered at not being awarded Hesione after he had rescued her, Heracles killed Laomedon and many of his sons.

Hesper (hes'-pur) or **Hesperus** (hes'-pur-us), G, the evening star, son of EOS and ASTRAEUS. Hesper was called VESPER by the Romans.

Hespere (hes'-pu-ree), G, one of the HESPERIDES. When the ARGONAUTS came, Hespere transformed herself into a poplar tree.

Hesperia (hes-pir'-ee-u), G, the western land, an early name for Italy and, later, for Iberia.

83

Hesperides, the (hes-per'-i-deez), G, the daughters of ATLAS and HESPERIS and guardians of HERA's GOLDEN APPLES in the Garden of the Hesperides. Some accounts make the Hesperides the daughters of NYX and EREBUS. Their names were AEGLE, HESPERE, and ERYTHEÏS.

Hesperus (hes'-pur-us), G. *See* HESPER.

Hestia (hes'-tee-u), G, the first child of CRONUS and RHEA and goddess of the hearth. Her Roman counterpart was VESTA. Hestia refused marriage with APOLLO and POSEIDON and vowed to remain unwed. She represented the hearthside, and each home had a shrine to Hestia, where she was worshiped daily. Each town had a public hearth, where a perpetual fire burned to Hestia, from which colonists carried coals to establish a hearth in the new colony. She was considered the most sacred of the twelve major deities.

Hey-Tau (hay'-taw, -tou), Ph, a deity of the woods who fostered the growth of trees. Hey-Tau was worshiped in the area around BYBLOS, where the products of the forests were of great value in ancient times. He was identified with OSIRIS by the Egyptians, who called him BA-TAU.

Hiawatha (hahy-u-wahth'-u, -waw'-thu, hee-), NA, a member of the Mohawk tribe, the leader in the formation of the Five Nations, a confederacy of peaceful alliance for mutual protection, known collectively as the Iroquois family. Hiawatha was a lawmaker and chieftain of the Iroquois. *The Song of Hiawatha* by Longfellow (1855) is a narrative poem based on the hero's deeds. Although Hiawatha was an Iroquois chief, the remainder of the material is Algonquin in origin.

Hina (hee'-nu) or **Hine** (-nay), O, the moon-goddess, protector of women, the home, and domestic arts. In Maori legend, Hina was the first woman, created from sand by TANE to be his wife. When Hina discovered Tane was her father as well as her husband, she sought refuge in the underworld, thus giving rise to death. Hina was worshiped as the goddess of death. In some areas of the Pacific she was known as SINA.

Hine (hee'-nay), O. *See* HINA.

Hinlil (hin-lil'), A-B, the goddess of crops and grain.

Hino (hin'-oh) or **Heno** (hee'-noh) or **Hinu** (hin-oo'), NA, the Iroquois thunder spirit, standing guard over the sky, protecting it from harm with his flaming arrows.

Hinu (hin-oo'), NA. *See* HINO.

Hiordis (hyawr'-dis), Sc, SIGMUND's second wife, the mother of SIGURD.

Hippodamia (hi-pahd-u-mahy'-u), G. the daughter of BUTES or Atrax. The battle of the CENTAURS and LAPITHAE took place at the marriage of Hippodamia and PIRITHOUS.

Hippolyte (hi-pahl'-i-tee), G, 1. the daughter of ARES and HARMONIA or Otrera and queen of the AMAZONS. Ares gave Hippolyte a splendid girdle, which she was asked to surrender to HERACLES so that he could give it to ADMETE. HERA's jealousy aroused the Amazons by spreading the report that their queen was being robbed. Heracles killed Hippolyte in the attack that followed and carried off the girdle.

2. a name sometimes given to Hippolyte's sister ANTIOPE, the mother of HIPPOLYTUS.

Hippolytus (hi-pahl'-i-tus), G, the son of THESEUS and ANTIOPE. When PHAEDRA, his stepmother, fell in love with Hippolytus and he denounced her to his father, she killed herself, and Theseus sent his son away. As Hippolytus drove along the sea, he was thrown to his death by a bull sent by POSEIDON. ASCLEPIUS restored Hippolytus to life, and he lived in immortality in Italy, where he was worshiped with ARTEMIS.

Hippomenes (hi-pahm'-u-neez), G, a suitor for the hand of ATALANTA, who won her in a running race by throwing three golden apples, given him by APHRODITE, to the ground and causing her to deviate from her course to pick them up. Hippomenes and Atalanta were the parents of PARTHENOPAEUS but were changed into lions by Aphrodite, because they forgot to offer thanks to her.

Hiranya-kasipu (hi-rahn'-yu-kahs'-i-poo), I, a king of the demons and holder of a boon of invulnerability granted to him by BRAHMA. He was the brother of HIRANYAKSHA. Hiranya-kasipu set himself up as the sole object of worship, in place of the gods, but his son Prahlada remained a fervent supporter of VISHNU, and all his father's attempts to do away with him were in vain. In disbelief at Prahlada's claim that Vishnu was omnipresent, Hiranya-kasipu kicked a pillar with his foot. When the pillar fell, NARASINHA, a lion-headed human incarnation of the god, appeared and tore him to bits.

Hiranyaksha (hi-rahn'-yuk-shu), I, a demon who was helped by BRAHMA's strength and a protecting boon until he became ruler of the universe by toppling INDRA from his throne and driving the gods from the heavens. The boar VARAHA, VISHNU's AVATAR, succeeded in destroying him, since that was the only animal to which Hiranyaksha, who was the first incarnation of RAVANA, was vulnerable.

Hochigan (hahsh-ee'-gun), Af, in the legends of the Bushmen, a being who had a hatred of animals. When Hochigan disappeared, never to return again, the animals lost the power of speech, which they had previously shared with man.

Hoder (hoh'-dur), Sc, the blind son of ODIN. Hoder was god of the night. LOKI persuaded Hoder to enter the sport of throwing things at BALDER, who was invulnerable to everything but mistletoe, and he guided Hoder in throwing the fatal plant. It was Hoder who sent HERMOD on his mission to bring Balder back from HEL's realm to ASGARD.

Hoenir (huh'-nir), Sc, the companion of ODIN and LOKI on their travels. Hoenir gave ASK and EMBLA reason and mobility when they were created. He was one of the AESIR and was sent as a peace hostage to the VANIR.

Homer (hoh'-mur), a Greek epic poet of the eighth century B.C. or earlier, reputed to be the author of the ILIAD, centering around the TROJAN WAR and the wrath of ACHILLES, and of the ODYSSEY, whose theme is the attempt of ODYSSEUS to reach Ithaca following the war, and his homecoming after a decade of wandering and adventure.

Horae, the (hoh'-ree), G, the hours, or seasons, daughters of ZEUS and THEMIS. These goddesses represented orderliness in nature and bore the names DIKE (Justice), Eirene (Peace), and Eunomia (Order). The Horae guarded the gates of OLYMPUS and were handmaidens of HERA.

Hornub (hawr'-noob), E, one of the sons of THOTH.

Horta (hawr'-tu), the Etruscan goddess of agriculture.

Horus (hoh'-rus, haw'rus), E, a solar- and sky-god who had attributes in common with RA. Called Hor by the Egyptians and Horos by the Greeks, but known by the Latin form of his name, Horus was the son, or sometimes the brother, of OSIRIS and ISIS. He was also called HARPOKRATES by the Greeks who associated him with APOLLO. Horus was worshiped in a number of places in various fashions and under different names, but he was almost consistently represented as a falcon or falcon-headed.

Hotei (hoh'-tay), J, the fat god of laughter and happiness and one of the gods of luck.

Hou-Chi (hoo'-chee'), Ch, a hero of royal birth who taught the Chinese the principles of farming and became one of the immortals. Hou-Chi was considered to be the founder of the dynasty of Chou, which began in about the twelfth century B.C., the time of the beginning of the large feudal estates.

Hreidmar (hrayd'-mahr), Sc, the father of FAFNIR and REGIN. His third son was turned into an otter. When LOKI killed OTTER, Hreidmar took the gods captive, setting a quantity of gold as the price of their release. Loki got the gold from ANDVARI, whom he found in a river in the shape of a fish, and gained the gods' freedom. Andvari, however, had set a curse on the ring and the gold. After Hreidmar got the treasure, he was slain by Fafnir, who then was killed by SIGURD.

Hrothgar (hrohth'-gahr), in the poem *Beowulf*, a Danish king whose men were being consumed by a monster named GRENDEL, and who lived in HEOROT HALL, his palace, always in terror of the creature.

Hrungnir (ruhng'-ner), Sc, a GIANT who flung a whetstone at THOR in a struggle with the god. Thor's powerful magic hammer fractured the stone in flight, then struck the giant, but a piece broken from the whetstone lodged in the god's forehead.

Hsi Wang Mu (shee' wahng' muh'), Ch, the Lady Wang or Queen Mother Wang. In her earliest manifestation, she was a tiger-toothed woman with a leopard's tail, who lived in a jade mountain to the west of KUN-LUN and ruled over spirits of evil, sending plague and affliction on mankind. She later, as consort of TUNG WANG KUNG, resided with the Jade Emperor in the palace on Kun-lun and was described as a gracious, young, and beautiful sovereign, the Queen of the West.

Hugi (hyoo'-gee, hoo'-), Sc, a youth who outstripped THIALFI in a race. He was a personification of thought.

Huitzilopochtli or **Uitzilopochtli** (wee-tsee-loh-pohch'-tlee), Az, the war-god, who sprang forth in full armor when the earth-goddess COATLICUE gave birth to him. His name means "hummingbird of the south." He was also the god of lightning and storms and the protector of travelers. As a sun deity, he was the conqueror of darkness. Humans in large numbers were sacrificed to Huitzilopochtli, who was generally represented with feathers and snakes.

Humbaba (huhm-bah'-bah), A-B. *See* KHUMBABA.

Hunab-ku (hoo'-nahb-koo), M, the supreme god of the Mayas. He was the father of ITZAMNA. Hunab-ku, who is analogous to the Aztec god OMETEOTL, was sometimes called Kinebahan.

Hun-tun (hoon'-doon'), Ch, the personification of chaos, a mythical emperor-god who held sway prior to the active forces, YIN AND YANG.

Hurakan (hoo-rah-kahn'), M, the god of wind, thunder, and storms, who brought fire to mankind. When the gods were angered by

87

the first race of men, they were destroyed in a flood sent upon the earth of Hurakan. Hurakan was worshiped especially in Guatemala and was associated with the Aztec god QUETZALCOATL.

Husheng (hoo'-sheng), Pe, the grandson of MASHYA AND MASHYOI who established justice and civilization in the world. Husheng was said to have invented irrigation and to have put animals to the plow to cultivate the fields.

Hvare-Khshaeta (hwah'-ru-kshah'-u-tu), Pe, a deity who was worshiped as the sun-god in the mythology of the period before Zoroastrianism.

Hyacinthus (hahy-u-sin'-thus), G, a beautiful young man of Sparta, loved by APOLLO, who, when they were throwing the discus, killed the youth by accident, perhaps brought about by the jealousy of ZEPHYRUS, who caused the discus to swerve. Apollo then brought forth the flower hyacinth, with *ai, ai* ("woe, woe") marked on its petals, from his friend's blood.

Hyades, the (hahy'-u-deez), G, the daughters of ATLAS and AETHRA and sisters of the PLEIADES. The Hyades, NYMPHS whose name meant Rainy Ones, nursed the infant DIONYSUS and were therefore placed in the heavens as stars.

Hydra, the (hahy'-dru), G, a water snake, offspring of TYPHON and ECHIDNA. The Hydra had nine heads, one of which was immortal, and wrought destruction in the vicinity of LERNA. EURYSTHEUS sent HERACLES to kill the Hydra, which he did with the aid of IOLAUS, who burned the necks, from which two new heads were capable of springing, as soon as Heracles struck off each head with his club. The immortal head was buried under a rock pile.

Hygea (hahy-jee'-u), G. *See* HYGEIA.

Hygeia or **Hygea** (hahy-jee'-u), G, the goddess of health and daughter of ASCLEPIUS. The Romans identified Hygeia with SALUS.

Hygelac (hig'-u-lahk), in the epic *Beowulf,* the king of the Geatas and uncle of BEOWULF.

Hylas (hahy'-lus), G, a favorite of HERACLES, who accompanied the hero on the expedition of the ARGONAUTS. When the Argonauts stopped in Asia Minor, Hylas was drawn into the water of a fountain by the NYMPHS, and Heracles stayed behind to search for him, but without success.

Hymen (hahy'-mun), G, the god of marriage and the wedding feast and an attendant of APHRODITE, whose son he was by DIONYSUS.

Hymir (hoo'-mir), Sc, a GIANT of the sea. THOR went in Hymir's boat to attempt to catch the MIDGARD SERPENT. Using an oxhead for bait, he caught the monster, but when Hymir cut the line, the serpent slipped back into the sea. Hymir perished at the hands of Thor before he could escape.

Hyperboreans, the (hahy-per-bawr'-ee-unz), G, those who lived beyond BOREAS, the north wind, in a land of bliss that could not be reached by land or sea and where there was eternal sun and springtime, with no old age or sickness, war or labor.

Hyperion (hahy-peer'-ee-un), G, the son of URANUS and GAEA. Hyperion was an early sun-god and the father by THEIA of HELIOS, the sun, EOS, the dawn, and SELENE, the moon.

Hypermnestra (hahy-perm-nes'-tru), G, the wife of LYNCEUS and the only one of the daughters of DANAUS who did not slay her husband on the wedding night.

Hypnos (hip'-nahs), G, the god of sleep, the twin brother of THANATOS, child of NYX, and father of MORPHEUS. His Latin name is Somnus.

Hypsipyle (hip-sip'-i-lee), G, the daughter of Thoas, king of Lemnos. When the women killed all the other men of the island, Hypsipyle spared her father and aided his escape by sea. When the ARGONAUTS landed on Lemnos, the women of Lemnos received them with hospitality, and Hypsipyle became the mother of JASON's twin sons.

Iapetus (ahy-ap'-i-tus), G, a son of URANUS and GAEA and father of ATLAS, EPIMETHEUS, PROMETHEUS, and Menoetius by CLYMENE.

Icarus (ik'-ur-us), G, the son of DAEDALUS. He flew too close to the sun in spite of his father's warning and, when the wax of his wings melted, fell into the sea near DELOS. The sea was henceforth called the Icarian Sea.

Ida (ahy'-du), G, the NYMPH who, with ADRASTEA, cared for the infant ZEUS on Crete.

Ida, Mt. (ahy'-du), G, 1. a mountain near Troy to which PARIS was taken as an infant and where he lived as a shepherd. It was the scene of the JUDGMENT OF PARIS.

2. the mountain on Crete where the infant ZEUS was cared for.

Idas (ahy'-dus), G, the brother of LYNCEUS, a hero of the CALYDONIAN BOAR hunt and the expedition of the ARGONAUTS, and the husband of Marpessa. Idas slew CASTOR in a dispute over some oxen and was struck down by a thunderbolt of ZEUS.

Idun (ee-thuhn) or **Iduna** (-thuhn-u), Sc, the wife of BRAGI. The goddess of spring and youth, she was the guardian of magic apples, which renewed the youth of the gods. When LOKI, acting as the accomplice of THIAZI, lured Idun into the forest, where the GIANT held her captive, the gods grew old and wrinkled, until, discovering who had kidnaped Idun, they ordered Loki to bring her back to ASGARD.

Iduna (ee'-thuhn-u), Sc. *See* IDUN.

Igerne (i-gurn'), Ce. *See* IGRAINE.

Igigi, the (ee-gee'-gee), A-B, divinities of the sky who were the offspring of ANSHAR and KISHAR. ISHTAR was their leader.

Igraine (i-grayn') or **Igerne** (-gurn'), Ce, the wife of the Duke of Cornwall who was loved by UTHER PENDRAGON. The latter, disguised as her husband by MERLIN's magic, made her the mother of ARTHUR.

Ihi (ee'-hee) or **Ahi** (ah'-), E, the Sistrum Player, son of the goddess HATHOR, to whom that musical instrument was sacred, and HORUS.

Ihoiho (ee-hoi'-hoh), O, the name given to the god IO in Tahiti.

Ilabrat (ee-lah'-braht), A-B, the messenger of ANU.

Iliad, the (il'-ee-ud), a Greek epic poem in twenty-four books, attributed to HOMER. The action, taking place during the end of the tenth and final year of the siege of Troy, revolves primarily around ACHILLES and the results of his actions.

Achilles, enraged at AGAMEMNON, leader of the Greeks, because of an argument over his captive girl, BRISEIS, withdraws from the fight. Emboldened by his absence, the Trojans under HECTOR press the Greeks hard, and—despite the valor of DIOMEDES, AJAX, and other Greek heroes—are at the point of winning a decisive victory. To avert this, PATROCLUS, dearest friend of Achilles, borrows his armor and enters the battle, and is slain by Hector. Frantic with rage and grief, Achilles returns to combat, kills Hector, and drags his body to the Greek ships. Finally, however, the corpse is mercifully surrendered to PRIAM, king of Troy and father of Hector. The story ends with the funeral of Hector.

Carefully drawn characters, realistic battle scenes, insight into human motivations, mixed narrative and dramatic style, beautiful poetic language, and skillful structure are among the many qualities that make the *Iliad* one of the finest literary works ever produced.

Ilithyia (il-u-thahy'-yu), or **Eileithyia** (ahy-lahy-), G, the goddess of childbirth, said to have been a daughter of HERA. It was she who hastened the birth of EURYSTHEUS and delayed that of HERACLES.

90

Ilmarinen (eel'-mah-ree-nun), F, a smith, the brother of VAINAMOINEN and LEMMINKAINEN. Ilmarinen forged a magic talisman, called the SAMPO, that produced food and wealth and won the Maid of the North, daughter of LOUHI, after Vainamoinen and Lemminkainen had both been unsuccessful. After his wife was slain by KULLERVO, Ilmarinen went again to POHJOLA in an attempt to win the hand of a second daughter of Louhi. There, when his suit failed, he conceived a plan to steal the Sampo, with the aid of his brothers, to gain its benefits for the land of KALEVALA. The Sampo was broken in the struggles that followed the theft.

Ilmater (eel'-mah-ter), F, the daughter of air who floated on the sea for seven centuries. She then created the world from eggs laid in her knee by a duck or an eagle. From the shells, the heavens were formed; from their color spots, the stars; from the yolks, the sun; and from the whites of the eggs, the moon. Ilmater was the mother of VAINAMOINEN.

Ilus (ahy'-lus), G, 1. a son of DARDANUS or, in some accounts, of TROS. When Troy was founded, it was named Ilium after him.

2. a name by which ASCANIUS, son of AENEAS, was known.

Ilya-Muromyets (il'-yu-muhr-oh-myetz'), Sl, a popular legendary hero who had a number of traits in common with the gods, most notably the god PERUN. His strength derived from a honey drink given him, when he was a young man, by two men passing by, for until that time he had been too weak to stand up. His bow sent powerful and swift arrows to accomplish incredible tasks, and his steed flew across the vault of heaven.

When he left his home after he was healed, Ilya-Muromyets came upon the home of the hero SVYATOGOR, and the two became friends. As he traveled toward Kiev, coming upon hordes of Tartars attacking a city to the north, he destroyed them easily with a giant oak. In later years, following many acts of prowess, when the Russians were defending Kiev against the Tartars, they bragged they could overcome the heavens, bringing quick defeat and death upon themselves. Ilya-Muromyets and his horse were turned to stone.

Ilya-Muromyets, whose exploits were largely those of a mythical hero, performed deeds representative of the Christianized Slavs, and his last accomplishment before his death was the construction of a cathedral at the orthodox Slavic city, Kiev.

Iment (i-ment'), E. *See* AMENTI.

Imhotep (im-hoh'-tep), E, a sage who was deified and worshiped as a god of medicine after his death. MEMPHIS was the seat of his worship.

Imhotep was the architect of King Zoser, the builder of the most ancient of the pyramids, who ruled in the Third Dynasty. In later times, Imhotep was said to be the son of PTAH and replaced NEFERTEM in the Memphis Triad of deities. He was known for his ability to heal, and he became the patron of medicine as well as of scribes and those dealing with the sciences. Imhotep was identified by the Greeks with ASCLEPIUS because of his healing powers. He was depicted as a man, with no royal or divine symbols but with the shaven head of a priest.

In (in), J. *See* YO AND IN.

Inachus (in'-u-kus), G, a river-god who was the son of OCEANUS and TETHYS and the father of IO. When Inachus decided in favor of HERA in her contest with POSEIDON for the possession of Argolis, Poseidon dried up the streams of Argolis.

Inanna (ee-nah'-nah), A-B, the war-goddess of Sumer and queen of the sky and heavens. She was also the goddess of love and an earth and mother goddess. She later became identified with ISHTAR. A hymn composed in the time of the Akkadian king Sargon furnishes us with descriptive details about Inanna.

Inari (i'-nah-ree), J, the god of agriculture, especially of rice, and of prosperity. He is depicted as an old man, with his attendants and messengers, two foxes. In some instances, Inari is regarded as a goddess and is portrayed as such.

Indra (in'-dru), Pe, 1. a minor deity in the mythology of ancient Persia with the characteristics of an evil spirit.

I, 2. the chief of the Vedic gods, called the mighty lord of the thunderbolt, cloud-gatherer, and bringer of rain and its fertility, who was invoked to send rain upon the parched earth of India. Indra was the son of DYAUS and PRITHIVI. He overcame VRITRA with the advice and aid of VISHNU and showed great courage against the demons.

Indra's consort was INDRANI; his son, SITRAGUPTA. His dwelling place, SWARGA, lay between heaven and earth on a mountain beyond the Himalayas. His attendants were the VASUS. With AGNI and SURYA, he formed a triad of the major Vedic gods. The greatest number of the Vedic hymns were in honor of Indra, who was often depicted with a thunderbolt in one hand and a bow in the other, or with a second pair of arms, holding lances.

Indrani (in-drah'-nee), I, the consort of INDRA and mother of SITRAGUPTA.

Innini (in-nee'-nee), A-B, one of the names given to the Sumerian goddess INANNA, representing the earth mother.

Innua (i-noo'-ah), NA, in Eskimo belief, the controlling force or spirit found in every object, creature, and phenomenon in the world of nature, and living within it. Thus, the sky, the sea, every stone, dog, whale, and bear has its innua dwelling in it as a governing force. Those that belong to bears and stones have special powers.

Ino (ahy'-noh), G, the daughter of CADMUS and HARMONIA, the wife of ATHAMAS, and mother of MELICERTES. Ino took care of the infant DIONYSUS. When Ino jumped into the sea with her child to escape from Athamas, a dolphin carried them ashore at the Isthmus of Corinth, after which she became a sea deity called LEUCOTHEA.

In-Shushinak (een-shush'-u-nahk), A-B, the local deity of Susa and the principal god of Elam, looked upon as creator of the world and ruler of gods and men. In-Shushinak had many attributes in common with both NINURTA and ADAD.

Inti (in'-tcc), SA, the Sun, from whom the Incas were descended. Inti, the supreme deity in the Incan pantheon, was the brother and husband of the moon, MAMA QUILLA. In his cycle, Inti brought dryness to the sea in the west and reappeared in the east after traveling beneath the earth. An eclipse of the sun was a sign of the wrath of Inti. He was represented as a man with his head in the form of the golden disk of the sun. At an annual festival held in his honor, animals and children were sacrificed. Inti was also known as Apu-Punchau.

Io (ahy'-oh), G, 1. the daughter of INACHUS. Because ZEUS loved Io, she was changed into a heifer through HERA's jealousy and was guarded by ARGUS. After HERMES slew Argus, Hera sent a gadfly to pursue Io until, finally, she reached Egypt, where she regained her original form and bore a son, EPAPHUS, to Zeus. Io was associated with the Egyptian goddess ISIS.

(ee'-oh), O, 2. the supreme deity of the Maoris, the creator of the world and all things in it. In time, Io became a god of a rather nebulous nature and was superseded to a great extent by other gods.

Iolaus (ahy-u-lay'-us), G, the son of IPHICLES, nephew and companion of HERACLES, whom he aided in his exploits, especially the slaying of the HYDRA of LERNA. In some versions, Heracles gave his wife MEGARA to Iolaus.

Iole (ahy'-u-lee), G, the daughter of Eurytus, who refused to give her to HERACLES, although the hero had won her in an archery contest. Heracles later killed Eurytus and took Iole captive. DEIANIRA's jealousy of Iole caused her to send the poisoned cloak to Heracles, thereby causing his death.

93

Ion (ahy'-ahn), G, the son of APOLLO and CREUSA, daughter of ERECHTHEUS. Ion was abandoned at birth and taken to DELPHI. Creusa wed Xuthus, but they were childless and went to the Delphic oracle, where they found Ion. Apollo revealed the truth to Creusa and Xuthus. Ion became the ancestor of the Ionians.

Ioskeha (yohs'-kay-hah) **and Tawiscara** (tah-wis-kah'-rah), NA, twin brothers in legends of the Huron tribe, who represented the dualistic principle of good opposed to evil. Their mother died when they were born, and Tawiscara blamed his brother for this. Ioskeha went to his father, who gave him corn and bow and arrows. After he had gained the tools of hunting, he created animals, then, placing the sun and moon in the sky, he created mankind. He taught man to make fire and brought skills and the arts of culture to the Huron tribe. Whatever Tawiscara made was monstrous and abnormal. Ioskeha became the spirit of the day; Tawiscara, the spirit of the night.

Ioskeha and Tawiscara correspond to ENIGORIO AND ENIGOHATGEA in Iroquois legend.

Iphicles (if'-u-kleez), G, the son of AMPHITRYON and ALCMENE and father of IOLAUS. Iphicles accompanied his half brother, HERACLES, on many of his adventures.

Iphigenia (if-i-ju-nahy'-u), G, the eldest daughter of AGAMEMNON and CLYTEMNESTRA. ARTEMIS, angered at Agamemnon for killing a sacred stag, becalmed the Greek fleet at Aulis and demanded that Iphigenia be sacrificed before the Greeks could sail for Troy. It was Agamemnon's sacrifice of their daughter that earned him Clytemnestra's undying hatred. In most versions, Artemis did not permit the girl to die but, instead, made her a priestess. The legend is the basis of works by Racine, Goethe, and Gluck.

Iris (ahy'-ris), G, the daughter of THAUMAS and the OCEANID ELECTRA. Iris was, like HERMES, a messenger of the gods, especially of ZEUS and HERA. She traveled between heaven and earth on a rainbow.

Iron Age, the, G, the last of the AGES OF MANKIND, before ZEUS sent the Deluge. It was a period of toil and difficulties, war and crime, when the virtues were abandoned and the baser qualities abounded.

Irra (eer'-ah), A-B, an ancillary of NERGAL, the ruler of the underworld, who brought diseases and pestilence to mankind.

Ise (ee'-say), J, the site, near the modern city of Nagoya, of a sanctuary of AMATERASU, established by the daughter of Emperor Suinin in the first century A.D. Since all repairs and restorations are carried out to produce an exact replica of the original, the appearance of the group of shrines dedicated to the sun-goddess has remained almost unchanged. The sacred mirror, used to attract Amaterasu from the cave where she hid, became an emblem of imperial sovereignty and was enshrined there. TSUKIYOMI, god of the moon and brother of Amaterasu, also has a shrine at Ise, the principal center of Amaterasu's cult.

Iseult or Yseult (i-soolt′), Ce, 1. the sister of MOROLD and queen of Ireland, who had great healing powers. TRISTRAM, as a minstrel named Tantris, sought her help and was cured by her of the wound inflicted by Morold.

2. the beautiful daughter of King Angush and Queen Iseult who became Tristram's pupil when he was at court in Ireland. Later, after Tristram successfully completed the mission he was sent on for this purpose, her hand was promised to King MARK of Cornwall. On the return voyage, however, Iseult and Tristram, by mistake, drank of a love potion intended for Mark, and they became lovers. When gossip drove them to part, Iseult gave Tristram a token ring to affirm her love and to be used if he needed her to come to him.

3. the daughter of a king of Brittany who became Tristram's wife.

Ishtar (ish′-tahr), A-B, a fertility and mother goddess who represented the planet Venus personified. Her symbol was a star. As the daughter of ANU, Ishtar was worshiped at URUK as the goddess of gentleness, love, and desire; as the daughter of SIN, the warlike side of her character was dominant. In her role as warrior, Ishtar rode into battle and sent the vanquished into the underworld, where her sister ERESHKIGAL reigned.

Ishtar's consort was TAMMUZ, but she was sometimes said to be the wife of ASSUR. After the death of Tammuz, she sought him in the underworld, but the demon NAMTAR was commanded to overpower her with disease, and she was held prisoner until she escaped through the efforts of EA.

When GILGAMESH scorned her love, Ishtar took revenge by sending a bull against him. After ENKIDU saved Gilgamesh from the bull, the goddess struck him down with a fatal illness.

Ishtar was identified with the Sumerian goddess INANNA and with ASTARTE of the Phoenicians. The seat of the worship of Ishtar was at Ninevah. The ZIGGURAT erected in her honor at Ur is in the best state of preservation among those that remain.

Isis (ahy′-sis), E, the daughter of GEB and NUT, mother of HORUS, and sister and wife of the god OSIRIS, whom she pieced together and revived by her life-giving powers after he had been murdered by SET. A mother goddess in whom the womanly virtues were incorporated, Isis was the personification of the fertility brought by the annual inundation of the Nile and of the verdant grainfield in ancient Egypt. In Hellenistic times, she came to be identified with the Greek goddess DEMETER.

Isis tricked RA by sending a serpent to poison him with its bite and making the revelation to her of his secret name the condition upon which she would cure him. As a result, her powers as a magician became even greater.

Isis, who was at times identified with HATHOR, was generally represented wearing the solar disk between the horns of a cow. Her worship spread through the ancient world to Rome, where it became one of the most popular of the MYSTERY religions and survived until the rise of Christianity under Constantine.

Isles of the Blessed, the, G, a land of happiness on the western edge of OCEANUS, the dwelling place after death of those favored by the gods.

Ismene (is-mee′-nee), G, a daughter of OEDIPUS and JOCASTA, the sister of ANTIGONE, ETEOCLES, and POLYNICES. Timidity kept Ismene from helping Antigone to bury Polynices in defiance of CREON.

Isthmian Games, the (is′-mee-un), G, a competition held at Isthmia, near Corinth, every two years in the spring in honor of POSEIDON, god of the sea. The first Isthmian Games were held early in the sixth century B.C. and were second only to the OLYMPIC GAMES in popularity, especially with the Athenians. They included races and gymnastics and poetry and musical contests.

Italpas (ee-tahl′-pas), NA, the name given by the Chinook Indians to COYOTE, who is in this case, however, of a more serious nature and not a trickster. Italpas made the land habitable by ridding it of inundating sea water, and established social and ritual laws.

Itzamna (eet′-sahm-nah) or **Zamna** (sahm′-nah), M, one of the chief gods, son of HUNAB-KU. He was the creator and father of both gods and men, identified at times with the Aztec god QUETZALCOATL. He brought a number of civilizing and cultural inventions to the people, including writing and the use of maize and rubber. Itzamna was the recipient of sacrificial squirrels and great quantities of gifts, in the belief he restored the dead to life. He was sometimes called Kabul.

Iulus (ahy-yoo′-lus), G, a name for ASCANIUS, linking him with Ilium (Troy) and the Julian family of Julius Caesar and Caesar Augustus.

Iusaas (ahy-yoos'-ahs), E, in later Egyptian mythology, believed to be the wife of ATUM.

Ixazalvoh (ees-ah-zahl'-voh), M, the goddess of weaving, said to have been her invention, and wife of the sun-god KINICH AHAU.

Ixion (ik-sahy'-un), G, a cruel king of the LAPITHAE, who was condemned in TARTARUS to be bound to a wheel that revolved forever, because he had tried to win HERA's love. According to some accounts, Ixion was the father of PIRITHOUS.

Ixtlilton (ees-tleel'-tahn), Az, the god of health and medicine. The medicine men were his priests.

Izanagi (ee'-zah-nah'-gee), J, the god who, although other deities had been born earlier, formed, with IZANAMI, the first divine couple of Japanese mythology. The island of Onokoro came into being from a drop of water falling from his lance, but Awa and the other islands of the Japanese archipelago and countless gods were born of Izanagi's union with Izanami.

After his wife, Izanami, died, Izanagi went to the kingdom of the dead to recover her, but it was too late, since she had eaten the food of the dead. He fled, horrified at the sight of her disintegrating body and pursued by his angered wife. To wash away the contamination, Izanagi then purged himself in a river and bathed in the sea, giving birth to numerous deities, among whom were the goddesses AMATERASU and TSUKIYOMI and the god SUSANOWO.

Izanami (ee'-zah-nah'-mee), J, the goddess wife of the god IZANAGI, sometimes considered to be his sister. She gave birth to Awa and to the rest of the islands in the Japanese chain, and to a great many gods of nature. Izanami died following the birth of the god of fire, KAGU-TSUCHI, but when the grieving Izanagi went to the dark kingdom below the earth to bring her back, she had eaten of the food of the dead, and she drove him out in anger at his having followed her.

Jade Emperor, the, Ch. *See* TUNG WANG KUNG.

Jamshid (jam-sheed'), Pe. *See* YIMA.

Janus (jay'-nus), R, the god of doors, entrances, and gateways. Janus was one of the earliest and most distinctive of the Roman deities. He was represented with two faces, looking in opposite directions. Also, he was worshiped as the god of good beginnings and was invoked first at all prayers and sacrifices. The doors of the Temple of Janus in the Roman Forum stood open in time of war and were closed during peacetime. His name comes down to us in January, the door or opening of the new year, which also looks back toward the old.

Jason (jay'-sun), G, one of the outstanding heroes in Greek mythology. The son of King AESON of Thessaly, Jason was brought up by the CENTAUR CHIRON and returned to find the throne had been usurped by PELIAS, his uncle, who promised to relinquish it on condition that Jason bring the GOLDEN FLEECE back from Colchis. Jason was leader of the expedition of the ARGONAUTS and carried out his task successfully with the help of MEDEA, whom he married.

Jikoku (ji-koh'-koo), J, one of the SHI TENNO and the guardian of the east.

Jocasta (joh-kas'-tu), G, mother and wife of OEDIPUS of THEBES, her son by LAIUS, and mother by him of ETEOCLES, POLYNICES, ANTIGONE, and ISMENE. She killed herself after learning she had unwittingly married her own son.

Jorojin (joh-roh'-jin), J, the white-bearded god of longevity and of good luck. He is accompanied by a tortoise or a crane, representing a happy old age.

Jotunheim (yoo'-tuhn-haym), Sc, the dwelling place of the GIANTS, a kingdom in an outer, snowy world near the ocean. YGGDRASIL had its roots in Jotunheim, which was sometimes identified with UTGARD.

Joukahainen or **Youkahainen** (you'-ku-hahy-nen), F, the brother of AINO. VAINAMOINEN overcame Joukahainen by means of incantations and the power of magic, and so Joukahainen promised Aino to Vainamoinen to save himself. After Aino was drowned, Joukahainen aimed an arrow at Vainamoinen, striking his horse and throwing him into the sea, where an eagle rescued him.

Jove (johv), R, another name for JUPITER.

Juck (yuk, juk), Af. *See* JUOK.

Judgment of Paris, the, G, the decision rendered by PARIS in the contest among APHRODITE, HERA, and ATHENA. A golden apple with the words "For the Fairest" on it was thrown by ERIS into the marriage feast of PELEUS and THETIS. All the goddesses contended for the prize, but when the choice was among Aphrodite, Hera, and Athena, ZEUS told them to seek the judgment of Paris on Mt. IDA. Each goddess offered bribes to Paris, who was the son of King PRIAM of Troy. Aphrodite promised him marriage with the most beautiful woman alive; Hera and Athena, power. Paris decided in favor of Aphrodite's gift and awarded her the golden apple. The Judgment of Paris led to the TROJAN WAR, because Aphrodite gave HELEN of Sparta to Paris.

Jumala (yoo'-mah-lah), F, the god of the heavens and the supreme deity of the Finns. The oak tree was sacred to Jumala.

Juno (joo'-noh), R, sister and wife of JUPITER and queen of the heavens and gods. She was the Roman counterpart of HERA in Greek mythology.

Juok (yoo'-awk, joo'-) or **Juck** (yuk, juk), Af, in the myth of the Shilluks, the creator of mankind. The god Juok created human beings from earth, using whatever color the clay or sand had in each area, with the result that some men were black, others white, and still others were brown. He gave man all the parts of his body to serve every use and purpose. The sacred white cow that rose up from the Nile was his creation and became the ancestor of UKWA.

Jupiter (joo'-pi-tur), R, the brother and husband of JUNO, king of the gods, god of light, and creator of lightning and storms. Jupiter was also called JOVE and was the Roman counterpart of ZEUS.

Jurupari (zhuh-roo-pa-ree'), SA, the chief deity of the Guarani and Tupi tribes of Brazil. Jurupari lived in the woods, where he watched over the animals, but he had a hatred for women, who were therefore excluded from the ritual of his worship. He is often pictured as a dreaded spirit or demon.

Juturna (joo-tur'-nu), R, a NYMPH whom JUPITER loved and made the goddess of lakes and springs. She tried in vain to save TURNUS, her brother, from death in his struggle against AENEAS. The sacred pool of Juturna in the Roman Forum was where CASTOR AND POLLUX were said to have watered their horses.

Kabul (kah'-buhl), M, another name for ITZAMNA.

Kachina (ku-chee'-nu), NA, among the Hopis, a deified ancestral spirit, represented and impersonated by masked dancers calling upon the spirits in ritual dance.

Kadi (kah'-dee), A-B, a goddess of the earth and its gifts. Kadi's emblem was a snake.

Kaggen (kah'-gun), Af, a clever, mischievous figure who appears in a number of the myths of the Bushmen and was quite possibly identified with CAGN. Kaggen's spirit entered and exists in the praying mantis.

Kagu-Tsuchi (kah'-goo-tsoo'-chee), J, the god of fire, whose birth brought about the death of IZANAMI.

Kalervo (kah-lur'-vaw), F, the father of KULLERVO.

Kaleva (kah'-le-vu), F, a hero and the ancestor of heroes. KALEVALA, an ancient name for Finland, was the land of Kaleva.

Kalevala (kah-lu-vah'-lu), F, 1. the Finnish national epic. Elias Lönnrot gathered oral accounts, such as folk songs, legends, poems,

99

and magic chants, and composed a heroic epic from them, which he published in a volume of fifty cantos in 1835. The work was expanded and reached its final form in the 1849 edition. The first part describes the creation of the world, the birth of the hero VAINAMOINEN, and the wooing of AINO and of LOUHI's daughter. An account of the adventures of KULLERVO, the Kullervo cycle, follows. The remainder and bulk of the cantos of the *Kalevala* center around the struggle to acquire the SAMPO and the related adventures of the heroes Vainamoinen and LEMMINKAINEN.

2. an ancient name for Finland, the land of KALEVA.

Kali (kah'-lee), I, a goddess of fertility and time, the personification of the opposing forces of creation and destruction. Kali was an aspect of SHIVA's consort.

Kalki (kal'-kee), I, the final AVATAR of VISHNU. At his appearance, still in the future, the wicked will be destroyed and the world will be created anew to enter an age of advancement. Kalki will appear in the form of a horse-headed giant, riding a white horse in the sky.

Kama (kah'-mu), I, the god of desire and love, son of VISHNU and LAKSHMI. Kama sometimes appears as an aspect of the god MARA.

Kame (kah'-mee) **and Keri** (ker'-ee), SA, in the legend of the Bacairi Indians, twin brothers who, after the Deluge, became the creators of mankind, making men out of reeds. In another version, they created animals from a tree trunk. Kame and Keri stole balls of feathers from a vulture to make the sun and the moon.

Kami (kah'-mee), J, the name given to a powerful natural force, such as a great river, lofty mountain, or venerable man, or a divinity or divine power. The kami fell into two groups, those of heaven and those of earth, Ama-Tsu-Kami and Kuni-Tsu-Kami respectively. As time went on, almost everything in nature and every locality had its kami, or spirit, and innumerable shrines and sanctuaries were erected to honor the kamis.

Kanaloa (kah-nah-loh'-ah), O, the name by which TANGAROA was known in Hawaii.

Kane (kah'-nay), O, the name by which the god TANE was known in Hawaii.

Kapo (kah'-poh), O, a fertility deity of Hawaii.

Karelia (ku-reel'-yu), F, a region lying to the east of Finland. MARJATTA's son was named king of Karelia.

Karliki (kahr-lyee'-ki), Sl, DWARFS of the underworld.

Karnak (kahr'-nak), E, that part of the ruined Theban complex that lay to the north of the ancient city, connected by a road with the temple at LUXOR. The Temple of AMON-RA, with a great avenue of SPHINXES with rams' heads leading to it, and the Temple of KHONS were erected there. Amenophis, a sage of the fifteenth century B.C., had supervised the building of many structures at Thebes, among them the temple of Amenhotep III, and was commemorated in statues at Karnak. Karnak was the place where a ram, considered to be the incarnation of AMON, was cared for.

Karttikeya (kahr-ti-kay'-yu), I, the war-god and god of bravery in late Vedic myth. When the gods were plagued by a demon, SHIVA created six children by the flame of his third eye to combat him. PARVATI, however, clasped them too tightly one day, and their bodies merged into one, but their heads remained multiple. In another version, Karttikeya was the son of AGNI and GANGA. Karttikeya, also known as Skanda, is depicted riding on a peacock.

Kathar (kah'-thahr), Ph, an inventor, also skilled in soothsaying, identified by the Greeks with HEPHAESTUS. When the temple of BAAL was built, ALEYIN gave Kathar control over the window he installed, so that Baal sent rain only when he opened the window, making it possible for Baal to leave his palace and fall on the earth below.

Kaukomieli (kou'-koh-mee-lee), F. *See* LEMMINKAINEN.

Kauravas, the (kou'-ru-vahz), I, in the MAHABHARATA, the enemies of their cousins, the PANDAVAS. They were also called Kurus, after their ancestor, KURU.

Keb (keb), E. *See* GEB.

Kebehut (ke'-be-hoot), E, goddess of freshness, the daughter of ANUBIS.

Keres, the (kee'-rees), G, the children of NYX and the personification of death by violence and in battle.

Keret (ke'-ret), Ph, a king of Sidon who was said to be the son of EL. He was in service to Sapas, a goddess and a daughter of El. When the moon-god ETERAH led an attack against the Phoenicians, El commanded Keret to withstand the enemy. After some hesitation due to cowardice, Keret carried out a sacrifice and began to plan his campaign. Eterah, however, had already made such inroads that the ensuing battle was indecisive. Keret then took a wife, by whom he had a fine son, as it had been revealed to him by El in a dream, who would be his heir.

Keri (ker'-ee), SA. *See* KAME AND KERI.

Kerikeri (ker'-i-ker'-i), Af, in Congo legend, a mortal who, in a dream, was instructed by BUMBA in the art of making fire, but performed his service only for a price. The daughter of a king, pretending to be in love with him, tricked Kerikeri into lighting a fire in her presence, then turned him away when she had acquired the treasured secret for the use of women.

Khenti Amenti (ken'-tee u-men'-tee), E, 1. a wolf-god of ABYDOS with whom OSIRIS was sometimes identified in his capacity as ruler of the dead.

2. a name, meaning "Ruler of the West," given to UPUAUT in connection with his worship as lord of the dead, especially at Abydos.

Khepera (kep'-u-rah), E. *See* KHEPRI.

Khepri (kep'-ree) or **Khepera** (-u-rah), E, one of the gods of the ENNEAD. He was believed to have been born of NUNU. Khepri was identified with RA as the morning sun, born again each day. He was often depicted with the face of a SCARAB, or with a scarab surmounting his head, a symbol, as was the sun, of creation and rebirth and everlasting life.

Khnum (khnoom), E, a deity of the upper Nile and its source. Khnum's temple was on the Isle of Elephantine near the First Cataract of the Nile. Here he was worshiped as lord of the upper river and as the god who watched over its powers of fertility and abundance. It was believed that Khnum molded the shapes of both gods and men on a potter's wheel. He was depicted as a ram or with a ram's head. Khnum was called Khnoumis by the Greeks.

Khons (kohns) or **Khuns** (koons), E, a moon-god worshiped at OMBOS, THEBES, and in the surrounding area. He was the son of AMON and MUT and gained a widespread reputation for his healing powers. He was usually represented wearing a crescent moon and disk surmounting a skullcap. One of the months of the Egyptian calendar was named Pakhons after him.

Khonvum (kahn'-vum), Af, the chief deity of the Pygmies, worshiped as a sky-god. Khonvum is the ruler of the forests and wild animals. His hunter's bow is seen as the rainbow, and the sun receives its light each morning when he throws the fragments of stars at it.

Khufu (koo'-foo), E, the ruler of Egypt in about 2650 B.C. The great pyramid of GIZEH was built as the tomb of Khufu, whom the Greeks called Cheops. HERODOTUS reported it took twenty years to build the pyramid, with 100,000 men working during that period.

Khumbaba (kuhm-bah'-bah), A-B, a monster and lord of the Mountain of Cedars. After ENKIDU dreamed he was hurled into the underworld, GILGAMESH made offerings to the god SHAMASH, who told him to overcome Khumbaba. The two friends made the long journey and succeeded in their task. He was also called Humbaba.

Khumban (kuhm'-bahn), A-B, a god of Elam who corresponded to the Babylonian god MARDUK. He was the husband of KIRIRISHA.

Khuns (koonz), E. See KHONS.

Ki (kee), A-B, a goddess of the Sumerians who personified the earth. Ki was analogous to the goddess ARURU.

Ki'i (kee'-ee), O. See TIKI, I.

Kinebahan (ki-nay-bah'-ahn), M. See HUNAB-KU.

Kingu (kin'-goo), A-B, one of the sons of APSU and TIAMAT. Tiamat made Kingu commander of the monsters she created to form an army that would free Apsu from the captivity imposed upon him by EA.

Kingu sided with Tiamat during the struggle between the gods, until they were overcome by MARDUK. He then helped Marduk imprison Tiamat's followers in the underworld after she was slain.

Kinich Ahau (kin'-ik ah-hou'), M, the sun-god, a deity of healing and medicine. He was the husband of IXAZALVOH.

Kintu (kin'-too), Af, in the myths of the Bantus, the first man on earth. After undergoing numerous trials, he was given the daughter of heaven to be his bride. They were told to descend to earth quickly to avoid her brother, Death, but went back to get corn for their hen. Death then went with them to earth, where he remained to take each of their children. Finally, Kintu gained a promise to have Death taken away, but this attempt to drive him off failed, and he stayed on earth.

Kiririsha (kee-ree-ree'-shu), A-B, a goddess of Elam who was the wife of KHUMBAN and queen of the gods.

Kishar (kee'-shahr), A-B, the wife and sister of ANSHAR, by whom she was the mother of ANU and EA. Offspring of LAKHMU and LAKHAMU, Kishar represented the earth.

Kitche Manitou (kich'-ee man'-i-too), NA, in Algonquin legend, the GREAT SPIRIT, who has always existed and is the father and benefactor of all living things, ubiquitous in nature.

Kittu (ki-too'), A-B, the personification of justice.

Knossos (nos'-us), G. See CNOSSUS.

Kojiki, the (koh-jeek'-ee, koh'-ji-ki), J, a book of ancient legends and traditions compiled by Hiyeda no Are in A.D. 712. It was written in a combination of Chinese writing and Japanese phonetically transposed into Chinese characters, resulting in considerable obscurity of meaning.

The book gives an account of the creation, and its purpose was to clarify the history of the imperial family by setting down the ancient myths associated with it and to give a set form to the legends of the official Shinto religion.

Komoku (koh-moh'-koo), J, one of the SHI TENNO, the guardian of the south.

Kore or **Core** (kohr'-ee) or **Cora** (-u), G, another name for PERSEPHONE. Kore means "the maiden."

Korwar (kawr'-wahr), O, the carved figure of an ancestor. The statue generally had a face of wood, but sometimes the actual skull was used, or it might be set into a surrounding wooden head.

Kriemhild (kreem'-hilt), T, GUNTHER's sister and the wife of SIEGFRIED, whose murder she avenged by the slaying of Gunther and HAGAN. Kriemhild married ETZEL, king of the Huns, after Siegfried's death, and she herself later met death at the hands of one of his knights. Kriemhild corresponds to GUDRUN in the VOLSUNGA SAGA.

Krishna (krish'-nu), I, the eighth AVATAR of VISHNU. Krishna grew up among shepherds, to whom he was entrusted by his parents because his uncle, the king, feared the prophecy he would be assassinated by one of his sister's children. He had prodigious strength even as a boy and won the jealous anger, then the admiration, of INDRA. He became a friend of Indra's son ARJUNA. Krishna's youth was filled with wondrous exploits and many pranks, but he bestowed his grace on all, winning love and affection.

When he was grown, Krishna returned to his home and brought safety to his family by killing his uncle, Kansa, and his cohorts in evil. After war broke out between the PANDAVAS and their cousins, the KAURAVAS, Krishna took the side of the five Pandavas and became Arjuna's charioteer. The answers of Krishna to the questions of Arjuna on the subject of the justice of war constitute the theme of the BHAGAVAD-GITA.

Although Krishna was among the few survivors of the war, he was accidentally killed by a hunter's arrow that struck the one spot where he was vulnerable, his heel.

Iconographically, Krishna is shown as slate-blue in color, often wrestling with a serpent or playing a flute.

Kronos (kroh'-nahs), Ph & G. *See* CRONUS.

Ku (koo), O, the name given in Hawaii to the war-god TU. Ku, however, held a more important position and wider powers and functions than did Tu.

Kuan-ti (gwahn'-ti'), Ch, the god of war. He had been a loyal and faithful general and was raised to the status of a god after his death. As patron of the people, he protected them by preventing or ameliorating war. Kuan-ti had many unusual experiences, related in the *Romance of the Three Kingdoms,* a Chinese historical novel set in the third century A.D. and based on folk tales and story cycles of the time.

Kuan-ti predicts the future to those suppliants who enter his temple for that purpose. He is depicted with a red face and green clothing.

K'uei-hsing (gway'-shing'), Ch, the god of examinations, who fulfilled an important function as assistant to the god of literature, WEN CH'ANG. Although very ugly, he was well liked, since it was he who selected the successful examination candidate.

He is usually depicted standing on a turtle, said to be the turtle that rescued him after he attempted to drown himself, when the emperor turned him down because of his ugliness, even though, in his mortal life, he took first place in his doctoral examinations. He carries a bushel basket to measure the talents of the candidates presented to TUNG WANG KUNG, the Jade Emperor. The bushel basket also represents his function as god of the constellation Big Dipper, since the dipper itself is called the "bushel" by the Chinese.

Kukailimoku (koo-kahy-lee-moh'-koo), O, the Hawaiian god of war.

Kukulcan (koo-kuhl-kahn'), M, an early god who came to be identified with the Aztec culture hero and deity QUETZALCOATL. He was the patron of artisans and was credited with instituting a system of laws, and with numerous inventions, among them the calendar.

Kullervo (koo'-lur-vaw), F, the son of KALERVO and nephew of UNTAMO, who made several attempts upon the boy's life. Kullervo was sold in slavery to ILMARINEN and finally set a pack of wolves and bears against his wife, who had tortured him unmercifully, to tear her to pieces. Fate led Kullervo back to his family when he fled, but delivered another cruel blow when a girl he seduced turned out to be his sister and committed suicide. Kullervo then sought revenge by the death of his uncle and ultimately ended his tragic life by his own hand.

Kumarbi (kuhm-ahr'-bee) or **Kumarbis** (-bis), a Hurrian god who was the father and king of the gods. When TESHUP defeated and replaced him, Kumarbi planned his revenge. He fathered a monstrous stone son, ULLIKUMMI, by lying with a huge rock. He then was successful in his struggle against Teshup, until Ullikummi was cut from UPELLURI's shoulder and lost his strength.

Kumarbis (kuhm-ahr'-bis). *See* KUMARBI.

Kun (kuhn), Ch, the one to whom the sovereign turned for help following a devastating, lasting flood.

Kung Kung (kuhng' kuhng'), Ch, a dragon or horned monster who struck down the pillars of the firmament with his head, causing tremendous earthquakes and the resulting great Deluge when the vault of heaven collapsed and fell.

Kun-lun Mountain (kuhn'-luhn'), Ch, the home of the immortals, located in the extreme west, extending to the heights of the sky and depths of the earth. It was the dwelling place on earth of the Lord of the Sky, TUNG WANG KUNG. In later mythology, it took on the features and quality of a heavenly paradise, and the Queen Mother, HSI WANG MU, lived there as well, acting as hostess at the feasts of immortality given for the gods.

Kunti (kun'-tee), I, a NYMPH's daughter who was granted a boon, by which she could bear five children by any god of her choosing. Her most important son was ARJUNA, son of INDRA.

Kupala (kuh-pah-lah'), Sl, a god whose worship involved the reverence of flowers and trees and of the river waters. Followers of the cult of Kupala bathed in the flower-strewn water and either burned or drowned an effigy of the god in the rites performed in his honor. The fern was especially sacred to Kupala, and its flower, one that bloomed only at midnight once a year, was a source of bounty and good fortune to its possessor, who had to pluck it from under the watchful eyes of guardian demons.

Kurma (koor'-mu), I, the second AVATAR of VISHNU, who appeared as a tortoise. When the gods were losing their strength after a RISHI laid a curse on INDRA, Vishnu instructed the DEVAS to join with the ASURAS and to churn the sea of milk, using Mt. Mandara as the churning stick and VASUKI, king of the snakes, as the churning rope. The rapid motion and the weight of the churn so threatened the sea and the earth below that only Vishnu, assuming the form of a giant turtle to support Mt. Mandara, could save them.

The efforts of the gods on one side of the churn and the demons on the other, at last, brought forth from the churning the treasures of the Vedic tribes lost in the Deluge. When Dhanvantari, the physician of the gods, appeared, he held the cup of ambrosia in his hands. After

Vishnu retrieved it from the asuras, the gods were restored to their former vitality and sovereign authority.

Kuru (kuhr'-oo), I, the common ancestor of the KAURAVAS and their cousins the PANDAVAS.

Kusanagi (koo-sah-nah'-gee), J, the marvelous sword SUSANOWO drew from the tail of an eight-headed serpent he killed after his arrival in Izumo province. He gave the sword to his sister AMATERASU, who presented it to her grandson, NINIGI, when she sent him to reign on earth. The sword Kusanagi became a symbol of imperial sovereignty.

Kuvera (koo'-vay-ru), I, the deity and protector of wealth.

Kvasir (kvah'-sir), Sc, an extremely wise GIANT who was created when the AESIR and VANIR made peace after their war, sealing it by spitting into a bowl. After BALDER's death, Kvasir succeeded in netting LOKI, then in the shape of a salmon, and turned him over to the gods for punishment. Kvasir was slain by DWARFS, who made a mixture from his blood and honey, the mead of knowledge and divine help.

Labdacus (lab'-du-kus), G, a son of POLYDORUS who became king of THEBES, the father of LAIUS, and grandfather of OEDIPUS.

Labors of Heracles, the (her'-u-kleez), G, twelve labors which HERACLES underwent to gain the gift of immortality. 1. He overcame the NEMEAN LION by strangling it in its cave and took it to EURYSTHEUS, who had assigned him the labors. 2. He slew the HYDRA of LERNA with the help of IOLAUS, who burned the necks as Heracles struck off the Hydra's nine heads, and then he buried the immortal head under a pile of rocks. 3. He chased the Erymanthian boar through the snow, captured it in a net, and brought it to Eurystheus alive. 4. He pursued the Cerynean hind for a year, then wounded it and carried it to Eurystheus. 5. With the bronze rattle given to him by ATHENA, he put the STYMPHALIAN BIRDS to flight and shot them with his arrows. 6. He cleaned out the Augean Stables by turning the the ALPHEUS and PENEUS rivers through them. 7. He carried the Cretan Bull to Eurystheus on his shoulders. The king freed the the bull, with the result that it ravaged the countryside until it was killed by THESEUS. 8. He was driving the wild mares of DIOMEDES back to MYCENAE when Diomedes attacked him. Heracles killed Diomedes and fed his body to the mares, thus taming them. 9. He was to bring back HIPPOLYTE's girdle for Eurystheus' daughter, ADMETE. He did so, but accidently killed Hippolyte. 10. While trying to capture the red oxen of GERYON in the west, Heracles placed the pillars of Heracles at the edge of Europe and Africa. He then killed the giant and the two-headed dog that guarded the oxen and slew Geryon when he attempted to follow. **11.** He was told by NEREUS where to find the GOLDEN APPLES of the HESPERIDES, and en route he freed PROMETHEUS. Heracles held the heavens on his shoulders while ATLAS got the apples for him. When Atlas wanted to take the apples to Eurystheus himself, Heracles asked him to hold the heavens while he adjusted a pad and then quickly departed. Eurystheus gave the apples to Heracles to keep, but he offered them to ATHENA, who restored them to the garden. **12.** He captured CERBERUS, the three-headed guardian of HADES, took him to EURYSTHEUS, and then returned him to the UNDERWORLD.

Labyrinth (lab'-u-rinth), G, a legendary maze associated with the Palace of MINOS at GNOSSUS, in Crete. Ascribed to the master builder DAEDALUS, the labyrinth was said to house the half man, half bull monster, called the MINOTAUR. The word has association with the word for double ax (*labrys*), a frequent symbol in Minoan art. Some scholars feel that the complexity of the construction of the Palace of Minos may have given rise to the legends of the Labyrinth.

Lacedaemon (las-i-dee'-mun), G, a son of ZEUS and TAYGETE, one of the PLEIADES. Lacedaemon was the founder of the city of Sparta, whose citizens were known as Lacedaemonians.

Lachesis (lach'-i-sis), G, one of the three FATES. Lachesis measured the length of each man's life and allotted him his destiny.

Laertes (lay-ur'-teez), G, ODYSSEUS' aged father, who grieved deeply at his son's long absence and helped him against PENELOPE'S suitors on his return.

Lagamal (lah'-gu-mahl), A-B, a deity of Elam who was believed to be the son of EA.

Laius (lay'-us), G, a king of THEBES, the husband of JOCASTA, and father of OEDIPUS. Because of a prophecy that his son would kill him, Laius had the infant's feet pierced and left him to die on Mt. Cithaeron. When he was grown, Oedipus killed a stranger, who was in fact Laius, in a quarrel on the highway, thus fulfilling the prophecy.

Lakhamu (luk'-u-moo) **and Lakhmu** (luk'-moo), A-B, huge serpents, the first deities to be born of APSU and TIAMAT. They, in turn, gave birth to ANSHAR and KISHAR.

Lakhmu (luk'-moo), A-B. *See* LAKHAMU AND LAKHMU.

Lakshmi (luksh'-mee), I, the beautiful goddess of fortune and prosperity, born of the churning of the sea. Lakshmi was the wife of

VISHNU, and KAMA was her son. During Vishnu's AVATAR as RAMACHANDRA, Lakshmi was incarnated as his wife, SITA.

Lamassu, the (lah-mas'-soo), A-B. *See* SHEDU.

Lancelot or Launcelot (lan'-su-lut, -laht, lahn'-), Ce, the most renowned of King ARTHUR's knights. He was the father of GALAHAD. Lancelot's love for Queen GUINEVERE inspired Lancelot to accomplish great deeds, but his illicit affair with her led to his failure to attain the GRAIL.

Lanka (lang'-kah), I, the kingdom of RAVANA, generally identified with modern Ceylon, and the name also of its capital city, built by VISVAKARMA.

Laocoon (lay-ahk'-oh-ahn), G, a priest of APOLLO and the son of PRIAM and HECUBA, who ran down from the citadel to warn the Trojans against the wooden horse, saying "I fear the Greeks even when they bear gifts." The Trojans did not follow his warning, because two serpents appeared and strangled Laocoon and his two sons to death, and this was taken as a sign of the anger of ATHENA, who was on the side of the Greeks during the TROJAN WAR and thus wished to see Troy fall.

Laodamia (lay-ahd-u-mahy'-u), G, the faithful wife of PROTESILAUS, who joined him in death after he was slain by HECTOR.

Laomedon (lay-ahm'-i-dahn), G, an early king of Troy, the father of PRIAM and HESIONE. POSEIDON sent a sea monster to plague Troy because Laomedon did not give Poseidon and APOLLO the horses he promised for their help in building the walls of Troy. When Laomedon broke a similar promise to HERACLES, who had rescued his daughter Hesione, Heracles murdered Laomedon and all his sons except Priam.

Lapithae, the (lap'-u-thee), G, a race of people who lived in Thessaly and whose named was derived from the fact that they used stone for building. The battle of the Lapithae and CENTAURS resulted when the latter became drunk and caused trouble at the wedding of the Lapith prince, PIRITHOUS, to HIPPODAMIA. The Lapithae, aided by THESEUS, who was a friend of Pirithous, overcame the Centaurs.

Lares (lehr'-eez) **and Penates** (pu-nay'-teez), R, the household gods, revered as protectors of each individual family and its servants, livestock, property, etc. The Lares were originally tutelary gods of farm lands and crossroads. The Penates were literally protectors of the pantry. Every Roman household regularly conducted domestic religious rites at its own private shrine, which always included statues, or representations, of these deities.

Larvae, the (lahr'-vee), R, those souls of the dead that were eternally restless because of evil or violence committed in life. Larvae, similar to ghosts and ghostly spirits, were thought to bring madness and fears to the living. They were also, at times, called LEMURES.

Latinus (lu-tahy'-nus), R, the king of Latium when AENEAS and the Trojans reached Italy. Latinus had been told in a dream that his daughter, LAVINIA, would wed a man from a foreign land and their descendants would rule the world. Aeneas married Lavinia and fulfilled the prophecy.

Latona (lu-toh'-nu), R, the counterpart of the Greek goddess LETO.

Laulaati (lou-lah-ah'-tee), O, in the mythology of the Loyalty Islands, the creator of the world.

Launcelot (lan'-su-lut, -laht, lahn'-), Ce. *See* LANCELOT.

Lavinia (lu-vin'-ee-u), R, the daughter of LATINUS, king of Latium. Because of a prophecy that Lavinia would marry a man from a foreign country, a war was fought between AENEAS and the Trojans and TURNUS, who had planned to marry her, and the Rutulians. The victorious Aeneas wed Lavinia and founded Lavinium, named for her. They became the parents of IULUS, founder of Alba Longa, and were the ancestors of the Roman race.

Leabhar Gabhala, the (lee'-bahr gu-bah'-lu), Ce, a narrative recounting the invasions of Ireland. Although the material is presented as historical fact, the work is based on myth and legend and is therefore a source of Irish mythology.

Leander (lee-an'-dur), G, the youth who loved HERO. Guided by a light shining from her tower, Leander swam across the Hellespont nightly to visit Hero in SESTOS. After Leander was drowned one night in a storm, Hero threw herself into the sea.

Leda (lee'-du), G, the wife of King TYNDAREUS of Sparta. ZEUS came to Leda in the form of a swan, making her the mother of two immortal children, HELEN and POLLUX. Her children by Tyndareus were CLYTEMNESTRA and CASTOR.

Legba (leg'-bu), Af, in Dahoman belief, the personal deity of each tribal member. The idol of this god receives regular sacrifice in the belief that Legba is a representative or messenger of the gods who intervenes on behalf of the individual worshiper.

Lei-kung (lahy'-guhng'), Ch, My Lord Thunder, the god of thunder. He is depicted as an ugly man with claws and wings and a blue body, carrying a mallet. At his side hang his drums. Lei-kung carries out punishment against the guilty who have escaped the law or whose crime was not discovered. At times, he solicits the aid of humans, rewarding them for furthering his work.

Lemminkainen (lem'-in-kai-nen), F, the brother of VAINAMOINEN and ILMARINEN and a carefree hero of the KALEVALA. When Lemminkainen tried to win the Maid of the North, daughter of LOUHI, after she refused Vainamoinen, Louhi told him he must first kill the swan of TUONELA with a single arrow. As he took aim, he was thrown into the river TUONI by the force of a water snake thrown at him by a blind shepherd. His mother, ILMATER, restored him to life with her magic powers. Lemminkainen learned many secrets of magic from his mother. He was also called Kaukomieli.

Le Morte d'Arthur (lu mawrt' dahr'-thur), Ce. *See* MORTE D'ARTHUR, LE.

Lemuralia (lem-yu-ray'-lee-u), R, the festival held annually in May to exorcise the LEMURES from the households, and celebrated with public games. It was also called Lemuria.

Lemures, the (lem'-yuh-reez), R, the ghosts of dead, similar to the LARVAE.

Ler (ler), Ce, the sea personified. He was the father of MANANNAN. Ler corresponds to the Welsh god LLYR.

Lerna (lur'-nu), G, a district in Argos plagued by the HYDRA.

Leshy (le'-shi), Sl. *See* LESIY.

Lesiy or Leshy (le'-shi), Sl, one of a group of forest satyrs or spirits who took delight in misleading those who entered the forest. They resembled humans, but had green beards and blue skin, and they were alive only in the spring and summer months. They reached the treetops when they were in the forest, and they shrank to the size of the grasses when they left the woods.

Leto (lee'-toh), G, a daughter of the TITANS Coeus and PHOEBE, and mother by ZEUS of APOLLO and ARTEMIS, whom she bore on DELOS to escape the unceasing jealous anger of HERA. Leto was called LATONA by the Romans.

Leucippus (loo-sip'-us), G, 1. the father of two daughters (the Leucippides), who were supposed to have married IDAS and LYNCEUS but were carried off by CASTOR AND POLLUX, to whom they bore sons.

2. the youth who, in love with DAPHNE, masqueraded as a girl in order to bathe with her. He was killed by APOLLO when the god, who also loved Daphne, discovered his true identity.

Leucothea (loo-koth'-ee-u), G, a sea deity who, as a mortal, was called INO. When ODYSSEUS' raft was destroyed in a storm, Leucothea gave him her veil and helped him reach Phaeacia.

Liber (lahy'-bur), R, an early Italian deity of wine and fertility, later identified with BACCHUS.

Libera (lib'-ur-u), R, an early Italian goddess of wine and fertility, sometimes associated with LIBER as his wife. Libera was later identified with the Greek goddess PERSEPHONE.

Libitina (lib-i-tahy'-nu), R, a goddess of the UNDERWORLD, whose worship corresponded to that of PERSEPHONE. As a goddess of love and fertility, Libitina was associated with APHRODITE.

Liod (lyawd), Sc, VOLSUNG's wife, the mother of SIGMUND and SIGNY.

Lissa (lees'-su), Af, a deity worshiped as the mother goddess among the Dahoman natives. Her sons were the SUN, MAOU, and the moon, GOU. Lissa was symbolized by the chameleon, her totem.

Livy (liv'-ee), a Roman historian, whose Latin name was Titus Livius and who lived from 59 B.C. to A.D. 17. His history, an inclusive work in 142 books spanning the entire period from the founding of Rome to 9 B.C., contains frequent references to the legends and myths of the Romans.

Llew Llaw Gyffes (hlahy' hlau' guh'-fes). Ce, an early Welsh mythical hero, the son of GWYDION by his sister ARIANRHOD. At his birth, his mother laid a triple curse on him, depriving him of a name, arms, and a wife. His father used his magic to circumvent the curse in each case, and Llew Llaw Gyffes attained each of the things his mother had denied him.

Llew met his death at the hands of his wife and her lover and changed into the form of an eagle, but Gwydion found his son and restored him to human shape.

Lloyd (loid, hloid), Ce, a friend of GWAWL who used his magic powers against PRYDERI out of revenge on behalf of Gwawl, RHIANNON's rejected suitor.

Lludd (hlood) or **Nudd** (nooth), Ce, a legendary king of Britain who saved his country from plagues and was sometimes considered to be a god.

Llyr (hloorr), Ce, a god of the sea who gave his name to Llyrcester, the modern Leicester, and was the Welsh counterpart of the Irish god LER. Llyr was the father of BRAN and BRANWEN by Iweridd and of

MANAWYDDAN by Penardun. He was a legendary king of Britain. *See also* CHILDREN OF LLYR.

Locha (loh'-kah), O, in legends of the Loyalty Islands, the deity of the dead, comparable to LOTHIA of the Fiji Islands.

Lokapalas, the (loh'ku-pah'-luz), I, the name given to the Vedic deities who became protective spirits under Brahmanism. They were guardians of the eight quarters of the world.

Loki (loh'-kee), Sc, one of the AESIR, the son of a GIANT. Loki personified fire and was clever but mischievous and malicious, and an opponent of the gods as well as their companion. He and ODIN were bound together in friendship.

It was Loki who urged HODER to throw the fatal mistletoe at BALDER and guided his aim. The gods then bound Loki to a rock with a poisonous snake above him, but his wife, SIGYN, saved him by catching the drops of venom. Loki then went over to the side of the giants and monsters, the perpetual enemies of the Aesir.

Loki was the father of FENRIR and HEL by ANGERBODA and of VALI by Sigyn. After Loki stole the necklace of FREYA, HEIMDALL struggled with him to recover it, incurring Loki's lasting hatred. Both were killed when they faced each other at RAGNAROK.

Lono (loh'-noh), O, the name given to RONGO in Hawaii, where he was an agricultural deity, honored by a joyous festival, the Makahiki. Because Lono left Hawaii promising to return, the people thought it was their god Lono when Captain Cook landed on their island.

Losna (los'-nu), the Etruscan moon-goddess, who was depicted with a crescent.

Loth (lohth), Ce, the Duke of Lothian and husband of ARTHUR'S sister, MORGAN LE FAY. GAWAIN and MODRED were their sons.

Lothia (law'-thi-u), O, in the Fiji Islands, the deity of the dead.

Lotus-Eaters, the (loh'-tus-ee'-turz), G, the inhabitants of a land on the north coast of Africa who lived on lotus fruit. Since the lotus made men forget their homes, ODYSSEUS had to pull his companions away from the land of the Lotus-Eaters and tie them to the ship's benches. They are also known as the Lotophagi (the Greek form of their name).

Louhi (loo'-hee), F, the ugly mother of the Maid of the North, who lived in POHJOLA. Louhi told VAINAMOINEN that if the SAMPO were forged and given to her, she would give him her daughter in marriage. In the end, however, she was won by ILMARINEN, the smith who forged the Sampo.

Later, when Ilmarinen returned to Pohjola with Vainamoinen and LEMMINKAINEN to seize the Sampo, Louhi caused a storm to arise, in which the Sampo was shattered and only a few pieces were salvaged. Then Louhi punished KALEVALA with pestilence until she was finally vanquished by Vainamoinen.

Lug or **Lugh** (luhKh), Ce, an early god of Ireland. It is possible that he was a solar deity, but this is not substantiated. Lug's spear had deadly accuracy and he was skilled in the arts of both war and peace. He became the hero of the TUATHA DE DANANN when he killed the leader of their enemies, the Fomorians, thus causing their defeat.

Lugal-banda (loo'-gahl-bahn'-du), A-B, a deity whose cult GILGAMESH honored. The hero kept the horns of the bull ISHTAR sent against him to hold the oil he used to anoint himself before paying homage to Lugal-banda.

Lugh (luhKh), Ce. *See* LUG.

Lu-hsing (loo'-shing'), Ch, the god of salaries, a human who was deified and given immortality. Lu-hsing was associated with the gods of happiness and long life.

Lukelong (loo-kay'-lawng), O, a god of the Caroline Islands, venerated as a sky deity and creator of the universe. His name has several variants, among them Luk and Lugeilang.

Luna (loo'-nu), R, the moon-goddess, the counterpart of SELENE, also identified with ARTEMIS.

Lupercalia, the (loo-per-kay'-lee-u), R, a festival held annually from very early times in honor of LUPERCUS. It was celebrated on February 15 and involved purification rites to renew life and vegetation.

Lupercus (loo-pur'-kus), R, a fertility-god, often identified with FAUNUS or with PAN, in whose honor the LUPERCALIA was celebrated.

Luxor (luk'-sawr), E, the site of a great sanctuary dedicated to AMON, MUT, and KHONS, the Theban triad of deities. The temple was connected to KARNAK by an avenue of SPHINXES. On its walls were carved bas-reliefs and hieroglyphics recounting the birth of Amenhotep III to the wife of Thutmose IV who was loved by the god Amon. A pair of OBELISKS, erected at the entrance to the temple, emphasized the connection between Amenhotep and the sun-god.

Lycus (lahy'-kus), G, 1. a son of PANDION, king of Athens and brother of AEGEUS, NISUS, and PALLAS. In a quarrel over the throne, Aegeus banished Lycus, who succeeded SARPEDON, king of Cilicia, changing the name of the country to Lycia.

2. a king in Asia Minor who welcomed both HERACLES and the

ARGONAUTS when they stopped in his kingdom and who was supported by them in military struggles.

3. a king of THEBES and husband of Dirce. ANTIOPE's sons, AMPHION and ZETHUS, slew Lycus, because he prepared to slay their mother, the former queen, and they tied Dirce to a bull, which dragged her to her death.

4. a son of Lycus and Dirce who killed CREON, making himself king of Thebes, and was slain by Heracles.

Lynceus (lin'-soos), G, 1. the brother of IDAS. When Lynceus and Idas killed CASTOR in a dispute either about oxen or over the daughters of LEUCIPPUS, Lynceus was slain by POLLUX in anger over the loss of his twin.

2. the husband of HYPERMNESTRA and the only bridegroom not slain by the DANAÏDS on the wedding night. Their son was ABAS, from whom PERSEUS was descended.

Maan-Emoinen (mahn'-u-muhi-nen), F, Mother Earth, the consort of the sky-god JUMALA or, in later mythology, of UKKO. The trees, and especially the mountain ash, were sacred to Maan-Emoinen, who was also known as Rauni.

Maat (mu-aht') or **Mat** (maht), E, a deity of creation and cosmic balance and order, worshiped as a mother goddess. Maat was the wife of THOTH and goddess of truth and honesty, a personification of the law. Her symbol was the feather, used to counterbalance the hearts of the dead in judgment before OSIRIS.

Mabinogion, the (mab-u-noh'-gee-un), Ce, the chief source of the myths and legends of the Welsh. It is an eleventh-century work, compiled from oral tradition by an able storyteller. It shows, however, the results of the composite nature of the material and the inadvertent inclusion of extraneous matter in a piece of literature whose primary purpose was not mythological accuracy but entertainment. The *Mabinogion,* whose tales were arranged in four parts or branches, was translated in the nineteenth century by Lady Charlotte Guest.

Macha (mah'-kah), Ce, an early fertility-goddess of Ireland, the eponym of Ulster's capital. She was also a warrior-goddess.

Machu Picchu (mah'-choo peek'-choo), SA, one of the chief cities of the ancient Incas. Its ruins are situated high in the Andes Mountains of Peru, about seventy miles north of CUZCO. Founded sometime in the fourteenth or fifteenth century, Machu Picchu was built on a series of terraces, connected by a myriad of steps and set against the sides of two mountains. The original name of the city is unknown. Built as a fortress with a strong stone defensive wall, and with numerous public buildings of stone, including palaces, temples, and barracks, Machu Picchu was connected to Cuzco by a stone-paved road. The almost inaccessible city apparently served as a stronghold for those Incas who were unwilling to submit to Spanish domination in the period immediately after the Spanish conquest. At an unknown date, for unknown reasons, Machu Picchu was abandoned by its inhabitants and eventually forgotten. It was rediscovered in 1911 by an archaeological expedition from Yale University led by Hiram Bingham. The following year excavations were started and have brought forth information of great importance in the study of almost all aspects of Inca history and culture.

Maenads (mee'-nadz), G, female attendants of DIONYSUS, who sang and danced in a bacchanalian frenzy. The Maenads were also called BACCHANTES.

Magna Mater (mahg'-nu mah'-ter), R, a name, meaning "the Great Mother," referring to CYBELE or RHEA.

Magog (may'-gahg), Ce. See GOG AND MAGOG.

Mah (mah), Pe, the god of the moon and ruler of time.

Mahabharata, the (mu-hah'-bahr'-u-tu), I, a long epic poem, concerned mainly with the struggle between the PANDAVAS, descendants of BHARATA, and their cousins, the KAURAVAS. It is one of the PURANAS, and the BHAGAVAD-GITA forms one part. In it are found myths of value and beauty. The Mahabharata, composed between about 1500 and 1000 B.C., received its final form around the fifth century A.D. It forms the source of the Vedic myths of the heroes and is a treasury of mythological information.

Mahadeva (mu-hah'-day'-vu), I, one of the names of SHIVA, meaning "the great god."

Mahiuki (mah-hee-oo'-kee), O, in Polynesian mythology, the creator of the world and father of the gods and mankind.

Mahou (mah'-hou), Af. See MAOU.

Mahrkusha (mahr-koo'-shu), Pe, a demon whose wickedness caused disastrous floods, with the destruction of all living creatures except for YIMA, whom AHURA MAZDA saved.

Maia (may'-yu), G, the daughter of ATLAS, and one of the PLEIADES. Maia was the mother of HERMES by ZEUS and came to be identified by the Romans with FAUNA and with BONA DEA.

Maira (mahy-rah'), SA, a culture hero of the Tupi-Guarani Indians, who brought civilization, farming skills, and social order to their lives. He was believed to have brought about the flood. The sur-

116

vivors became the ancestors of the tribes of the Tupi-Guarani Indians. As a young boy, Maira bestowed the blessings of edible plants, vegetables, and fruits on the people. These all appeared when he was beaten by some children he happened to meet. He met his death in a trial by fire imposed on him by the same Indians, a pattern that was not unusual in myths of tribal culture heroes. After death, he lived in a place of pleasure and happiness, the home also of all who died without sin.

Mama Allpa (mah'-mah ahl'-pah), SA, an Incan earth deity and goddess of the harvest.

Mama Cocha (mah'-mah koh'-chah), SA, the Incan mother goddess, sister and wife of VIRACOCHA, the creator of mankind. She was a goddess of rain and of water, associated especially with Lake Titicaca.

Mama Occlo (mah'-mah oh-kloh'), SA, the sister and wife of MANCO CAPAC who made the trek with him in search of CUZCO. Mama Occlo instructed the Inca women in the domestic arts.

Mama Quilla (mah'-mah kwi-lay'), SA, the Incan goddess of the moon, sister and wife of INTI, the sun. With the exception of the planet Venus, the planets and stars were her attendants. One of the chief deities of the Incas, Mama Quilla was represented as a disk of silver with the face of a human.

Mami (mah'-mee), A-B, the goddess who, according to the beliefs held at ERIDU, molded man out of clay, softened by the blood from a god slain by EA. Mami aided mothers in childbirth.

Mammitu (mah'-mi-too), A-B, the goddess who plotted the destiny of the newborn child's life.

Manabozho (man-u-boh'-zhoh) or **Winabojo** (win-u-boh'-joh), NA, the culture hero and trickster of the Algonquins. When the world was flooded by the waters of a huge lake, Manabozho, taking refuge on a mountain, survived to become the tribal ancestor. He was the defender of the human race, guardian and protector of man, and the one who found the plants that were to be the food of mankind.

Manala (mah'-nu-lu), F. See TUONELA.

Manannan (mah-nu-nahn', man-u-nan'), Ce, the son of LER and one of the TUATHA DE DANANN, for whom he furnished food by keeping pigs that constantly came to life again to be eaten the next day. He was the god of the sea that lay above the underworld and was associated with the Isle of Man. Manannan corresponds to the Welsh MANAWYDDAN.

Manawyddan (man-u-wid'-un, -wuh'-thun), Ce, the son of LLYR by Penardun and the brother of BRAN and BRANWEN, and stepbrother of EVNISSYEN, whose mother was Iweridd. He was RHIANNON's second husband. Manawyddan went to PRYDERI's aid to save him from the spells LLOYD had put upon him. He corresponds to the Irish MANANNAN, the son of LER.

Manco Capac (mahn'-koh kah-pahk'), SA, the brother and husband of MAMA OCCLO. In one version of the legend, he and his sister were children of the sun-god, who told them to travel until a gold rod would sink into the earth. They became the mythical founders of CUZCO and the first rulers of the Inca empire.

Manes, the (may'-neez), R, the spirits of the dead. The Manes had immortality and lived in the UNDERWORLD, where they were ruled by the goddess Mania, who was identified with PERSEPHONE. They returned to earth thrice yearly, when a religious festival was held in their honor, and on certain other occasions.

Manitou (man'-i-too), NA, among the Algonquins and a number of other Indian tribes, a supernatural being or spirit, found in all natural phenomena and holding power over them. The manitou corresponds to the ORENDA of the Iroquois.

Mantus (man'-tus), an Etruscan god who was equated with the god HADES. With his wife Mania, Mantus was the tutelary deity of the UNDERWORLD.

Manu (man'-oo), I, the name of a number of sages, among them Vaivasvata, the survivor of the Deluge, and the progenitor and lawgiver of mankind.

Maou (mah'-ou) or **Mahou** (-hou), Af, in Dahoman belief, the sun-god, the supreme spirit, son of LISSA, and the creator of all things.

Mara (mahr'-u), I, a demon who tempted and attacked the BODHISATTVA, while he meditated under the tree of wisdom, but failed to divert him. Mara sometimes appears as an aspect of the god KAMA.

Marduk (mahr'-duhk), A-B, the son of EA and NINKI. In early mythology, he was a deity of fertility and agriculture. Marduk, however, had the quality of invincible courage, and he became lord and ruler of the gods as his price and reward for doing battle against TIAMAT. Thenceforth, Marduk took on many of the attributes and functions of the other gods. In another version, Marduk was said to have been given his divine supremacy by ANU after he recovered the TABLETS OF FATE from ZU.

Marduk created mankind from clay with the aid of the goddess ARURU, or, in a different account, from the blood of KINGU. When the god SIN was threatened by evil spirits, it was Marduk who fought off his oppressors and routed them, restoring Sin's light.

Marduk took on many of the characteristics of ENLIL and became the chief god of the Babylonian pantheon. The worship of Marduk became the official cult during King Hammurabi's reign. He was often called BEL-Marduk in this later period.

Marduk's consort was ZARPANIT, and he was the father of NABU. He was often depicted holding a scimitar.

Marjatta (mahr′-jah-tu), F, the mother of the hero who succeeded VAINAMOINEN. Her son was conceived after she ate a berry, and, while still an infant, he displayed a superiority to which Vainamoinen was forced to bow.

Mark (mahrk), Ce, a king of Cornwall and the brother of TRISTRAM's mother. Mark sent Tristram to Ireland as his deputy to bring back the king's lovely daughter ISEULT to be his wife.

Mars (mahrz) or **Mavors** (may′-vawrs), R, the god of war and of country life. As guardian of the state, he was the avenger who punished the foes of Rome. Mars was the father of ROMULUS and REMUS by RHEA SILVIA. His name meant "bright" or "shining," and March, the first month of the Roman calendar, was named for him. DISCORDIA preceded his chariot and the wolf, horse, and raven were sacred to him. Mars was the Roman counterpart of the Greek ARES.

Maruts, the (mu′ruhtz), I, genii who were deities of storm and wind. They were the sons of RUDRA and were also called Rudras, especially in early texts. Happy and brave warriors, the Maruts were companions of INDRA.

Mashya (mahsh′-yu) **and Mashyoi** (-yoi), Pe, the first human pair, born of the seed of GAYOMART's body after it lay in the earth for forty years. They, in turn, bore seven couples, one of which gave birth to FRAVAK AND FRAVAKAIN, the forefathers of the fifteen races of humans.

Mashyoi (mahsh′-yoi), Pe. See MASHYA.

Maslum (mahs′-lum), NA. See GLUSKAP AND MASLUM.

Mat (maht), E. See MAAT.

Math (math), Ce, a skillful magician and the uncle of GWYDION, to whom he taught his art. Math's feet were held in the lap of a girl during peacetime.

Matholwych (math-ahl′-oh-iKh), Ce, a king of Ireland and the husband of BRANWEN, who was maltreated by him at the instigation of EVNISSYEN out of hatred and spite. Matholwych and most of his supporters were killed in the battle that followed BRAN's attack on Ireland in defense of his sister.

Mati-Syra-Zemlya (mah'-ti-seer'-ah-zem'-lyu), Sl, Mother Earth, a goddess who dispensed justice in land disputes. She was believed to have clear knowledge of the future and could foretell the results of a peasant's work, if he heard and understood her.

Matsya (mat'-syu), I, the first AVATAR of VISHNU. A tiny fish came into the hand of MANU Vaivasvata, begging to be allowed to live, but it grew so swiftly, soon only the sea was big enough to contain it. Warning of the approaching Deluge, he told Vaivasvata to save himself in a ship loaded with a pair of all living creatures and the seeds of all plant life. When the flood came, and only a great horned fish, the avatar of Vishnu, could be seen, Manu Vaivasvata moored his ship on it and was saved.

Maui (mah'-oo-ee, mou'-ee), O, an outstanding and popular hero of the Polynesians. Repudiated by his mother, Maui was brought up and taught by the gods. He grew into an epitome of bravery, but he was a law unto himself, fond of pranks and mischief, and had an untold number of adventures. He was said to have raised the sky to its present position, because its damaging weight was too near the earth. Another of his exploits was to fish for and bring a number of islands from the bottom of the ocean. When his brothers, who were helping him, started to cut them up, the valleys appeared.

Maui gave mankind numerous gifts, including fire, which he gained from the underworld, its source. His final undertaking was his attempt to win immortality for man by his plan to go to the underworld and kill HINA. Instead, however, the goddess took Maui's life, and mankind was thus condemned to suffer death.

Maui-tikitiki (mah'-oo-ee-tee'-kee-tee'-kee), O, a name by which MAUI was often called. Tikitiki was an epithet referring to the fact that he was so small at infancy, his mother could put him in her hair.

Maut (mawt), E. *See* MUT.

Mavors (may'-vawrs), R. *See* MARS.

Maya (mah'-yah, -yu), I, the queen of the Sakyas, rulers of a district in the Himalayas. The BODHISATTVA appeared in a dream, entering her womb in the form of a pure white elephant. The son born to her was named SIDDHARTHA. It was predicted that the child's destiny would lead him to the life of an ascetic.

Mazda (maz'-du), Pe. *See* AHURA MAZDA.

Medea (mi-dee'-u), G, the daughter of King AEËTES of Colchis. Medea wed JASON, helped him to get the GOLDEN FLEECE, and strewed the dismembered body of her brother APSYRTUS on the sea to delay her father's pursuit of them. Medea, skilled in magic and sorcery, restored AESON, father of Jason, to youth, but she tricked the daughters of PELIAS, Jason's uncle, who had usurped the throne, into killing their father by giving them a false promise of renewing his youth. When Jason later deserted her to marry GLAUCE of Corinth, Medea sent a poisoned cloak to Glauce and slew her own two sons. Medea then fled to Athens, where she married AEGEUS, THESEUS' father, to whom she bore MEDEUS. When Theseus returned to Athens, Medea fled to Asia with Medeus.

Medeus (mee'-dee-us), G, the son of MEDEA and AEGEUS, king of Athens. When Medea's plan to poison THESEUS failed, she fled with her son to Colchis, where they restored AEËTES to the throne. The kingdom was enlarged by Medeus, whose subjects were then called Medes. In some versions, JASON was the father of Medeus.

Medusa (mu-doo'-su), G, one of the GORGONS, who turned to stone all who looked upon them. Formerly a lovely maiden, Medusa's hair had been changed to snakes by ATHENA, because she had dared to think she was equal to the goddess in beauty. At the order of POLYDECTES, PERSEUS succeeded in cutting off Medusa's head with the help of Athena by watching the monster's reflection in his shield, thus avoiding her gaze. The winged horse PEGASUS arose from Medusa's blood. Her head was placed in the center of Athena's AEGIS.

Megara (meg'-ur-u), G, a daughter of CREON and the wife of HERACLES, who, when he was driven mad by HERA, killed their children.

Mehit (me-it'), E, the wife of ANHUR. She was identified with TEFNUT and was depicted with the head of a lioness.

Melampus (mu-lam'-pus), G, an early Greek soothsayer, who not only had the gift of prophecy but had been taught the language of the birds by serpents.

Melanion (mu-lay'-nee-un), G, an Arcadian youth, identified with HIPPOMENES as the husband of ATALANTA.

Meleager (mel-ee-ay'-jur), G, a son of OENEUS and ALTHAEA of Calydon and brother of DEIANIRA. Althaea extinguished a burning log when the FATES prophesied her child's life would end as soon as the log was consumed. Meleager went on the expedition of the

ARGONAUTS and took part in the CALYDONIAN BOAR hunt. He killed the boar after ATALANTA had wounded it and gave the victor's prize, the hide and head, to Atalanta, slaying his mother's brothers when they opposed this. His mother, therefore, finished burning the fateful log, and Meleager perished with the flame.

Melicertes (mel-i-sur'-teez), G, the son of ATHAMAS and INO and grandson of CADMUS. He was transformed into a sea-god, named PALAEMON, when his father, maddened by HERA, tried to kill him.

Melkart or **Melqart** (mel'-kahrt), Ph, in early mythology, a sun-god who was the BAAL of the city of Tyre. As a deity of the sea in later times, he was given the epithet Melkart, meaning "God of the City."

Melpomene (mel-pahm'-u-nee), G, the MUSE of tragedy, depicted with a tragic mask.

Melqart (mel'-kahrt), Ph. See MELKART.

Memnon (mem'-nahn), G, the son of TITHONUS and EOS, and the king of Ethiopia. Memnon led his troops in the TROJAN WAR until he was slain in battle by ACHILLES. Eos had his body borne home, and Memnon was made immortal. The dewdrops are said to be the tears of Eos, weeping for her son.

Memphis (mem'-fis), E, a city, now in ruins, south of Cairo on the Nile River. It was an ancient capital of Egypt and a religious center of importance. The Memphis triad, those deities closely associated with the city of Memphis, was composed of PTAH, his wife SEKHMET, and their son NEFERTEM, who was replaced by IMHOTEP in later mythology.

Mendes (men'-deez), E, a ram in whose form OSIRIS was sometimes incarnated.

Menelaus (men-u-lay'-us), G, the son of ATREUS and AËROPE, king of Sparta, husband of HELEN, and father of HERMIONE. With his brother AGAMEMNON, Menelaus led the Greeks against the Trojans. After the war, Menelaus underwent eight years of wandering before he reached Sparta to live happily again with Helen. In other versions, he was reunited with Helen right after the fall of Troy.

Menoeceus (mu-nee'-see-us), G, 1. the father of CREON and JOCASTA. When a plague fell upon THEBES, Menoeceus hurled himself from the city walls after TIRESIAS told him only the sacrifice of a descendant of the SPARTI could end the plague.

2. the son of Creon of Thebes. Tiresias prophesied the city could be saved from the attack of the SEVEN AGAINST THEBES, if a descend-

ant of the Sparti offered his life. Menoeceus sacrificed himself, fulfilling the prophecy.

Menrva (men'-er-vu), the Etruscan goddess of wisdom, who was depicted armed and, like ATHENA, wearing a breastplate with the AEGIS. She was the predecessor of the Roman goddess MINERVA, whose name was derived from hers.

Menthu (men'-too), E. *See* MONT.

Mentor (men'-tur), G, the loyal friend and counselor of ODYSSEUS who taught TELEMACHUS in Odysseus' absence. ATHENA assumed the guise of Mentor to stop the revenge and bloodshed after PENELOPE's suitors were slain. The word "mentor" refers to a trusted friend and adviser.

Mentu (men'-too), E, the god RA in the form of the rising sun.

Mercury (mur'-kyu-ree), R, the god of trade and commerce and the protector of merchants. He represented peace and prosperity. Mercury was the Roman counterpart of HERMES.

Merlin (mur'-lin), Ce, a magician and bard who had powers of divination. He was an early Celtic mythical hero, known as Myrddin, who was later associated with the Arthurian legends. Merlin gave ARTHUR his magic sword EXCALIBUR.

Merope (mer'-oh-pee), G, 1. the daughter of King OENOPION of Chios who was loved by ORION. Oenopion blinded Orion, because he tried to seize Merope.

2. one of the PLEIADES, who were daughters of ATLAS. Merope was the wife of SISYPHUS and mother of GLAUCUS.

3. the wife of Polybus, king of Corinth, who raised the young OEDIPUS.

Merseger (mer'-se-gur), E. *See* MERTSEGER.

Mertseger (mert'-se-gur) or **Merseger** (mer'-), E, a Theban goddess who was closely associated with OSIRIS and represented silence. She was depicted as a snake with the head of a woman, often surmounted by the solar disk, or with the heads of a vulture and a snake on either side of her human head.

Meru, Mt. (may'-roo), I, a mountain at the world's center where the cities of the gods were located. Mt. Meru corresponded to the Mt. OLYMPUS of Greek mythology.

Merwer (mer'-wer), E, a bull sacred to ATUM. The sun-god RA was said to assume the shape of Merwer at times. His Greek name was Mneris.

Meshlamthea (mesh-lahm'-thee-u), A-B. *See* NERGAL.

Meskhenit (mes-ken'-it), E. *See* MESKHENT.

Meskhent (mes'-kent) or **Meskhenit** (mes-ken'-it), E, like TAU-ERET, a deity of childbirth, who assisted at the mother's confinement and the baby's delivery. She had the power to prophesy the future of the newborn. Meskhent was often identified with HATHOR in her role as a mother goddess.

Metis (mee'-tis), G, the daughter of OCEANUS and TETHYS and wife of ZEUS, who swallowed her because of a prophecy that she would give birth to a son who would overcome him. As a result, ATHENA was born full-grown from the head of Zeus.

Meztli (mes'-tlee), Az, the goddess of the moon and night. She was a benevolent deity of agriculture and a fearful deity of darkness. Meztli was burned in flames, symbolic of the consuming of night and the birth of the light of day.

Mictlan (meek-tlahn'), Az, the underworld, land of the dead, ruled by MICTLANTECUHTLI and his queen, Mictlancihuatl. It was also known as Apochquiahuayan.

Mictlantecuhtli (meek-tlahn-tay-koo'-tlee), Az, the king of the dead and god of death. He was king of MICTLAN, the dark land of death. His wife, queen of the dead, was Mictlancihuatl.

Midas (mahy'-dus), G, a king of Phrygia, son of Gordius and CYBELE. When SILENUS, the friend and teacher of DIONYSUS, became lost, Midas took care of and entertained him and then delivered him safely to Dionysus. As a reward, Dionysus promised to grant whatever Midas wished for. Midas asked that all he touched be turned to gold. When even his food and drink became gold, however, Midas begged that the gift be revoked. The god of wine told Midas to bathe in the PACTOLUS RIVER. When he did so, Midas' power entered the sands, which were henceforth golden. In the musical contest between PAN and APOLLO, Midas awarded the prize to Pan. Apollo then gave Midas the ears of an ass. The king kept his shame covered but could not refrain from whispering his secret into a hole, from which reeds then grew and spread the news abroad. "The touch of Midas" means the ability to acquire money with ease.

Mider (mid'-er), Ce, the son of DAGDA and BOANN and god of the underworld. Mider had a magic cauldron that was stolen from him by CUCHULAINN.

Midewiwin (mi-day'-wi-win), NA, the name of a society of shamans among the Chippewa Indians. MANABOZHO was the first to be initiated into the Midewiwin.

Midgard (mid'-gahrd), Sc, the world of mankind, created with the heavens and sea from the body of YMIR. Midgard was the middle of the universe, located between the world of light, MUSPELHEIM, and the world of mist, NIFLHEIM, and was connected to ASGARD by the rainbow bridge BIFROST.

Midgard Serpent, the (mid'-gahrd), Sc, a serpent, the offspring of LOKI and ANGERBODA, that lay in the lower regions of the sea, coiled around the world and holding its tail in its mouth. THOR tried without success to catch the serpent from HYMIR's boat, but the GIANT thwarted him. At RAGNAROK, Thor faced the great Midgard Serpent again and struck him down with his infallible hammer, but fell dead himself, victim of the monster's terrible venom.

Milu (mee'-loo), O. See MIRU.

Mimingus (mee'-min-gus), Sc, the guardian of a magic sword HODER used to slay BALDER. This version of Balder's death, that he could be killed only by this sword, appears in a twelfth-century work by the Danish writer Saxo Grammaticus.

Mimir (mee'-mir), Sc, a god of inland waters and ponds and springs who was full of wisdom. One tradition said ODIN exchanged his eye for knowledge that was kept in Mimir's well, the fountain of inspiration. Another myth relates that Mimir was decapitated by the VANIR in their war against the AESIR, and his head was given to Odin, who held it as a source of knowledge and advice for the Aesir.

Mimming (mee'-ming), Sc, the name of a magic sword, guarded by MIMINGUS, which, in one version, was the sole means of bringing about BALDER's death.

Min (min), E, a deity of growth and the fertility of crops, associated especially with eastern Egypt. The main center of Min's worship was at Koptos, a town from which caravans departed, since he was a god and protector of those who traveled in the desert. Min was identified with AMON.

Minerva (mi-nur'-vu), R, the goddess of wisdom and mental activities, and protective deity of the arts and crafts, who granted talents to mankind. Minerva came to be identified with ATHENA, her Greek counterpart.

Minos (mahy'-nus), G, the son of ZEUS and EUROPA, brother of RHADAMANTHUS and SARPEDON, king of CNOSSUS in Crete, husband of PASIPHAË, and father of ARIADNE. A white bull, born from the sea, was given to Minos by POSEIDON to be sacrificed. When Minos kept the bull and sacrificed another in its place, Poseidon made the bull mad and caused Pasiphaë to fall in love with it and give birth to the MINOTAUR. After his death, Minos became a judge in the UNDERWORLD with AEACUS and Rhadamanthus and decided which souls should dwell in the ELYSIAN FIELDS and which should receive punishment in TARTARUS.

Minotaur (min′-u-tawr), G, a monster, half bull and half human, the offspring of PASIPHAË, wife of MINOS, by a white bull, which POSEIDON had made mad because Minos had not sacrificed it to him. Minos employed DAEDALUS to construct the LABYRINTH to restrain the Minotaur and keep it from escaping. Because ANDROGEUS, Minos' son, had met death when AEGEUS of Athens sent him out against the Bull of Marathon, Minos demanded a periodic tribute of seven girls and seven boys from Athens. This sacrifice of the Athenian youths and maidens to the Minotaur was ended only when THESEUS slew the Minotaur with the help of ARIADNE.

Miolnir or **Mjolnir** (myuhl′-nir), Sc, THOR's magic hammer that always flew true and struck its mark, returning to his hand again. Marriages were consecrated by Thor's hammer.

Miru (mee′-roo) or **Milu** (-loo), O, the Polynesian god of one of the sections of PO, the underworld, where evildoers met lasting torture by fire.

Misharu (mi-shah′-ru), A-B, the representation of law and order.

Mithraeum (mi-three′-um), Pe & R, a temple dedicated to MITHRAS, generally a sanctuary in the form of a man-made cave hollowed out of the rock. Those at Ostia and Capua in Italy are good examples of such structures, which were numerous when Mithraism was at its height.

Mithras (mith′-ras) or **Mithra** (-ru), Pe, one of the most important gods during the era preceding Zoroastrianism and the worship of AHURA MAZDA. Mithras was venerated as a deity of light and purity. In later mythology, he was a sun-god and guided the sun's chariot. Mithras was also a mighty warrior who held the power of victory in his hands. The cult of Mithras spread into Europe, where he was widely worshiped in the time of the Roman Empire.

Mitra (mee′-tru), Pe, 1. an early Aryan deity who was a god of justice and agreements, later regarded as the defender of truth.

I, 2. the Vedic god of justice, guardian of friendship and contracts. He was a sun deity, protector of the daylight. Mitra was a son of ADITI and was one of the ADITYAS.

Mixcoatl (meeks'-koh-aht'l), Az, originally the god of the hunt, who hurled thunderbolts and was often depicted as a deer, but, at a later date, a stellar deity. His mother was CIHUATCOATL.

Mjolnir (myuhl'-nir), Sc. *See* MIOLNIR.

Mnemosyne (nee-mahs'-u-nee), G, a TITANESS, the daughter of URANUS and GAEA. She was the personification of memory and was the mother of the MUSES by ZEUS.

Modred (moh'-drid) or **Mordred** (mawr'-dred), Ce, King ARTHUR's nephew, son of MORGAN LE FAY. While Arthur and his troops were attacking the Romans on the continent, Modred usurped Arthur's kingdom and GUINEVERE committed adultery with him. Modred was killed in the battle that followed Arthur's hasty return, and Arthur himself was mortally wounded.

Moerae, the (mee'-ree), G, the three FATES, offspring of EREBUS and NYX or ZEUS and THEMIS; called the PARCAE by the Romans.

Monan (moh-nahn'), SA, an ancient Tupi-Guarani hero who created mankind. He later attempted the destruction of the world by fire to punish men for their evil ways, but a great flood saved it.

Mont (mawnt) or **Menthu** (men'-too), E, a war-god of THEBES who went into battle against the enemies of the pharaoh. He lived mainly at the "City of Mont," Hermonthis, in Upper Egypt and not far from Thebes. He was, for a time, adopted by AMON and MUT and called their son.

Worshiped as a sun-god at KARNAK, Mont was identified with APOLLO by the Greeks. He was depicted as falcon- or bull-headed, wearing the disk of the sun and two long plumes on his head.

Mordred (mawr'-dred), Ce. *See* MODRED.

Morgan le Fay (mawr'-gun lu fay'), Ce, the sister of ARTHUR and mother of GAWAIN and MODRED. She was a fairy or a priestess of water and used her power of healing to heal Arthur's injuries.

Morold (mawr'-uld), Ce, a supporter of the Irish king, who yearly exacted a round of duty from the young men of Cornwall. He was slain by TRISTRAM, who was wounded in the combat.

Morpheus (mawr'-fee-us), G, god of dreams, the son of HYPNOS. He was sometimes called the god of sleep, hence the phrase "in the arms of Morpheus."

Morte d'Arthur, Le (lu mawrt' dahr'-thur), Ce, a fifteenth-century prose narrative by Sir Thomas Malory, who combined and translated into English most of the existing French versions of the legends surrounding King ARTHUR.

Mot (maht), Ph, a god of the harvesting of crops, especially corn. He was the son of EL. Since Mot held sway over the drying sun that came at harvest time, BAAL fought and overcame him at the start of the rains.

In a poem found at RAS SHAMRA, the perennial struggle between Mot (dry) and Baal (wet) is described. After the death of Mot at the hands of Baal, the goddess ANAT sought revenge by slaying Baal and applying all the processes of the harvest to his body as though it were grain. With Baal's return from the underworld, the rains fell and the rejuvenation of the earth began, starting the new cycle of growth.

Mu King (muh' jing', king'), Ch, the god and ruler of the immortals. Mu King was the first living creation, born of primeval vapor.

Muluku (moo-loo'-koo), Af, the supreme god in the mythology of Mozambique. Muluku created a man and a woman from holes he made in the ground, then gave them instructions on how to use the tools and seeds he gave them. When they did as they pleased and had no success in supporting their own lives, Muluku gave the same counsel and implements to two monkeys, who carried out his recommendations. Then, putting monkeys' tails on the man and woman, he told them to be monkeys and told the monkeys to be humans.

Mummu (moo'-moo), A-B, the personification of the waves of the ocean, created from the union of APSU and TIAMAT.

Muses, the (myooz'-uz), G, the nine daughters of ZEUS and MNEMOSYNE who inspired and guided creative and intellectual activity. They were CALLIOPE, muse of epic poetry (represented with a parchment roll or tablet); CLIO, history (a partially opened scroll); ERATO, love poetry (small lyre); EUTERPE, music and lyric poetry (double flute); MELPOMENE, tragedy (tragic mask); POLYHYMNIA, hymns and sacred music (veiled figure); TERPSICHORE, dance (lyre); THALIA, comedy (comic mask); URANIA, astronomy (a rod in one hand and a globe in the other).

Muspelheim (muhs'-pul-haym), Sc, a land of fire, south of the abyss of space, that existed in the very beginning, before the creation of the world, and whose fire sent forth warming winds, melting NIFLHEIM's ice to mist. Muspelheim was ruled by SURT.

Mut (moot) or **Maut** (mawt), E, a goddess of motherhood and the womanly arts, worshiped at THEBES as the consort of AMON. Mut was depicted as lioness- or vulture-headed.

Mycenae (mahy-see'-nee), G, a city located on a rock ridge high above the plain of Argos, the home of ATREUS, THYESTES, and

AGAMEMNON, among others. The ACROPOLIS was fortified by great Cyclopean walls, said to have been built by PERSEUS with the help of the CYCLOPES. Archaeologists, starting with Heinrich Schliemann's excavations between 1874 and 1876, have uncovered the palace, smaller but similar to that of MINOS at CNOSSUS, many tombs, and numerous fine artifacts of gold and other precious metals, all pointing to a civilization parallel to that of the Minoan Age of Crete.

Myesyats (mi-us-yahtz'), Sl, the moon. In some myths, Myesyats is depicted as the young wife of the sun-god, a summer bride who was deserted each winter. In others, Myesyats was considered to be a male, the uncle of the sun, or the sun's husband and father of the stars, their offspring.

Myrddin (mur'-thin), Ce, a name by which MERLIN was known in early Welsh legend.

Myrmidons, the (mur'-mi-dahnz), G, the followers of ACHILLES in the TROJAN WAR. In jealousy, HERA sent a plague against Aegina, where AEACUS, son of ZEUS and AEGINA, was king. When Aeacus called on Zeus for help, he saw a colony of ants and begged that they become men. Zeus changed the ants into men, called Myrmidons from the word *myrmex*, meaning "ant," to repopulate the island. During the period of the wrath of Achilles, PATROCLUS led his friend's warriors and defeated the Trojans in battle but lost his own life.

Myrtilus (mur'-ti-lus), G, the charioteer of Oenamaus, king of Elis. In a chariot race against Oenamaus for the hand of his daughter, HIPPODAMIA, PELOPS won, because he bribed Myrtilus with the promise of half of his kingdom to remove the pins from Oenamaus' chariot wheels, killing him. When Pelops cast him over a cliff into the sea, Myrtilus pronounced a curse on the House of Pelops.

Mysteries, the, G & R, secret religious ceremonies which led to the purification of those individuals taking part. The most popular were those associated with the worship of DIONYSUS and DEMETER; the most famous, the ELEUSINIAN MYSTERIES, honoring Demeter and her daughter, PERSEPHONE. The mysteries were in the charge of priests, and their secrets were known only to their initiates. Much of the ritual was symbolic. The mysteries later spread throughout the Roman Empire, and numerous foreign elements, especially those connected with the worship of ISIS and MITHRAS, were introduced.

Nabu (nab'-oo), A-B, the son of MARDUK. Nabu was god of wisdom and intelligence and patron of writing and scribes. The TABLETS OF FATE were in his charge, and he inscribed the judgments made by the gods. Nabu was the husband of TASHMETUM, or, in some versions, of

NISABA. He was represented, as was Marduk, with a dragon and also with the tools of engraving.

Nagas, the (nah'-guz), I, a group of serpents, appearing sometimes with human shape or as monsters, but generally simply as snakes, who were known for their strength and deception. The Nagas lived under the earth in a kingdom of magnificent palaces, temples, and great buildings of all sorts. Their ruler was VASUKI.

Nagenatzani (nah-gu-naht-zah'-nee) and Thobadestchin (thoh-bad-est'-chin), NA, twin sons of ESTANATLEHI who were highly revered warrior heroes of the Navaho Indians. Their father was the sun.

Nah-Hunte (nah-hun'-tu), A-B, the sun-god of the Elamites. He was also a deity of law and order and of light.

Naiades, the (nay'-u-deez), G. See NAIADS.

Naiads, the (nay'-adz), or Naiades (nay'-u-deez), G, deities who were nymphs of the rivers, springs, brooks, and fountains.

Nala (nul'-u), I, the son of VISVAKARMA by a monkey queen. Nala was the designer of the bridge to LANKA that was erected for RAMA, and directed the monkeys in its construction.

Namtar (nahm'-tahr), A-B, an evil spirit who brought plagues to mankind and carried out the destructive plans of NERGAL. His abode was ARALLU, and he acted as the messenger of ERESHKIGAL. When ISHTAR sought TAMMUZ in the underworld, Namtar was ordered to strike her with disease and later restored her to health upon her release.

Nanna (nah'-nah), A-B, 1. the moon-god of the Sumerians. He was the counterpart of the Babylonian god SIN. Nannar is a variant of his name.

(nahn'-nah), Sc, 2. the moon-goddess, wife of BALDER and the mother of FORSETI. Nanna died of heartbroken grief, when she saw the body of her husband, slain by the mistletoe thrown by HODER, and was placed beside him on his funeral pyre.

Nanshe (nahn'-shu), A-B, a goddess of the waters of springs who had the ability to interpret the dreams sent by ZAQAR. A daughter of EA, she was, like her father, worshiped at ERIDU and at Lagash, where a yearly festival was held in her honor.

Narasinha (nu-ru-sin'-hu), I, the fourth AVATAR of VISHNU, who appeared in the form of a man-lion, a human with the head of a lion, and killed the demon HIRANYA-KASIPU.

Narayana (nah-ru-yah'-nu), I, a name given at times to an aspect of BRAHMA and, in other versions, to an aspect of VISHNU. Narayana was born from the primordial egg floating on the waters before the creation. The universe and everything in it then sprang into being from his will.

Narcissus (nahr-sis'-us), G, a handsome youth, loved by the NYMPH ECHO, whom he scorned because she could only repeat his words. Narcissus was punished by NEMESIS, who made him fall in love with his own reflection. Narcissus wasted away with love of himself, and the flower narcissus came into being where he had lain.

Nataraja (nah-tu-rah'-ju), I, a manifestation of SHIVA as the master of rhythm and dancing and a name by which he was sometimes called.

Nauplius (naw'-plee-us), G, the son of POSEIDON and AMYMONE and the founder of the city of Nauplia on the Gulf of Corinth.

Nausicaä (naw-sik'-ay-u), G, the daughter of ALCINOUS and ARETE, king and queen of the PHAEACIANS, who found ODYSSEUS asleep on the shore, after he had been borne to their island by a storm, and took him to the palace, where he recounted his adventures. In some versions, she later married Odysseus' son TELEMACHUS.

Naxos (nak'-sahs), G, an Aegean island favored by DIONYSUS. It was here that ARIADNE was deserted by THESEUS.

Ndriananahary (undree-ah-nah'-nah-hah'-ree), Af, the supreme god in the legends of the Madagascans and the father of ATAOKOLOINONA. When his son went down into the earth, Ndriananahary sent men from heaven to search for him, but without success. The god, however, gave mankind rain to make the earth fertile and to cool them, as their reward for their unending search. Men travel to heaven continually to report on their efforts to find his son, but they fail to return, since they have become the dead.

Nebhet Hotep (neb'-et hoh'-tep), E, in later Egyptian mythology, the mother of SHU and TEFNUT and wife of ATUM.

Nebmerutef (neb-mer'-u-tef), E, a scribe who was inspired by THOTH, the patron god of writing and the keeping of records.

Nebthet (neb'-thet), E. See NEPHTHYS.

Nectar (nek'-tur), G, the drink of the gods, poured by their cupbearer, HEBE or GANYMEDE.

Nefer Hor (nef'-ur hohr), E, a son of the god THOTH.

Nefertem (nay'-fer-tem) or Nefertum (-tum), E, the son of PTAH and SEKHMET. Nefertem was associated with the setting sun and he was believed to be a personification of Ptah as the lotus of the god RA. One of his attributes was a saber. He was represented with a lotus flower, containing two long stalks, surmounting his head. Nefertem was called Iphtimis by the Greeks.

Neheh (nee'-hee) or **Heh** (hee), E, a god who was the personification of eternity, representing unending time and a long, happy life.

Nehmauit (nee-maw'-it), E, a wife of THOTH. Her name means "Uprooter of Evil."

Neit (nee'-it), E. See NEITH.

Neith (nee'-ith) or **Neit** (-it), E, a goddess who was worshiped from the earliest times, especially in the Nile Delta. Femininity personified, Neith was a skilled weaver and was the patron deity of the arts of domestic life. In addition, Neith was a goddess of war, identified by the Greeks with ATHENA, and was generally depicted with a shield and arrows or with a bow and arrows. Neith was also equated with SELKET in her role as a deity of the dead, and with ISIS and HATHOR, and was sometimes said to be the mother of RA.

Nekhbet (nek'-bet) or **Nekhebet** (-u-bet), E, a goddess, guardian of Upper Egypt, often depicted as a serpent or a vulture, protecting the pharaoh as she hovers over his head with her wings outstretched.

Nekhebet (nek'-u-bet), E. See NEKHBET.

Nemean Games, the (ni-mee'-un), G, one of the great national festivals, held every two years at Nemea, a site in the northeastern part of the Peloponnesus.

Nemean Lion, the (ni-mee'-un), G, a fierce creature, born of TYPHON and ECHIDNA, that lived in the hills near Nemea in Argolis. As one of his Labors, HERACLES strangled the lion and took it to MYCENAE on his shoulders. Heracles, thereafter, wore the lion's skin as a cloak. See also LABORS OF HERACLES.

Nemesis (nem'-u-sis), G, the child of EREBUS and NYX who represented divine vengeance and righteous anger. It was the aim of Nemesis to preserve moderation and a middle course in the activities of mankind.

Neoptolemus (nee-ahp-tahl'-u-mus), G, the valiant son of ACHILLES and Deidamia. After the death of his father in the TROJAN WAR, he went to Troy and killed PRIAM. He was also, in some accounts, the one who hurled ASTYANAX from the walls of Troy. Neoptolemus received ANDROMACHE as his prize of victory, but soon deserted her. In some versions, he later married HERMIONE, daughter of MENELAUS and HELEN. Neoptolemus, sometimes called PYRRHUS, died in DELPHI.

Nephele (nef'-u-lee), G, a cloud shaped in the form of HERA by ZEUS to ward off IXION's lust for the goddess. She was the mother of PHRIXUS and HELLE by ATHAMAS. Nephele put Phrixus and Helle on a ram with a GOLDEN FLEECE so they could escape from the jealousy of INO, then the wife of Athamas, who planned the sacrifice of the children to end a famine.

Nephthys (nef'-this), E, one of the early deities of Egyptian mythology, the daughter of GEB and NUT, goddess of death, and sister and wife of SET. She was generally said to be the mother of ANUBIS. Nephthys, who was also known as Nebthet, had magical powers, especially the ability to restore life to the dead.

Neptune (nep'-toon), R, the god of the sea, wed to Salacia, a goddess of salt water, who corresponded to AMPHITRITE, Neptune was the Roman counterpart of POSEIDON.

Nereids, the (neer'-ee-idz), G, the fifty nymphs of the sea who came to the aid of sailors. They were the daughters of NEREUS and the OCEANID DORIS. The best known were AMPHITRITE, wife of POSEIDON, THETIS, PELEUS' wife and the mother of ACHILLES, and GALATEA.

Nereus (neer'-ee-us), G, a god of the sea, the son of PONTUS and GAEA, and father of the NEREIDS by DORIS. Nereus, called the Old Man of the Sea, lived in a cave in the Aegean Sea. It was from Nereus that HERACLES learned the location of the GOLDEN APPLES.

Nergal (nehr'-gahl), A-B, in early myth, a god of war. Nergal led a company of evil spirits into the underworld, forcing its queen, ERESHKIGAL, to marry him and appoint him sovereign of her kingdom as the price of peace. Nergal's attribute was a sword or the head of a lion. He was sometimes called Meshlamthea.

Nerthus (nur'-thus), Sc, a fertility- and earth-goddess who, in an account by the Roman historian TACITUS, traveled through Denmark in a wagon, dispensing peace, prosperity, and happiness.

Nessus (nes'-us), G, the CENTAUR whom HERACLES killed with one of his poisoned arrows because of his attentions to DEIANIRA. As he was dying, Nessus gave Deianira the poison from his blood, which she later put on the robe that led to Heracles' death.

Nestor (nes'-tur), G, king of Pylos in southern Greece, the only one of the twelve sons of Neleus and Chloris not to be killed by HERACLES. Nestor took part in the expedition of the ARGONAUTS and the CALYDONIAN BOAR hunt. He was considered the wisest of counselors among the Greeks during the TROJAN WAR, as well as the oldest.

Ngendei (ng-gen'-day), O, a deity of the Fiji Islands who upholds the earth, causes earthquakes, and is ruler of the land of the dead. Comets are believed to be his children. In some accounts, Ngendei is called the creator of the world and of mankind. His form is half snake and half man.

Nibelungenlied, the (nee'-bu-luhng-un-leet), T, an epic written in about the thirteenth century and corresponding to the VOLSUNGA SAGA. The poem, centering around the hero SIEGFRIED, son of SIEGMUND and SIEGLINDE, narrates the main events of his life and relates his exploits and those of the other heroes involved. The gods, who played a major part in the Volsunga Saga, appear in a minor role in the *Nibelungenlied*.

Nibelungs, the (nee'-bu-luhngz), Sc & T, a race of DWARFS, also known as "children of mist," who had the famous treasure and magic ring which SIEGFRIED took from them. The Nibelungs lived below the earth, in Nibelungenland, or Nibelheim. After Siegfried overcame the Nibelungs, his warriors were also known by that name. Richard Wagner wrote a series of four operas, *The Ring of the Nibelung*, comprising the entire legend of the gold of the Nibelungs.

Nidhogg (need'-hawg), Sc, a serpent who lived in NIFLHEIM and continually gnawed at the roots of YGGDRASIL.

Niflheim (niv'-ul-haym), Sc, the underworld, where the souls of the dead went. Niflheim, lying north of the gaping abyss of space, was a region of ice and mist out of which twelve rivers flowed and turned to ice. The goddess HEL was queen of Niflheim, and YGGDRASIL had some of its roots there.

Nihongi, the (nyee'-hong-gi), J, a history of Japan completed in A.D. 720. It was written in Chinese, for lack of a Japanese system of writing at that date. The first section of the chronicles contains the various versions of Japanese myths and legends then known. It gives an account of the emperors of Japan, showing that the first emperor descended directly from the sun-goddess AMATERASU, and it emphasizes the people of Yamato over those of Izumo province.

Nike (nahy'-kee), G, the daughter of PALLAS and STYX who was the goddess of victory. Nike aided ZEUS and the other Olympian gods against the TITANS. She was usually depicted as winged and often held a branch of palm as a symbol of victory. Her Roman counterpart was VICTORIA.

Nina (nee'-nah), A-B, 1. a daughter of EA and goddess of the city of the same name, later called Ninevah. She uttered oracular responses from the temple at Nina, dedicated to her brother NINURTA. SA, 2. the Incan deity of fire.

Ninazu (nin'-ah-zoo), A-B, the grandfather of TAMMUZ.

Ningal (nin'-gal), A-B, a sun-goddess, the wife of SIN, and mother of SHAMASH.

Ningirsu (nin-gir'-soo), A-B. *See* NINURTA.

Ningishzida (nin-gish-zee'-dah), A-B, the father of TAMMUZ, with whom he guarded the gate of ANU's dwelling place.

Ninhursag (nin-huhr'-sag), A-B. *See* NIN-KHURSAG.

Ninib (nee'-nib), A-B. *See* NINURTA.

Ninigi (nee-nee'-gee), J, the grandson of AMATERASU, who sent him to dwell on earth and gave him the mirror with which the gods had enticed her to the mouth of the cave where she was hiding. The sacred mirror was set in the sun-goddess' principal shrine at ISE. Ninigi came to the throne after ONAMUJI, the son of SUSANOWO, was forced to abdicate. He had in his possession the three symbols of power, the mirror, jewels, and a sword, which continued thereafter to be the imperial emblems.

Ninigiku (nin-u-gee'-koo), A-B, a name, meaning "King of the Sacred Eye," given to EA because of his omniscience and wisdom.

Nin-Karrak (nin-kahr'-rahk), A-B, a goddess of health, considered to be a daughter of ANU, and sometimes given the role of consort of NINURTA.

Nin-khursag (nin-kuhr'-sag) or **Ninhursag** (-huhr'-), A B, a name under which NINLIL was sometimes worshiped.

Ninki (nin'-kee), A-B, the consort of EA. She was also called Damkina.

Ninlil (nin'-lil), A-B, the main wife of ASSUR. In early mythology, Ninlil was considered to be ENLIL's consort, who assisted him in bestowing kingship upon earthly monarchs. Ninlil was a goddess of fertility.

Ninsun (neen-soon'), A-B, the mother of the hero GILGAMESH. Ninsun was a goddess of URUK and was considered omniscient.

Nintud (nin'-tuhd), A-B. *See* BELIT-ILI.

Ninurta (ni-nuhr'-tah), A-B, the son of ENLIL. Primarily a war-god and hunter, he was also a fertility deity and the south wind personified. The world of nature went to war, taking sides against and for him. After Ninurta vanquished his foes, he cursed them, while he favored with his blessing those who had taken his side, thus dividing the common stones from the valued ones.

Ninurta's wife was BAU and their anniversary was celebrated each New Year's Day. In some localities, GULA or NIN-KARRAK was said to be his wife.

The center of Ninurta's cult was Lagash, where a temple to him was built after an apparition came to the king, instructing him to erect it. Ninurta's symbol was an eagle and he was sometimes represented as lion-headed. He was known also as Ninib or Ningirsu.

Niobe (nahy'-oh-bee), G, the daughter of TANTALUS and wife of King AMPHION of THEBES to whom she bore seven sons and seven daughters. Because Niobe boasted she was superior to LETO, the latter had her two children, APOLLO and ARTEMIS, kill all of Niobe's children with their arrows. Amphion then took his own life, and Niobe wept until the gods turned her to stone, always damp with her tears.

Niord or **Njord** (nyawrd), Sc, one of the VANIR. He was the husband of SKADI, daughter of THIAZI, and the father of FREY and FREYA. Niord was the god of fertility and of the sea, over which he ruled as king of the winds and the protective deity of sailors.

Nisaba (ni-sah'-bu), A-B, the Sumerian goddess of grain crops and the harvest, corresponding to the Greek goddess DEMETER. Nisaba, the sister of NANSHE, was considered to be the wife of NABU.

Nisus (nahy'-sus), G, the king of Megara, which could not fall so long as the lock of purple hair was not cut from Nisus' head. His daughter, SCYLLA, cut off the lock when MINOS, whom she loved, was attacking Megara. Nisus was changed into an eagle of the sea by the gods.

Njord (nyawrd), Sc. *See* NIORD.

Nobu (noh'-boo), O, in legends of the New Hebrides, the creator of the world.

Nokomis (noh-koh'-mis), NA, in Algonquin legend, Mother Earth, dwelling in the sky below the clouds and nourishing all living things. She was the grandmother of MANABOZHO.

Noncomala (non-coh-mah'-lu), in Costa Rican myth, the father of the sun and the moon and the creator of the earth and mankind. When he saw men had become evil, he wiped them out by sending a deluge upon the world.

Norns, the (nawrnz), Sc, the three goddesses who took care of

YGGDRASIL, the sacred tree, and ordained the fate and destiny of mankind and the gods. URD, the past, and VERDANDI, the present, were beneficent and formed the web of fate. SKULD, the future, was maleficent and tore the web.

Notus (noh'-tus), G, the south wind, offspring of ASTRAEUS and EOS. The Romans called the south wind AUSTER.

Nox (noks), R, goddess of night, the counterpart of NYX.

Nuada (noo'-u-thu), Ce, a god and king of the TUATHA DE DANANN. He lost his hand in battle and was fitted with an artificial silver one. Nuada was the possessor of a mighty sword, an all-powerful weapon.

Nubu (noo-boo'), a benevolent deity in Costa Rican legend, who rescued the seeds of mankind from the flood sent upon them by NONCOMALA and planted them to produce a new generation of men. Those seeds that did not ripen fully became monkeys.

Nudd (nooth), Ce. See LLUDD.

Nu-kua (noo'-kwah'), Ch, the one who, after the formation of heaven and earth, molded mankind of yellow clay and is credited with helping to bring civilization to China. She was said to have replaced the overturned poles of the world with the feet of a giant turtle and to have repaired the widespread damage that accompanied the catastrophic flood and fire, restoring order to heaven and earth.

Nun (noon), E. See NUNU.

Nunu (noo'-noo) or **Nun** (noon), E, a god who was the personification of the ocean and the waters of chaos, the primordial source from which the world was shaped.

Nurrundere (nur-run-de-ray'), O, the name given in the Murray River area of Australia to the hero who brought crafts and skills to his people and established tribal customs and religious rituals. In Victoria, he was known as PUN-GEL, in northern Australia as BIRAL, and elsewhere as BUN-JIL.

Nusku (nuhs'-kuh), A-B, a god of fire, son of SIN or of ANU. It was he who burned the sacrificial offerings to the gods. In early mythology, Nusku was the minister of ENLIL, and he sometimes acted as a god of justice.

Nut (noot), E, the sky-goddess, the child of SHU, dryness, and TEFNUT, water, and one of the deities of the ENNEAD. Nut and her brother GEB were the parents of OSIRIS, ISIS, SET, and NEPHTHYS. She was comparable to the Greek goddess RHEA. It was Nut who, in the form of a cow, carried RA to the heavens, where she became the support of the sky. Nut, sometimes represented bearing a vase on her head, was usually depicted with her hands and feet planted on the earth and her body arching up to form the vault of heaven.

Nyambe (nyahm'-bee), Af, in the mythology of the Zambezi, the sun. When men attempted to slay Nyambe, they were punished for it.

Nyame (nyahm'-ee), Af, the sky-god and ruler of the storms and lightning, the chief god or supreme being of the Ashanti, who was driven from earth to the upper reaches of the sky by the noise of the pounding of grain. Nyame gave mankind the moon and sun, rain, and other blessings, after the spider ANANSE reported man's needs to him.

Nymphs, the (nimfs), G, goddesses of nature who presided over the streams, mountains, fountains, caves, fields, woods, and the like. There were some groups of nymphs who had special provinces within their power. They were the DRYADS and HAMADRYADS, woods and trees; NAIADS, springs and rivers; OCEANIDS, the sea; and OREADS, the hills.

Nyx (niks), G, the goddess of night, born of CHAOS and sister of EREBUS. Nyx bore AETHER, HEMERA, NEMESIS, and numerous other children to her brother-husband Erebus.

Nzambi (unzahm'-bee) or **Nzame** (-ee), Af, in legends of the Bantu tribes, the supreme deity and creator of the human race. The first man created by Nzambi became evil and destructive. As a result, he was buried, and another man was created. He shaped a wife from wood, and they were the ancestors of mankind.

Nzame (unzahm'-ee), Af. *See* NZAMBI.

Obelisk (ob'-u-lisk), E, a tall, slender, and tapered four-sided shaft, usually a monolith, rising to a pyramidlike point at its top. Generally connected with the worship of RA, the sun-god, and representing the sun's ray in a petrified form, the peaks were covered with copper or gold to catch and reflect the light of the sun. They ranged from about fifty to ninety feet in height, and the four sides were carved with hieroglyphics. The highest of the obelisks, now in Rome, was taken from HELIOPOLIS by Emperor Constantine. Obelisks, often in pairs, were erected at the entrance to a temple, or were even placed inside the temple.

Oceanids, the (oh-see'-u-nidz), G, the three thousand NYMPHS of the oceans and rivers, daughters of the TITANS OCEANUS and TETHYS.

Oceanus (oh-see'-u-nus), G, 1. a TITAN, the son of URANUS and GAEA, who was only one not to rise up against Uranus. Oceanus was married to his sister TETHYS, and they were the parents of the OCEANIDS.

2. the personification of the ocean, which was believed to surround the entire earth and bound the limits of the world, and from which all streams, fountains, and rivers sprang.

Ocyrrhoë (oh-sir'-oh-ee), G, the daughter of the CENTAUR CHIRON, who prophesied the future fame of the infant ASCLEPIUS. She was turned into a mare by the gods, who were angered over her powers of prophecy.

Odin (oh'-din), Sc, the god of war, magic, and poetry. BURI's son Bor was Odin's father by a giantess. Odin set the sun and moon on their courses at the creation of the world and brought ASK and EMBLA, the first man and woman, to life. Odin, the chief Scandinavian deity and king of the AESIR, was wed to FRIGG, lived in VALHALLA with the heroes fallen in battle, and had as his attendants and messengers the VALKYRIES. Two ravens kept him informed on everything. He had an eight-legged horse named SLEIPNIR; a great spear, GUNGNIR; and a magic ring, DRAUPNIR. Odin was the father of BALDER, BALI, BRAGI, HODER, THOR, TYR, and VIDAR.

By the skill of his magic powers, Odin gained the mead of inspiration, source of the poet's skill, for the gods and, in turn, for mankind from the GIANT SUTTUNG, who had stolen it from the DWARFS and closed it up in a mountain. Odin, with the help of Suttung's brother BAUGI, whom he tricked, pierced the mountain, transformed himself into a serpent, slipped inside, and spent three nights with Suttung's daughter. She gave him the mead and, holding it in his mouth, Odin, in the shape of an eagle, flew with it to ASGARD, where he spat it out for the gods to have for their use and to give to men.

Odin was consumed at RAGNAROK by the wolf FENRIR. He was identified with the Anglo-Saxon Woden and the Teutonic WOTAN.

Odomankoma (oh-doh-mahn-koh'-mu), Af, in myths of the Ashanti, the creator of mankind and all things of the earth, including death. Death not only controlled living creatures but ultimately overcame even Odomankoma himself.

Odudua (oh-doo'-doo-u), Af, the earth-goddess of the Yoruba tribe of West Africa and mother of AGANJU and YEMAJA. Their father was Obatala, the sky-god and ruler of the heavens, or, in another version, Orishako, the patron god of farming.

Odysseus (oh-dis'-ee-us), G, king of Ithaca, son of LAERTES and Anticlea, husband of PENELOPE, and father of TELEMACHUS; his Roman name was Ulysses or Ulixes. At first unwilling to take part in the TROJAN WAR, Odysseus pretended to be mad, but he turned his plow aside when he saw that Telemachus had been placed in its path as a test, thus revealing his sanity. He was a wise and crafty leader of the Greeks in the war. After the death of ACHILLES he held the Trojans back, and he won the contest for the armor of Achilles over AJAX. His extended journey home to Ithaca after the Trojan War is the subject of HOMER's ODYSSEY, in which he is depicted as a paragon of shrewdness, perseverance, and endurance. His character has been variously interpreted from ancient times to the present: to some, he has appeared as a craven schemer; to others, as an ingenious and resolute victim of misfortune; and to still others, he is the representative of mankind wandering through the vicissitudes of life.

Odyssey, the   (od'-i-see), Greek epic poem in twenty-four books of dactylic hexameter verse, attributed to Homer. The work begins with an account of the last fifty days of the decade of wandering by ODYSSEUS as he tries to return home from the TROJAN WAR. ATHENA, in accordance with the gods' decision to allow Odysseus to return home, appears in disguise at Ithaca to advise TELEMACHUS, Odysseus' son, to seek news of his father in NESTOR's kingdom of Pylos and from MENELAUS at Sparta. Menelaus informs Telemachus that Odysseus was reputed to be at OGYGIA with the nymph CALYPSO. At HERMES' command, Calypso assists Odysseus to prepare for his departure. POSEIDON wrecks the craft with which Odysseus left and casts him ashore on the island of Phaeacia. Courteously received and promised safe passage by the Phaeacian king ALCINOUS and his daughter NAUSICAÄ, Odysseus is reminded of his sufferings by the song of a court minstrel. Thereupon, he relates the many incidents of his wanderings.

When his men ate the fruit in the land of the LOTUS-EATERS, Odysseus dragged them to the ships and tied them. One of the CYCLOPES, POLYPHEMUS, ate some of his men and kept Odysseus and his remaining companions imprisoned, but they escaped by burning out the giant's eye with a sharpened tree trunk and clinging beneath his sheep when he rolled the tremendous rock away from the entrance of his cave to let his sheep out to pasture. King AEOLUS sent Odysseus off with all the winds in a bag, with the exception of a favoring westerly breeze, but the men opened the bag and their ships were blown back to Aeolia, delaying their journey. In the land of the Laestrygonians, all the ships and men were destroyed, except for Odysseus' own ship, which had not entered the small harbor. CIRCE turned his men to swine, but Hermes helped him persuade her to restore them to human form. He visited HADES, where TIRESIAS explained to him how he could reach Ithaca. On his second visit to Aeaea, Circe gave him a favorable wind. They passed the island of the SIRENS safely when Odysseus stuffed his comrades' ears and tied himself to the mast. Some of his men were lost when they passed SCYLLA and CHARYBDIS. ZEUS struck the ship with lightning and all but Odysseus were drowned, because they had killed the oxen of HELIOS. Odysseus then went to Ogygia, where he spent eight years with Calypso.

When they hear his story, the PHAEACIANS take Odysseus back to Ithaca, where, after concealing his identity in the guise of a beggar, he finally slays the suitors of his faithful wife PENELOPE, regains mastery of his house, and reasserts his claim to leadership in Ithaca. To all the qualities of the ILIAD (except extensive battle scenes) are added more varied episodes, a more complex hero, and a more sophisticated theme. A source of literary and artistic inspiration through the ages, the *Odyssey* theme has been most recently reinterpreted and extended in Joyce's *Ulysses* and Kazantzakis' *Odyssey*.

Oedipus (ed'-u-pus), G, the tragic hero of a saga antedating the TROJAN WAR. LAIUS, king of THEBES, received a prophecy that any child he sired by his wife JOCASTA would commit patricide and be guilty of incest with his mother. When Oedipus was born to the couple, Laius bound his feet together and ordered a shepherd to leave him on Mt. Cithaeron to die. The shepherd pitied the child and handed him over to a friend. The friend gave him to Polybus and MEROPE, king and queen of Corinth, who raised him as their son. When Oedipus grew to manhood, he heard a rumor that he was an adopted child. Seeking the truth from the Delphic Oracle, he was ordered from the temple because he was destined to kill his father and marry his mother, but his real parents were not identified. To avoid the dismal fate foretold, and assuming that his parents were Polybus and Merope, Oedipus resolved never to return to Corinth and journeyed to Thebes. En route, he met and killed an old man whom he did not know, but who turned out to be Laius, thus fulfilling the first part of the prophecy.

Oedipus saved the city of Thebes by solving the riddle of the SPHINX, and as a result became king of Thebes and married Jocasta, completing the prophecy. They had four children, ANTIGONE, ISMENE, ETEOCLES and POLYNICES. When a plague fell upon the city because of the unavenged murder of Laius, Oedipus undertook to identify and punish the killer. Though warned by the prophet TIRESIAS that the quest would have dire results, Oedipus continued the search until his acts of patricide and incest were revealed. Jocasta then committed suicide, and Oedipus blinded himself.

The tragedy of Oedipus has inspired many literary works. SOPHOCLES, Seneca, and Voltaire have all interpreted the theme. Freud employed its psychological aspects in his theories.

Oeneus (ee'-nee-us), G, a king of Calydon, husband of ALTHAEA, father of MELEAGER and DEIANIRA. A wild boar was sent to plague the countryside, because Oeneus had neglected to sacrifice to ARTEMIS. This led to the CALYDONIAN BOAR hunt.

Oenone (ee-noh'-nee), G, the NYMPH who lived on Mt. IDA and who married PARIS prior to his abduction of HELEN. Having foretold that Paris would desert her and bring ruin to Troy, Oenone killed herself when Paris succumbed to the wounds he incurred when he was struck by one of the arrows of PHILOCTETES.

Oenopion (ee-noh'-pee-ahn), G, the father of MEROPE. He was the son of ARIADNE, in some versions by DIONYSUS, in other versions by THESEUS.

Oeta, Mt. (ee'-tu), G, the place of HERACLES' death. After DEIANIRA gave him the fatal robe, Heracles died on Mt. Oeta on a funeral pyre lighted by PHILOCTETES at his command.

Ogma (og'-mu), Ce, the son of DAGDA and BOANN. He was the eloquent god of learning and poetry, credited with the invention of the alphabet. Ogma was one of the TUATHA DE DANANN.

Ogygia (oh-jij'-ee-u), G, a Mediterranean island, the home of the nymph CALYPSO. *See also* ODYSSEY.

Oileus (oh-il'-ee-us), G, the father of AJAX the Lesser and king of the Locrians.

Okuninushi (aw-koo'-nee-noo'-shee), J, the son born to SUSANOWO after he went to dwell in Izumo province. He was an earth-god and god of healing and medicine. Okuninushi underwent numerous trials and labors after he made Susanowo's daughter Suseri-Hime his wife and was ultimately made ruler of Izumo.

Olokun (oh-loh'-kun), Af, the sea-god of the Yoruba tribe of West Africa.

Olorun (oh'-law-run), Af, the chief deity of the West African Yoruba tribe, whose pantheon included a relatively large number of gods, most of whom quite possibly had been early tribal leaders who received worship after death. Olorun was the lord and ruler of heaven, who, according to one myth, was born of the primordial ocean, OLOKUN. His role appears to be a passive one, and he is not the focus of either myth or worship.

Olympia (oh-lim'-pee-u), G, a site in the northwestern part of the

Peloponnesus, sacred to ZEUS and one of the most important Panhellenic shrines. The sanctuary of Zeus was a walled precinct and sacred grove, situated at the foot of the Hill of CRONUS. In it were the seventh century B.C. Doric Temple of HERA, where the HERMES of Praxiteles was found, numerous statues and votive offerings, twelve treasuries built on a terrace along the north side to hold the wealth and offerings dedicated to the gods, and the Doric Temple of Zeus, built in the fifth century B.C. A great altar stood in front of the temple, and the large chryselephantine statue of Zeus seated on his throne, the Olympian Zeus by Phidias, was within.

Beyond the sanctuary were structures connected with the OLYMPIC GAMES. A vaulted entrance passage led to the stadium, which seated twenty thousand people. The hippodrome, scene of the horse and chariot races, has disappeared due to the flooding of the ALPHEUS River, which ran beside it.

Olympia was excavated in the latter part of the nineteenth century by German archaeologists under the direction of Ernst Curtius. At present, the stadium is being reconstructed, and a fine museum has been erected near the site.

Olympic Games, the (oh-lim-pik), G, Panhellenic athletic and dramatic competitions held in the summer every four years at OLYMPIA as a religious offering to ZEUS and other major deities. Participants came from all over the Greek world to take part in the competitions, which included the pentathlon (five events: jumping, javelin and discus throwing, wrestling, and a foot race), chariot races in the hippodrome, and contests in music, poetry, and drama. The Olympic Games, started in 776 B.C., soon became a major national festival of the Greeks, providing a social and religious bond among the citizens, and were held regularly until they were ended by the Roman emperor Theodosius in A.D. 392. The games were revived in modern times at Athens in 1896.

Olympus, Mt. (oh-lim'-pus), G, a lofty, and often cloud-covered, mountain in Thessaly, the home of the principal gods of the Greek pantheon.

Omacatl (oh-mah-kah't'l), Az, the god of happiness and feasting, who demanded lavish feasts in his honor.

Ombos (awm'-baws), E, the site of a sanctuary in Upper Egypt where the god HORUS was worshiped and where his wife, HATHOR, was also honored. Ombos was the early center of the cult of SET.

Ometeotl (oh-may-tay-oh't'l) or **Ometeuctli** (-ook'-tlee), Az, the supreme being and creator of the universe. Ometeotl was the em-

143

bodiment of two persons, both god and goddess, representing dualistic, opposite forces within one deity. Thus, the god was male and female, darkness and light, positive and negative. Ometeotl corresponds to HUNAB-KU, the principal god of the Mayas. He was sometimes called TLOQUE NAHUAQUE.

Ometeuctli (oh-may-tay-ook'-tlee), Az. *See* OMETEOTL.

Omphale (ahm'-fu-lee), G, the queen of Lydia to whom HERACLES was in service for three years after he killed his friend Iphitus in a seizure of madness. She later became his mistress and had several children by him, according to some accounts.

Omphalos, the (ahm'-fu-lus), G, the sacred stone disgorged by CRONUS. The Omphalos, located at DELPHI in the temple of APOLLO, was thought to be the navel or center of the earth.

Omumbo-rombonga (oh-mum'-boh-rahm-bahng'-gu), Af, in the legends of the Bushmen, the tree that gave birth to mankind and cattle.

Onamuji (oh-nah-moo'-jee), J, the son of SUSANOWO, and an earth-god. Onamuji was forced to abdicate in order that AMATERASU's grandson, NINIGI, might take his place on the throne.

Onnophris (oh-naw'-fris), E, a name, meaning "Good One," by which OSIRIS was known as god-ruler of Egypt.

Ono (ohn'-oh), O, the name by which RONGO was known in the Marquesas Islands, where he was a god of farming and of festive celebration and singing.

Onouris (oh-noo'-ris), E. *See* ANHUR.

Onuphis (oh-noo'-fis), E, the name of a bull whose shape OSIRIS sometimes assumed.

Opet (oh'-pet), E. *See* TAUERET.

Opochtli (oh-pohch'-tlee), Az, the god who presided over the catching of birds and fish.

Ops (ahps), R, the wife of SATURN and goddess of fertility and plenty, sowing and reaping. *Ops* is a Latin word for plenty. Ops was identified with RHEA and with CYBELE.

Oracles (awr'-u-kulz), G, the prophetic utterances of the gods. Priests interpreted the words of the gods given in answer to those who came to consult them and ask their advice. The Oracle of ZEUS at DODONA, where the rustle of oak leaves gave forth prophecies through priests, was the oldest of the Greek oracles. The famous Oracle of APOLLO at DELPHI revealed the future through the priestess PYTHIA.

Orcus (awr'-kus), R, 1. the god of the UNDERWORLD, identified with DIS and with the Greek deities HADES and PLUTO. 2. the underworld itself, also called Dis and analagous to TARTARUS.

Oreads, the (ohr'-ee-adz), G, mountain NYMPHS, who were immortal and who attended ARTEMIS. The most famous Oread was ECHO.

Orenda (oh-ren'-du, aw-), NA, among the Iroquois, a supernatural spirit, a magic power making its force known to all men and enabling man to attain his goals. The orenda, existing in all things, both animate and inanimate, corresponds to the MANITOU of the Algonquin Indians.

Orestes (oh-res'-teez), G, the son of AGAMEMNON and CLYTEMNESTRA, and brother of ELECTRA and IPHIGENIA. Orestes avenged Agamemnon's death by killing Clytemnestra and her lover AEGISTHUS with the help of Electra. Wed to HERMIONE after slaying NEOPTOLEMUS, Orestes was pursued by the ERINYES until he finally received purification through ATHENA, who pardoned him because he had acted on the advice of the DELPHIC ORACLE. With his purification, the curse put on the house of ATREUS by THYESTES was lifted.

Orion (oh-rahy'-un), G, a hunter, the son of POSEIDON. Orion loved MEROPE, daughter of OENOPION, and was blinded by Oenopion when he tried to seize her. Orion found his way to APOLLO, with the help of the CYCLOPES and HEPHAESTUS, and regained his sight. ARTEMIS loved Orion, but unwittingly caused his death by killing him with an arrow at the challenge of Apollo, who pointed out to her an object in the water. Artemis then placed Orion in the heavens as a constellation.

Orithyia (awr-u-thahy'-u), G, the daughter of ERECHTHEUS, king of Athens. She and BOREAS were the parents of Calais and Zetes, who participated in the expedition of the ARGONAUTS.

Ormazd (awr'-muzd), Pe. *See* AHURA MAZDA.

Oro (oh'-roh), O, the Polynesian war-god, worshiped especially in Tahiti, where the king was believed to be the human manifestation of the god. In the Society Islands, Oro, son of TA'AROA, assumed most of the activities of the war-god TU, who, along with the other deities, became subordinate to Oro.

Orpheus (awr'-fee-us), G, the son of the MUSE CALLIOPE. Orpheus, a poet and skillful musician, was taught by Apollo to play the lyre, with the result that all the gods, men, and nature were moved by his music. Orpheus went to HADES, to recover his beloved wife, EURYDICE, and stirred the entire UNDERWORLD with his pleading and sad song. Hades granted that Eurydice could return to the upper world, provided that Orpheus did not look back at her on their journey out. Just before they reached the earth, however, Orpheus glanced at his wife in concern and love, and she was lost to him. Orpheus wandered alone, singing his melancholy song, until he reached Thrace, where he was torn apart by women in a bacchanalian frenzy. Orpheus was buried by the Muses, and ZEUS placed his lyre in the heavens. The legend forms the basis of operas by Monteverdi and Gluck.

Orthia (awr'-thee-u), G, another name for ARTEMIS. Orthia means "upright."

Orunjan (oh-ruhn'-juhn), Af, the sun-god of the Yoruba tribe, deity especially of the sun in its noontime aspect. He was the son of AGANJU and YEMAJA. In one version, Orunjan was said to have been the father of the other deities in the pantheon of the Yorubas by YEMAJA, his mother.

Osiris (oh-sahy'-ris), E, the god of vegetation and fertility, son of GEB and NUT. Osiris, one of the most important members of the ENNEAD, was the brother and husband of ISIS, and the father, or, in some cases, the brother, of HORUS, who avenged the death of Osiris by slaying SET. He succeeded his father as lord of Egypt.

According to legend, Osiris was killed and mutilated by his brother Set, the god of darkness, out of jealousy and hatred, then was reassembled by Isis and became ruler of the afterlife and the judge before whom the dead appeared. The ritual that re-enacted the legend of Osiris' immortality was believed to be effective in ensuring immortality for man.

Through fertility associations in the Greco-Roman period, the bull-god APIS came to be viewed as a reincarnation of Osiris, and the fertility cult of SERAPIS became one of the important MYSTERY religions of the Roman Empire. His sanctuary at ABYDOS was the chief seat of the worship of Osiris.

Ossa, Mt. (ahs'-u), G, a mountain in Thessaly. The TITANS piled Mt. PELION on Mt. Ossa in their attempt to reach OLYMPUS, but were driven back each time by ZEUS's thunderbolts. The CENTAURS were also said to have lived there.

Otter (ot'-ur), Sc, HREIDMAR's son, the brother of FAFNIR and REGIN, who, in the shape of an otter, was killed by LOKI.

Ovid (ahv'-id), a Roman poet who lived from 43 B.C. to about A.D. 17. One of his major works was the *Metamorphoses*, fifteen books of

146

dactylic hexameter forming a compendium of Roman mythology. His Latin name was Publius Ovidius Naso.

Oya (oh-yah'), Af, a water-goddess and a deity of fertility, worshiped by the Yoruba tribe. She was the consort of SHANGO and the priestess of the Niger River. After Shango's death, Oya became the personification of the Niger.

Pachacamac (pah-chah-kah-mahk'), SA, a pre-Incan god who was a creator deity and was incorporated into the pantheon of the Incas. It was he who was believed to have made the men and women who were their ancestors and to have given them all the necessities as well as the fine things of life. A great temple, erected to him on a hillside near the modern city of Lima, was the center of the cult of Pachacamac. It was looted of its treasures by Pizarro and his men.

Pachamama (pah-chah-mah'-mah), SA, an Incan deity, the representation of mother earth.

Pactolus River (pak-toh'-lus), G, the river in which MIDAS bathed, at the instruction of DIONYSUS, to rid himself of the golden touch. The sands of the river then turned to gold.

Paean or **Paeon** (pee'-un) G, 1. a name given both to ASCLEPIUS, the physician of the gods, and to APOLLO, the healer.

2. a chant or song of praise, victory, and rejoicing. The paean was first sung by Apollo, in prayer and thanksgiving, after he had slain the serpent PYTHON.

Paeon (pee'-un), G. See PAEAN.

Pakht (pahkt), E, a goddess with the head of a lioness, who was identified with BAST, or was sometimes considered to be that goddess in another form.

Palaemon (pu-lee'-mun), G, the name given to MELICERTES when he became a god of the sea after INO jumped into the sea with him in her arms to escape the pursuit of her husband ATHAMAS. Palaemon was often represented with a dolphin, and he was associated with POSEIDON and with the ISTHMIAN GAMES.

Palamedes (pal-u-mee'-deez), G, the son of NAUPLIUS and CLYMENE. Palamedes was believed to be the inventor of the alphabet and of the discus and dice. ODYSSEUS feigned madness when Palamedes tried to induce him to join the Greek leaders starting off to the TROJAN WAR. Palamedes tested Odysseus by placing his infant son TELEMACHUS in the way of his plow, and Odysseus turned aside.

Pales (pay'-leez), R, the deity of pastures and cattle and protective deity of shepherds. Pales, whose festival was held on April 21, the traditional anniversary of the founding of Rome, was sometimes considered to be a god analogous to FAUNUS; sometimes, a goddess, identified with VESTA.

Palinurus (pal-u-nuhr'-us), R, the pilot of AENEAS. Palinurus was overcome by sleep and fell overboard near Sicily as a sacrifice to the god of the sea, so that Aeneas could continue safely on his journey toward Italy. Palinurus was murdered when he reached the shore of Italy. He was later buried by Aeneas, giving his name to Cape Palinurus.

Palladium, the (pu-lay'-dee-um), G, a wooden statue of PALLAS ATHENA sent from heaven by ZEUS to protect Troy. It was believed that Troy would stand as long as the Palladium was safe within the city walls. Toward the end of the TROJAN WAR, the Palladium was stolen by DIOMEDES and ODYSSEUS with the help of HELEN and taken to the camp of the Greeks.

Pallas (pal'-us), G, 1. a GIANT, son of GAEA and URANUS, who was overthrown by the Olympians, aided by HERACLES, in the war of the Giants.

2. a daughter of TRITON and playmate of the goddess ATHENA when they were young. After Athena accidentally killed her friend, she assumed the name Pallas and made a wooden effigy of the girl, which was revered at Troy as the PALLADIUM.

R, 3. the son of EVANDER who welcomed AENEAS and the Trojans when they landed at the Tiber River and fought with them against TURNUS.

Pan (pan), G, the son of HERMES and a NYMPH, or of ZEUS and CALLISTO. Pan, meaning "all," was the god of all the countryside and nature, especially of shepherds and the woods. He possessed prophetic powers. The pipes of Pan, or shepherd's pipes, invented by him, were fashioned from reeds and called the SYRINX. In the contest between Pan, playing the pipes, and APOLLO, playing the lyre, MIDAS gave the prize to Pan. He was the father, or the brother, of the SATYR SILENUS. He was represented with the horns and hoofs of a goat and with a snub nose and beard. Pan's name led to the word "panic," because of the fear of woods at night and because the Persians were said to have been routed at the Battle of Marathon by the panic Pan was believed to have instilled in them. Pan was associated by the Romans with FAUNUS.

Panathenaea, the (pan-ath-u-nee'-u), G, an annual religious festival held in Athens every four years in honor of ATHENA. It was celebrated by musical and athletic contests and by a procession to the top of the ACROPOLIS to make sacrifices to Athena and present her with a new robe. The Panathenaic Procession is depicted on the PARTHENON frieze.

Pandavas, the (pun'-du-vuz), I, the family to which ARJUNA belonged and whose struggles are described in the MAHABHARATA. They were the cousins and enemies of the KAURAVAS.

Pandion (pan'-dee-ahn), G, the son of ERICHTHONIUS and father of PHILOMELA and PROCNE, who died of grief when his daughters were transformed into birds. He was also the father of ERECHTHEUS and BUTES.

Pandora (pan-dohr'-u), G, the first woman, fashioned from clay by HEPHAESTUS at the direction of ZEUS in order to punish PROMETHEUS for having stolen fire from the heavens. Pandora meant "the gift of all," because all the gods gave her gifts symbolic of their powers (e.g., ATHENA gave her feminine skills, APOLLO the talent to sing, and so on). Zeus gave her a box, which she was not to open. HERMES led Pandora to earth, where Prometheus rejected her. EPIMETHEUS, however, married Pandora. In spite of the warnings of the gods, Pandora opened the box Zeus had given her, and all the sins and evils that have plagued mortals since sprang forth. By the time Pandora closed the lid of the box, only Hope was left within. In modern usage, a "Pandora's box" refers to a gift that appears to have value but brings bad luck.

Pandrosos (pan'-dru-sus), G, the daughter of CECROPS and AGRAULOS and sister of HERSE. A priestess of ATHENA, she was worshiped on the ACROPOLIS with Athena in the Pandroseum, her shrine.

P'an-ku (pahn'-koo'), Ch, a cosmological being appearing from the primeval substance. According to one account, P'an-ku was born in the egg of primordial chaos and, after many thousand years, YIN AND YANG came from the division of the egg to form the earth and the sky. As the world grew, so did P'an-ku, until his body reached from heaven to earth, supporting the firmament. Other versions describe the belief that, after his death, the parts of P'an-ku's body became the mountains, rivers, wind, stars, and all else in the world.

P'an-t'ao (pahn'-tou'), Ch, the peaches of the orchard of heaven that ripened only once in three thousand years and bestowed immortality. To the Chinese, the peach became a symbol of long life, as did the tortoise.

Papa (pah'-pu), O, the earth, mother of the gods in union with RANGI, the sky. When the sky was lifted and they were separated, Papa promised Rangi she would show her sorrow, which appears as

mists in the summertime. Among Papa's sons were the gods
TANGAROA and RONGO, sometimes considered to be twins, TANE and
TU.

Paphos (pay'-fahs), G, a city sacred to APHRODITE, named for
Paphos, the son of PYGMALION, located on the island of Cyprus.

Parashurama (par-u-shuh-rah'-mu), I, the sixth AVATAR of VISHNU,
as RAMA with the ax. When Parashurama's father, believing his wife
lacked purity, wanted her killed, he beheaded her with an ax, given
him by SHIVA and named Parashu, the source of his own name. As
a boon, Parashurama was granted his wish that his mother be
brought back to life.

Parcae, the (pahr'-see), R, the name given by the Romans to the
three FATES, identified with the Greek MOERAE.

Paris (par'-is), G, the son of PRIAM and HECUBA. Paris was left as
an infant to die on Mt. IDA because of a prophecy that he would be
the cause of the destruction of Troy. He was found and brought up
by shepherds. Paris was a shepherd on Mt. Ida when he was called
upon to render the decision in the contest over who was the fairest of
the goddesses. APHRODITE offered Paris the most beautiful woman
(HELEN) as his wife; ATHENA promised wisdom and glory; and HERA,
wealth and power. The JUDGMENT OF PARIS declared Aphrodite to be
the fairest of the three, and Paris, although he was wed to the NYMPH
OENONE, took Helen to Troy as his wife, which led to the TROJAN
WAR and to the fulfillment of the original prophecy. In the contest between MENELAUS and Paris, which was to decide and end the war,
Menelaus was almost victorious, but Aphrodite carried Paris off in a
cloud and the war continued. It was Paris who killed ACHILLES by
striking him in the heel with an arrow. Wounded in combat with
PHILOCTETES by HERACLES' arrow, Paris went to Oenone, who refused to care for his wounds, but took her own life following his
death. Paris was the twin of CASSANDRA and was sometimes called
Alexander.

Parnassus, Mt. (pahr-nas'-us), G, a lofty mountain in Phocis on
which DELPHI was located. During the Deluge only the top of Mt.
Parnassus remained dry, and DEUCALION and PYRRHA were carried
there safely as the sole survivors. Parnassus was sacred to APOLLO and
the MUSES as well as to DIONYSUS.

Parthenon, the (pahr'-thu-nahn), G, the great temple of ATHENA
Parthenos (the maiden), the patron goddess of Athens situated on
the Athenian ACROPOLIS, generally regarded as one of the finest mas-
terworks of ancient Greek architecture. Designed by the architects

Callicrates and Ictinus under the over-all supervision of the sculptor Phidias, it was begun in 447 B.C. and completed in about 438 B.C. The Parthenon, built of pentelic marble, is of the Doric order with certain Ionic stylistic elements. Inside there stood a monumental chryselephantine statue of Athena by Phidias. The sculptures on the east pediments depicted the birth of Athena; those on the west, the contest between Athena and POSEIDON for possession of Athens. The frieze, which ran around the entire cella wall, more than five hundred feet, showed the Panathenaic Procession. On the outer side of the Parthenon was a Doric frieze: The relief sculptures of the ninety-two metopes represented the battle of gods and giants, the battle of the LAPITHAE and CENTAURS, and other mythological battles. The Parthenon was continuously used as a temple until the fifth century A.D. when it was converted into a Christian church, and in the fifteenth century the Turks converted it into a mosque. Subsequently the Turks used part of the building as a powder magazine, and during the Venetian bombardment of Athens in 1687 it blew up, doing extensive damage and ruining many of the sculptures. In the nineteenth century most of the pedimental sculptures and some of the panels from the frieze and the metopes were taken to England and later sold to the British Museum by Lord Elgin; other sections are in the Louvre, and a few remain in Athens.

Parthenopaeus (pahr-thu-noh-pee′-us), G, the son of ATALANTA, whose father is variously given as HIPPOMENES, ARES, or MELEAGER. He took part and was killed in the expedition of the SEVEN AGAINST THEBES.

Parthenope (pahr-then′-u-pee), G, one of the SIRENS who cast herself into the sea when ODYSSEUS did not succumb to the singing of the Sirens. Her body came ashore at present-day Naples, sometimes called by her name.

Partholon (pahr-thoh′-lun), Ce, the leader of a band of forty-eight men and women who began a new race of people in Ireland, after the early inhabitants were wiped out in the flood of biblical times. They retained their power by winning a victory over the Fomorians, monsters with evil and magic powers. Partholon brought agriculture, crafts, and civilization to Ireland.

Parvati (pahr′-vu-tee), I, the lovely young wife of SHIVA in her manifestation as a goddess of the mountains, the daughter of the Himalayas. Parvati was an unrelenting opponent of the demons. She was the mother of GANESHA and KARTTIKEYA. Shiva's wife had a variety of aspects and names, including DURGA, DEVI, KALI, and SATI.

Pasiphaë (pu-sif'-u-ee), G, the daughter of HELIOS and wife of King MINOS of Crete. She was the mother of ARIADNE by Minos. POSEIDON caused Pasiphaë to fall in love with the white bull of Minos, as a result of which she gave birth to the MINOTAUR.

Patala (pu-tu'-lu), I, the lowest region of the underworld, lying beneath Mount MERU. Patala, the dwelling place of the ASURAS, was guarded by the NAGAS.

Patroclus (pu-troh'-klus), G, the companion of ACHILLES who, clad in Achilles' armor, led the MYRMIDONS in the TROJAN WAR after Achilles withdrew from the fighting. When Patroclus was slain by HECTOR, the infuriated Achilles reentered the fighting and killed Hector in revenge.

Pausanias (paw-say'-nee-us), a Greek geographer and author of the second century A.D. who traveled extensively throughout the Graeco-Roman world. His work, entitled *Description of Greece,* gives a detailed account of Greece in his day, including details of customs, religion, and mythology of great interest and value.

Pax (paks), R, the goddess of peace. She was also identified with CONCORDIA.

Pegasus (peg'-u-sus), G, the winged horse that sprang up from the blood of MEDUSA when she was beheaded by PERSEUS. Pegasus appeared to BELLEROPHON at Corinth, and ATHENA showed him how to tame the steed. Mounted on Pegasus, Bellerophon met and overcame the CHIMAERA, but when he attempted to climb to OLYMPUS, ZEUS sent a gadfly to sting his mount, and Bellerophon was thrown. Pegasus was taken to Olympus and was later transformed into a constellation.

Pelasgus (pu-laz'-gus), G, the grandson of INACHUS. He was the eponymous founder of the Pelasgians, a group of Greek people in the Peloponneseus. Among his descendants were ARCAS, ATALANTA, and CALLISTO.

Peleus (pee'-lee-us), G, the son of AEACUS, brother of TELAMON, father of ACHILLES, and king of the MYRMIDONS. It was at the wedding feast of Peleus and THETIS that ERIS threw the golden apple among the guests, leading to the JUDGMENT OF PARIS and the TROJAN WAR. Peleus took part in the expedition of the ARGONAUTS and the CALYDONIAN BOAR hunt.

Pelias (pee'-lee-us), G, JASON's uncle, who seized the kingdom of Iolcus from his half brother AESON, Jason's father, and sent Jason off to bring the GOLDEN FLEECE back from Colchis. Even when Jason accomplished his mission, Pelias would not surrender the throne to him. MEDEA then tricked Pelias' daughters (among whom was ALCESTIS) into murdering him and refused to restore him to life with her magic powers.

Pelion, Mt. (pee'-lee-un), G, the mountain in eastern Thessaly that was piled on Mt. OSSA by the GIANTS in their attempt to scale the heights of OLYMPUS and overthrow the gods. The expression "to pile Pelion on Ossa" means to add one difficulty to another.

Pelopia (pu-loh-pahy'-u), G, the daughter of THYESTES and mother of AEGISTHUS. She was also said to be the mother of CYCNUS by ARES.

Pelops (pee'-lahps), G, the son of TANTALUS and father of ATREUS and THYESTES. Tantalus served Pelops to the gods at a feast, but all except DEMETER refused the human flesh. HERMES restored Pelops to life, and Demeter, who had consumed a piece of his shoulder, replaced it with one of ivory. The ivory shoulder of Pelops was handed down to his descendants. Pelops won HIPPODAMIA and the kingdom of Elis in a chariot race against her father, Oenomaus, by getting MYRTILUS to pull out the pin of Oenomaus' chariot. Because Pelops cast Myrtilus into the sea instead of giving him half his kingdom as he had promised, Myrtilus cursed the House of Pelops as he died. The curse was handed down through generations (the House of Pelops became known as the House of Atreus) until it was expatiated following ORESTES' murder of CLYTEMNESTRA. Pelops gave his name to the Peloponnesus, "the island of Pelops."

Penates, the (pu-nay'-teez), R. See LARES AND PENATES.

Penelope (pu-nel'-u-pee), G, the loyal wife of ODYSSEUS and mother of TELEMACHUS. Penelope wove a cloak for LAERTES, Odysseus' father, to ward off her many suitors during her husband's absence, saying she could not wed until it was finished. Penelope then ripped out her work each night. Thus, a "web of Penelope" is something that is continually worked on but never finished. By the rejection of her suitors and her concern for her son, she stands as a figure of matronly virtue.

Peneus (pu-nee'-us), G, a river-god, the father of DAPHNE. HERACLES directed the Peneus and ALPHEUS rivers through the Augean Stables to clean them as one of his labors. See also LABORS OF HERACLES.

Penthesilea (pen-thu-su-lee'-u), G, the daughter of ARES and Otrera, who, as queen of the AMAZONS, led her warriors against the Greeks on the side of the Trojans in the TROJAN WAR. Penthesilea was slain by ACHILLES, who regretted having done so.

Pentheus (pen'-thoos), G, son of Echion and AGAVE, and king of THEBES, who was torn to pieces during a bacchanalian orgy by his mother and other women, who had mistaken him for a wild boar.

Perceval (pur'-su-vul), Ce. *See* PERCIVAL.

Perchta (perch'-tah), Sl, a goddess of fertility, who was celebrated by festival and feasting in the spring, honoring her beauty.

Percival or **Perceval** (pur'-su-vul), Ce, a young man who was taken by his mother to Wales, where he lived in the mountains, until he joined ARTHUR's court. Percival, the counterpart of the German Parsifal, became a chivalrous knight and vowed to seek the GRAIL.

Perdix (pur'-diks), G, the sister of DAEDALUS and mother of TALOS. When her son was killed by Daedalus, who was envious of his skill, Perdix took her own life and was transformed into a partridge (the meaning of the word *perdix*) by ATHENA.

Peris, the (pee'-riz), Pe, evil female creatures who were attractive in appearance but demons in actions.

Persa (pur'-su) or **Perse** (-see), G, a daughter of OCEANUS and TETHYS, the mother by HELIOS of AEËTES, PASIPHAË, and CIRCE.

Perse (pur'-see), G. *See* PERSA.

Persephone (per-sef'-u-nee), G, the goddess of spring, the daughter of ZEUS and DEMETER. Her Roman counterpart was PROSERPINA. While picking flowers in a field in Sicily, she was seized by HADES and carried off to the UNDERWORLD and made his wife and queen. At Demeter's behest, Zeus granted that Persephone could spend two thirds of the year in the upper world and one third in the underworld. Thus the year was divided into the seasons of growth and harvest, and of winter. Persephone was also known as KORE. She was generally represented with a cornucopia.

Perseus (pur'-see-us), G, the son of ZEUS and DANAË. ACRISIUS, father of Danaë, cast his daughter and her son into the sea in a chest because of a prophecy that his grandson would cause his death. The mother and child were carried to the island of Seriphus, where POLYDECTES was king. When Perseus had grown up and Polydectes fell in love with Danaë, Polydectes sent Perseus off to get the head of MEDUSA, hoping he would not return. Perseus got an invisible helmet, winged sandals, and a bag from the GRAEAE, a shield from ATHENA, and a sword from HERMES. With this help he cut off Medusa's head, while he looked in his shield to avoid her gaze that turned men to stone, and then fled with the head. When he reached the west and encountered ATLAS, Perseus turned Atlas to stone with Medusa's head, because Atlas opposed him. Thus the Atlas Mountains were created. In Ethiopia, Perseus freed ANDROMEDA and married her. PHINEUS, Andromeda's uncle, was turned to stone by the head of Medusa, when he tried to kill Perseus. Upon his return to Seriphus, Perseus turned Polydectes to stone and then gave the head of Medusa to Athena, who used it on her breastplate. Perseus went to Thessaly, where he took part in games being held there. As he threw his discus, it struck and killed a man who was Acrisius, his grandfather, thus fulfilling the original prophecy. Perseus and Andromeda were the parents of Alcaeus, father of AMPHITRYON, of Electryon, father of ALCMENE and of Perses, legendary ancestor of the Persians.

Perun (pu-roon') or **Pyerun** (pi-u-roon'), Sl, a sun-god and deity of lightning, whose worship continued well into the Christian era. As the god of war and lord of the thunderbolt, Perun was held in high regard, especially in the area around Kiev, the center of his cult. Perun's weapon was the bow.

Phaeacians, the (fee-ay'-shunz), G, people who dwelt on the island of Phaeacia or Scheria and lived in wealth and peace. The Phaeacians had swift and intelligent ships that were pilotless. ALCINOUS was their king when ODYSSEUS was driven to their shores by a storm.

Phaedra (fee'-dru), G, the daughter of MINOS and PASIPHAË and sister of ARIADNE. Phaedra became the wife of THESEUS, after the death of ANTIOPE, and fell in love with her stepson HIPPOLYTUS. When he spurned her incestuous love, she killed herself, leaving a note falsely accusing Hippolytus of attacking her. Theseus returned and in his rage called upon POSEIDON to destroy his own son.

Phaëthon (fay'-u-thun), G, the son of HELIOS and CLYMENE. When Phaëthon doubted that Helios was really his father, the sun god promised to grant him any wish. Phaëthon asked to drive the chariot of the sun. His father objected, but Phaëthon was determined, and Helios kept his promise. The youth, however, lost control and the chariot ran way off course, setting fire to the world. ZEUS struck Phaëthon down with a thunderbolt to prevent total destruction of the earth. His name has survived in an open carriage called a *phaeton*.

Phaon (fay'-un), G, a young boatman who lived on the Aegean island of Lesbos. When he was an old man, APHRODITE gave him youth and beauty as a reward for carrying her in his boat. The poetess Sappho wrote many poems of love to Phaon and is said to have thrown herself into the sea because he did not love her.

Philae, Island of, the (fahy'-lee), E, an island in the upper Nile near the First Cataract, site of the Temple of ISIS and other sanctuaries. It was said that KHNUM fashioned both gods and men on his potter's wheel at Philae.

Philemon (fi-lee'-mun), G, the husband of BAUCIS. A poor and aged couple, they were hospitable to ZEUS and HERMES, when other humans had turned them away as they traveled in disguise through Phrygia. Because of this, when a flood later destroyed their village, their small cottage became a temple and they the priest and priestess. Because they asked never to be separated, they were together even after death: Philemon became an oak tree and Baucis a linden, with branches intertwining.

Philoctetes (fil-ahk-tee'-teez), G, the friend who set fire to HERACLES' funeral pyre at the request of that hero, who was suffering from the poisoned robe given him by DEIANIRA. As he was dying, Heracles gave Philoctetes his bow and arrows. When he was en route to the TROJAN WAR, Philoctetes was left behind on Lemnos because he had been accidentally injured by one of Heracles' poisoned arrows. At the urging of ODYSSEUS, he later joined the Greeks at Troy and slew PARIS, an act that led to the conquest of Troy.

Philomela (fil-u-mee'-lu), G, the sister of PROCNE. Tereus, husband of Procne, fell in love with Philomela and, telling her Procne had died, married her. He then cut out Philomela's tongue to hide his crime. Philomela, however, informed Procne of the truth by weaving the information for her to see. The sisters then cooked Tereus' son by Procne and served him to his father, after which they fled. The gods changed Philomela into a nightingale, Procne into a swallow, and Tereus became a hawk, ever pursuing them.

Phineus (fin'-ee-us), G, 1. the uncle of ANDROMEDA. When Phineus tried to kill PERSEUS, because he had hoped to marry Andromeda himself, Perseus turned him to stone with MEDUSA's head.

2. a king of Thrace, brother of CADMUS and EUROPA, whom ZEUS sent the HARPIES to punish because he had blinded his sons by his first wife, sister of Calais and Zetes. Phineus was rescued from the Harpies by the ARGONAUTS and, in gratitude, showed them how to get through the SYMPLEGADES by sending a dove through first.

Phlegethon (fleg'-u-thahn), G, the river of fire, a branch of the ACHERON, in HADES.

Phoebe (fee'-bee), G, 1. a TITANESS, the mother by Coeus of ASTERIA and LETO.

2. another name for ARTEMIS, meaning "shining."

3. one of the daughters of LEUCIPPUS.

156

4. in some versions, a daughter of LEDA and TYNDAREUS, sometimes known as Timandra.

Phoebus (fee'-bus), G, another name for APOLLO. Phoebus means "shining" or "bright."

Phoenix (fee'-niks), E, 1. a long-lived bird which, after several hundred years, burned in its nest, became ashes, and then was reborn, in a continuous cycle. The phoenix is a symbol of immortality.

G, 2. the son of AGENOR and TELEPHASSA, brother of CADMUS, PHINEUS, and EUROPA. Phoenix searched without success for Europa and then went to live in Phoenicia, which was said to have been named for him.

3. a teacher of ACHILLES. Phoenix taught Achilles the skills of war and accompanied him to the TROJAN WAR.

Phorcys (fawr'-sis), G, an early god of the sea, son of PONTUS and GAEA. Phorcys was the father by Ceto of the GORGONS and the GRAEAE.

Phosphor (fos'-fur), G, the morning star, son of ASTRAEUS and EOS. Phosphor was the father of Ceyx, husband of ALCYONE. His Roman counterpart was Lucifer.

Phrixus (frik'-sus), G, the son of ATHAMAS and NEPHELE. When Athamas' second wife, INO, created a famine in the land, the Delphic oracle told Athamas that Phrixus must be sacrificed. Phrixus and HELLE, his sister, were taken by Nephele and were carried away on a ram with the GOLDEN FLEECE. Phrixus arrived safely in Colchis, where he sacrificed the ram to ZEUS and gave the Golden Fleece to King Aeëtes.

Phtah (ptah), E. See PTAH.

Pierides, the (pahy-eer'-i-deez), G, 1. a name for the MUSES, whose legendary birthplace was Pieria, a district of Thessaly.

2. nine maidens of Thessaly who challenged the Muses to a singing contest. The boastful challengers were changed into magpies after they insulted the Muses, who were judged the winners.

Pilan (pahy-lahn'), SA. See PILLAN.

Pillan or Pilan (pahy-lahn'), SA, the thunder-god and supreme deity of the Araucanian Indians of Chile. Lightning and earthquakes were due to his activities. Tribal chiefs were received by Pillan after death and assumed the form of volcanoes. Pillan had many spirits of evil under his command to bring drought, disease, and other disasters to mankind.

Piltzintecutli (pilts-in-tay-koo'-tlee), Az. See TONATIUH.

157

Pindar (pin'-dur), a Greek lyric poet of the fifth century B.C. whose poems are richly enhanced by his frequent use of legends and myths. Among his works are the *Hymns* and *Paeans,* addressed to various deities, and the *Odes,* immortalizing the victors of the games held at ISTHMIA, NEMEA, OLYMPIA, and DELPHI.

Pinga (pin'-gah), NA, in Eskimo myth, the one who watches over hunting and game animals, the caribou in particular. Pinga resides in the sky and shares some of the activities of ALIGNAK and SEDNA, such as supervising the souls of the dead.

Pirene (pahy-ree'-nee), G, 1. a daughter of the river-god ACHELOUS or Asopus who was transformed into a fountain when she wept bitterly after ARTEMIS, by accident, killed her son by POSEIDON.

2. a fountain at Corinth, from which PEGASUS was drinking when BELLEROPHON awoke to find him.

Pirithous (pahy-rith'-oh-us), G, the son of IXION and Dia, and king of the LAPITHAE. Pirithous was a close friend of THESEUS, and it was they who kidnaped HELEN from Sparta, but CASTOR AND POLLUX rescued her soon after. He took part in the hunt for the CALYDONIAN BOAR. The battle of the CENTAURS and Lapithae broke out at his marriage to HIPPODAMIA. Later, when he went to the UNDERWORLD in an attempt to get PERSEPHONE for his wife, he was fastened to a chair in eternal punishment.

Pittheus (pit'-thee-us, -thoos), G, a son of PELOPS and HIPPODAMIA and the father of AETHRA, mother of THESEUS. Pittheus was king of Troezen and noted for his wisdom.

Plato (play'-toh), a Greek philosopher who lived from 428 to 347 B.C. and founded the Academy, a school of philosophy and related disciplines, in Athens. Plato's *Dialogues,* outstanding for their literary merit as well as for philosophical insight, contain frequent references to mythological topics.

Pleiades, the (plee'-u-deez), G, the daughters of ATLAS and the OCEANID Pleione and sisters of the HYADES. The Pleiades were seven nymphs, named ALCYONE, Celaeno, ELECTRA, MAIA, MEROPE, Sterope, and TAYGETE, whom ZEUS placed in the heavens when ORION fell in love with them and pursued them. It was believed that the one not clearly visible was either Electra, who hid so that she could not see the destruction of Troy, founded by her son DARDANUS, or possibly Merope, ashamed because she wed SISYPHUS, a mortal.

Plutarch (ploo'-tahrk), a Greek scholar and biographer who lived from about A.D. 46 to 120. His literary works, chiefly in the form of essays, dialogues, and biographies, are widely interspersed with myth-

158

ological subject matter and references shedding graphic light on the religion and archaeological remains of the ancient Greeks.

Pluto (ploo'-toh), G, a name of HADES, identified with ORCUS and DIS by the Romans.

Plutus (ploo'-tus), G, the son of DEMETER and Iasion. Plutus was the god who personified wealth. ZEUS was said to have blinded him so that his gifts would go to the deserving and undeserving alike.

Po (poh), O, 1. the underworld, a place of eternal darkness.
2. the god of the realm of the dead.

Pohjola (paw'-hyaw-lu), F, the kingdom to the north of Finland, the realm of the sorceress LOUHI. Pohjola is generally identified with Lapland.

Pollux (pol'-uks), G, the Latin name of POLYDEUCES. *See also* CASTOR AND POLLUX.

Polydectes (pahl-i-dek'-teez), G, a king of Seriphus, where DANAË and her small son PERSEUS landed. Later, when Polydectes fell in love with Danaë, he sent Perseus to get the head of MEDUSA, thinking the youth would be killed. Perseus, however, returned with the GORGON's head, with which he turned Polydectes to stone.

Polydeuces (pahl-i-doo'-seez), G, the Greek name of CASTOR's twin brother, more commonly known by his Latin name, Pollux. *See also* CASTOR AND POLLUX.

Polydorus (phal-i-dawr'-us), G, 1. the son of CADMUS and HARMONIA who became king of THEBES.
2. a son of PRIAM and HECUBA. Priam sent the young Polydorus to Thrace to be safe from the TROJAN WAR, but the king, Polymnestor, murdered him and seized his wealth.

Polyhymnia (pahl-i-him'-nee-u), G, the MUSE of sacred music and poetry. She was depicted as thoughtful and veiled.

Polynices (pahl-i-nahy'-seez), G, the son of OEDIPUS and JOCASTA, and brother of ETEOCLES, ISMENE, and ANTIGONE. Eteocles and Polynices were to rule THEBES in alternate years, but Eteocles would not give up the throne at the end of his year of rule. This led to the expedition of the SEVEN AGAINST THEBES, in which seven heroes fought bitterly to regain the throne for Polynices. In the end, in a duel between Eteocles and Polynices to decide the issue, the brothers slew each other. Polynices was buried by his sister Antigone, who lost her life as a result.

Polyphemus (pahl-i-fee'-mus), G, a one-eyed GIANT, one of the CYCLOPES, who lived in Sicily. Polyphemus captured ODYSSEUS and his men when they landed there, but they escaped from his cave by putting out his eye with a sharpened pole and holding on underneath the sheep when Polyphemus rolled away the great stone at the entrance of his cave to let his flock out to pasture. Polyphemus fell in love with GALATEA and, in jealously, slew Acis, whom she loved.

Polyxena (pu-lik′-su-nu), G, a daughter of PRIAM and HECUBA. Polyxena was loved by ACHILLES and was sacrificed on his tomb at the end of the TROJAN WAR.

Pontus (pon′-tus), G, an early god of the sea, the son of URANUS and GAEA. Pontus was the father of Ceto, NEREUS, and PHORCYS.

Popol Vuh, the (poh-pohl′ voo), M, the title of a "Book of Advice," written in the sixteenth century, following the Spanish conquest, the principal source of our knowledge about the mythology of the Mayas. The language is that of the Quiches, the Mayas of Guatemala, and it is transposed to the Latin alphabet.

The *Popol Vuh* deals basically with the early creation of man and his destruction by flood, the struggles of the gods and giants, and the new creation of mankind. It suffers, however, from being dependent on a long oral tradition and from the often almost hopeless intertwining of myth and historical and subjective material.

Poseidon (poh-sahy′-dun), G, a son of CRONUS and RHEA, god of the sea, and one of the twelve Olympians. His Roman counterpart was NEPTUNE. Poseidon dwelt at the bottom of the sea with his queen, AMPHITRITE. TRITON was their child. Poseidon was also the father by other mothers of other children, among them, THESEUS, in some versions, POLYPHEMUS, ORION, and ANTAEUS. He was the father of the winged horse PEGASUS by MEDUSA. Poseidon sent a monster to plague LAOMEDON after that king declined to pay him the reward promised for his help in building Troy. This led to the sacrifice of HESIONE to the sea monster. A rival of ZEUS in most matters, Poseidon favored the Greeks in the TROJAN WAR. He rode over the sea in a horse-drawn chariot and brought forth steeds and fountains on land with his TRIDENT. Poseidon was also called the Earth-Shaker, because he was thought to cause earthquakes. The chief center of the worship of Poseidon was Isthmia, where the ISTHMIAN GAMES were held. The horse and dolphin were sacred to him.

Priam (prahy′-um), G, 1. the king of Troy at the time of the TROJAN WAR. The only son of LAOMEDON not slain in vengeance by HERACLES, he was the husband of HECUBA and father of fifty sons and twelve daughters, the more important of whom were CASSANDRA, PARIS, DEÏPHOBUS, CREUSA, HECTOR, POLYDORUS, and TROILUS. Priam met his death at the hands of NEOPTOLEMUS on the altar of his palace, where he had sought refuge with his wife and daughters when Troy fell to the Greeks.

2. a grandson of King Priam, a friend of ASCANIUS and his companion on the voyage to Italy following the Trojan War.

Priapus (prahy-ay'-pus), G, the son of DIONYSUS and APHRODITE and a god of fertility and vegetation. Priapus was a protective deity of farmers and shepherds.

Prithivi (pri-tee'-vi), I, a Vedic goddess of the earth, a personification of fertility. She was the consort of DYAUS and the mother of INDRA.

Procne (prahk'-nee), G, PHILOMELA's sister, who was wed to Tereus. After Procne learned that Tereus had cut out Philomela's tongue to keep her silent after he raped her, she slew her son by him and served him to Tereus. Procne escaped with Philomela and was changed into a swallow.

Procris (proh'-kris), G, the daughter of Erechtheus and wife of CEPHALUS. EOS, who was in love with Cephalus, led Procris to doubt Cephalus. Procris hid in a bush when Cephalus was out hunting, and he, hearing a noise, killed her by mistake.

Proetus (proh-ee'-tus), G, the twin brother of ACRISIUS and ruler of Tiryns.

Prometheus (pru-mee'-thee-us), G, the son of the TITAN IAPETUS and the OCEANID CLYMENE. Prometheus, whose name meant "forethought," was the brother of ATLAS, EPIMETHEUS, and Menoetius. When Prometheus and Epimetheus were entrusted by ZEUS with the creation of mankind and other animals, they fashioned them out of clay and water in the likeness of the gods. Because Epimetheus had endowed the other animals with all that man had, Prometheus gave fire to man to make him superior to animals. Prometheus espoused the cause of man against the Olympian gods. Zeus, therefore, took fire away from man. Prometheus then stole fire from the heavens in a reed and restored it to mankind. As a result, Zeus had HEPHAESTUS fashion PANDORA as a punishment to man. Prometheus was chained to a mountainside by Zeus, and an eagle was set over him to consume his liver daily. HERACLES rescued Prometheus from this plight. It was Prometheus who warned DEUCALION, his son, and PYRRHA to build an ark to escape the Deluge. Prometheus was considered to be a giver of thoughtful advice and wisdom.

Proserpina (proh-sur'-pi-nu), R, the daughter of CERES, and wife of

PLUTO. She was the queen of the UNDERWORLD and was the Roman counterpart of PERSEPHONE.

Protesilaus (pro-tes-u-lay'-us), G, the son of a king of Thessaly. Protesilaus was the first to step ashore at Troy and was, therefore, according to a prophecy, the first of the Greeks to be killed in the TROJAN WAR. After HERMES led Protesilaus back to the upper world to see his wife, LAODAMIA, the two joined each other in death.

Proteus (proh'-tee-us), G, an early god of the sea, the son of OCEANUS and TETHYS. Proteus had the gift of prophecy and was able to assume different shapes and forms at will. He was thought to dwell at times on the island of Pharos in Egypt.

Pryderi (pri-dehr'-ee), Ce, the son of PWYLL and RHIANNON on whom LLOYD cast magic spells to avenge his friend GWAWL, Rhiannon's rejected suitor. Gwawl stole the infant Pryderi, but the child was restored to his parents after a few years. Pryderi accompanied BRAN on his expedition against MATHOLWYCH.

Psyche (sahy'-kee), R, the maiden whose beauty caused jealousy on the part of VENUS. Venus sent her son CUPID to make Psyche fall in love with someone unattractive, but Cupid himself fell in love with the beautiful Psyche. Cupid and Psyche were wed, but Cupid came to Psyche only at night and was not seen by her. Psyche asked to have her two sisters in the palace with her, but they became envious and led Psyche to learn who her husband was. Taking a lamp, Psyche saw Cupid, but he awoke and left her. Venus then punished Psyche with many tasks, such as being sent to HADES to bring back some of PROSERPINA's beauty. On the way back, Psyche opened the box and fell asleep. Cupid found Psyche asleep and took her to JUPITER, who bestowed immortality on her. Psyche, meaning "soul," represented the human soul and its relationship to love.

Ptah or **Phtah** (ptah), E, an early deity, considered to be the creator of the universe. Ptah was worshiped as the chief god of the ancient capital of MEMPHIS. In early mythology, Ptah was looked upon as the father and creator of all. His wife was SEKHMET; his son, NEFERTEM.

Puhsien (poo'-shyen'), Ch, the name given to the Vedic sun-god PUSHAN in Chinese mythology.

Pun-Gel (pun'-jel), O, the form of the name BUN-JIL that was preferred in the Victoria district of Australia.

Purana (puh-rah'-nu), I, one of a collection made up of epic poems, myths and legends, and stories connected with Hinduism. These had

162

been preserved by oral tradition for centuries until they were put into written form. The MAHABHARATA and the RAMAYANA are the most famous of the puranas.

Pushan (poo'-shun), I, a solar diety who was one of the ADITYAS. Pushan was a guardian of roads and of cattle, and he guided the dead to the underworld.

Pwyll (pool), Ce, the husband of RHIANNON, whom he had taken from his rival, GWAWL, and the father of PRYDERI.

Pyerun (pi-u-roon'), Sl. *See* PERUN.

Pygmalion (pig-mayl'-yun), G, 1. the creator of a statue of a beautiful woman with which he fell in love. In answer to his prayer, APHRODITE gave the statue life, and they became the parents of PAPHOS.

R, 2. the son of BELUS and brother of DIDO. Pygmalion slew SYCHAEUS, Dido's husband, for his riches, causing Dido to flee from Tyre with a band of followers and found the city of Carthage.

Pylades (pil'-u-deez), G, the son of Strophius, king of Phocis, and companion of ORESTES. Pylades became the husband of ELECTRA, sister of Orestes.

Pyramid Texts, the, E, engravings and paintings on the inner walls of sarcophagi and pyramid burial chambers, giving instructions concerning the journey into the world of the dead, and including detailed descriptions of the daily life of the god RA. These texts, dating from the period of the Old Kingdom, are the earliest records of their kind and form a valuable source of mythological information. They were later written on long papyrus rolls, collectively called the BOOK OF THE DEAD.

Pyramus (pir'-u-mus), G & R, a youth in love with THISBE. Pyramus and Thisbe, who lived in Babylon, fell in love and spoke to each other through a hole in a wall between their adjoining houses because their parents would not permit their marriage. One night they ran way to a planned meeting place at a mulberry tree. Thisbe arrived first, but a lioness with fresh blood at its mouth frightened her away. In her flight, Thisbe dropped her cloak, which the animal tore to pieces. Pyramus saw only the cloak when he arrived, and killed himself. Thisbe then found Pyramus and followed him in death. Their blood turned the mulberries, previously white, to red.

Pyrrha (pir'-u), G, 1. the daughter of EPIMETHEUS and wife of DEUCALION.

2. the name ACHILLES assumed when he hid at the court of

Lycomedes in the guise of a maiden in order to avoid joining the Greeks en route to the TROJAN WAR.

Pyrrhus (pir'-us), G, another name for NEOPTOLEMUS, the son of ACHILLES.

Pythia (pith'-ee-u), G, the priestess of APOLLO in his temple at DELPHI. Pythia uttered the oracular sayings and prophecies of Apollo to all who consulted her.

Pythian Games, the (pith'-ee-un), G, Greek national games, second only to the OLYMPIC GAMES, held every eight, and later every four, years at DELPHI in honor of the slaying of the serpent PYTHON by APOLLO. The Pythian Games, held from the early sixth century B.C. to the end of the fourth century A.D., included athletic, dramatic, and musical contests, as well as foot and chariot races.

Python (pahy'-thahn), G, a huge serpent, the offspring of GAEA, that dwelt near DELPHI in the caves of Mt. PARNASSUS. Python was slain by the arrows of the young APOLLO. In some versions, Python arose from the stagnant waters which remained after the Deluge.

Qat (kaht), O, a culture hero of the Banks Islands. Qat was said to have fashioned the first men and women out of wood, bringing them to life by dancing and beating his drum. In another account, he created both mankind and pigs, with no difference between them, until he gave pigs four legs. Qat also gave the earth its changing seasons and the rains to bring fertility.

Quetzalcoatl (ket-sahl-kaw-ah't'l), Az, a hero or early deity of the Toltecs who became one of the major deities of the Aztec pantheon, the god of the atmosphere and of civilizing influences. Quetzalcoatl, whose cult dates back to sometime before A.D. 300, was the god of wind, life, fertility, wisdom, and practical knowledge. He was held to be the inventor of agriculture, the calendar, and the various arts and crafts. Quetzalcoatl was ruler of the sun of the second universe, which was destroyed by violent winds. He also represented the planet Venus as the morning star, as his twin, XOLOTL, did the evening star. He was sometimes represented in art as a feathered serpent, sometimes as a bearded man. Quetzalcoatl was identified in legend with a semihistorical priest-king, who had sailed away, promising to return. At the landing of Cortes and his conquistadors, many of the Mexican peoples welcomed them, thinking Quetzalcoatl had at last returned to his homeland.

Quirinus (kwi-rahy'-nus), R, an early Italian god of war. After his deification, ROMULUS was worshiped under the name of Quirinus, as the son of MARS.

Ra (rah) or **Re** (ray), E, the sun-god, chief deity of the Egyptian pantheon. The center of his worship was HELIOPOLIS, where he was said to have first appeared as an OBELISK. The father of SHU and TEFNUT, he was the principal deity of the ENNEAD and was generally known as RA-HORAKTE in that capacity.

Protected by a lotus, he lay in the embrace of NUNU and had the name ATUM before he was born as lord of the sky and was called Ra. The world came into being when NUT, transforming herself into a cow, transported Ra to the heavens on her back, and he received the title of lord and creator of the world. Ra was believed to travel across the sky in his bark much as though he were journeying over the sea or on a celestial Nile, a symbol of life and rebirth as he was born each dawn, reached the zenith of his life at midday, and his life's end at sunset, to be born anew the following morning.

Ra called upon the goddess HATHOR to destroy mankind because the human race was plotting against him. He relented, however, after all but a few mortals had been killed, although he then ceded his place as ruler to SHU.

The pharaohs claimed descent from Ra. He was analogous to the Greek god HELIOS and was assimilated into the pantheon of the Phoenicians. He was represented wearing the solar disk on his head and often with the URAEUS, the sacred asp.

Rabefihaza (rab-u-fee-hah'-zu), Af, in the legends of the Madagascans, the inventor of snares and the one who taught men to fish and hunt.

Radha (rah'-dah), I, a pretty milkmaid who became the consort of KRISHNA.

Ragnar Lodbrok (rahg'-nahr lawd'-brahk), Sc, a hero who was sacrificed to ODIN in a snake pit as he sang in eulogy of the god, who would receive him in VALHALLA.

Ragnarok (rahg'-nu-rahk), Sc, the day of doom, the time of the destruction of the gods and of the universe and all its inhabitants. Ragnarok, the last battle against the powers of evil that led to the destruction of all things, was caused by ODIN's inability to prevent BALDER's death. When Balder died, Odin led his army out of VALHALLA to save the earth from the consuming fire that followed. All the gods, the AESIR and VANIR alike, fought side by side against the GIANTS. The gods and monsters were destroyed together, the heavens fell, and all was consumed by the holocaust.

From Ragnarok there would come a new world, a new race of men, a new pantheon of gods, formed around the nucleus of a few surviving gods, among whom was Odin's son VIDAR.

Ragnarok, which is described in the *Völuspa,* a poem used as a source by Snorri Sturluson, corresponds to the Germanic GÖTTERDÄMMERUNG.

Ra-Harakhte (rah-hahr-ahk'-tee), E. *See* Ra-Horakte.

Ra-Horakte (rah-hawr-ahk'-tee) or **Ra-Harakhte** (-hahr-), E, the name given to the sun as ruler of Egypt and chief of the gods of HELIOPOLIS. As Ra-Horakte, the sun-god RA was usually shown with the head of a falcon and wearing the solar disk wreathed by the URAEUS. Horakte means "Horus of the horizon."

Raiden (rahy'-den, ray'-), J, the thunder-god. Raiden is generally depicted as a demon, often with claws on his feet and carrying a drum.

Rakshasas, the (ruk'-shu-suz), I, beings, with some characteristics of the gods, who were violent and malevolent. They had magic powers and could take on any form at will. The Rakshasas are comparable to the ASURAS in that they were powers of evil and darkness and were opposed to INDRA. In the RAMAYANA, RAVANA was king of the Rakshasas, who were also called YAKSHAS.

Rama (rah'mu), I, any one of the three AVATARS of VISHNU, as he appears in the RAMAYANA incarnated as RAMACHANDRA, PARASHURAMA, and BALARAMA. Ramachandra was often known simply as Rama.

Ramachandra (rah-mu-chun'-dru), I, the seventh AVATAR of VISHNU, as the hero of the RAMAYANA and the destroyer of RAVANA, his inexorable enemy. He also played a role in the MAHABHARATA. Ramachandra, more generally known as RAMA, was the representation of the ideal hero, courageous and virtuous. His consort was the lovely SITA, who went with him into the exile forced upon him by his jealous stepmother's schemes.

Soon, however, Sita was abducted by Ravana and held captive in LANKA. An eagle pointed out the way to Sita, and the monkeys came to Rama's aid. HANUMAN even managed to reach Sita's side. Rama, soliciting the ocean's help, was advised to build a bridge to Lanka with the assistance of NALA. Thus, a great bridge soon stretched to the island, and the army of monkeys crossed over. Rama's troops proved superior to Ravana's, and the rival leaders met in single combat. New heads grew where Rama struck Ravana's ten heads one by one with his arrows, but at last a mighty arrow, piercing the monster's chest, killed him.

Thus the god Vishnu triumphed over the demon king. The freed

Sita proved her chastity by fire, and Rama's joy was complete when INDRA restored his fallen comrades to life.

Ramayana, the (rah-mah'-yu-nu), I, an epic poem of India, relating the romantic tale of the recovery by Prince RAMA, aided by a force of monkeys, of his lovely wife SITA, after her abduction by the demon king RAVANA. The Ramayana is one of the PURANAS, and VALMIKI is credited with its composition in about the sixth century B.C.

Rangi (rahng'-ee), O, the sky, father of the gods and all creatures. Rangi loved PAPA, the earth, and their offspring were nature gods, deities of wind, sea, trees, and storm, and also gods of peace, war, and evil. Their crushing embrace was ruinous to all living things and necessitated the lifting of the sky to a lofty, light-giving position. When Rangi weeps at his separation from Papa, his tears are the dew, and his sighs in the wintertime are the ice.

Ras Shamra (rahs sham'-ru), Ph, the modern name of the ancient city Ugarit. Archaeological excavations, carried out there in 1928–29 and thereafter, have revealed important cuneiform tablets that give us valuable information about the main points of their mythology, legends, and the rites and ceremonies connected with their cults. The material gathered from Ras Shamra, however, is sometimes of a local nature, and the myths often varied in different parts of the areas inhabited by the Phoenicians. *See also* UGARIT TABLETS.

Rat (raht), E, in later Egyptian mythology, the wife of RA.

Rati-mbati-ndua (rah-tee-mbah'-tee-ndoo-u), O, in Fiji myth, the god of the realm of the dead, whom he consumed with his one tooth.

Rauni (raw'-nee), F. *See* MAAN-EMOINEN.

Ravana (rah'-vu-nu), I, a demon who was king of the RAKSHASAS in the kingdom of LANKA. Ravana had three incarnations as VISHNU's enemy, the first, in the form of HIRANYAKSHA; the second, RAVANA; and the third, SISUPALA. Ravana, the unrelenting foe of RAMA, abducted his wife, SITA, and was ultimately felled in combat by an arrow from Rama's mighty bow.

Raven, NA, the name given to the trickster or COYOTE by the Indians of the Pacific Northwest. When nothing existed but primeval water, Raven made the dry land by dropping stones, thus giving himself perching places. Then he brought every living thing into being, fashioning a man and a woman from wood and clay after other materials proved unsuitable. In a myth of the Haida Indians, Raven underwent a series of metamorphoses to get daylight from the sky chieftain and bestow its blessings on man.

Re (ray), E. *See* RA.

Regin (ray'-gin), Sc, the brother of FAFNIR, son of HREIDMAR, who acted as foster father to SIGURD. Regin urged Sigurd to kill Fafnir in the expectation of gaining the treasure the dragon guarded. Sigurd later decapitated Regin, on the advice of the birds, whose language he learned from feeding on Fafnir's heart.

Remus (ree'-mus), R, the son of MARS and RHEA SILVIA and twin brother of ROMULUS. He was killed by Romulus in an argument at the time of the building of Rome.

Renenet (ray-nen'-ut) or **Renenit** (-it), E, a deity represented sometimes as lion- or snake-headed and with some of the same functions as SHAI. She fed the newborn infant and named him, and also attended him when he was judged after death. One of the months of the Egyptian calendar was named for Renenet. She was associated with MESKHENT.

Renenit (ray-nen'-it), E. *See* RENENET.

Renpet (ren'-pet), E, a deity of the springtime of life and of the yearly calendar. She was a goddess of the eternity of time.

Rerir (ray'-rir), Sc, the son of ODIN's son Sigi and the founder and king of the VOLSUNGS. Rerir prayed to FREYA for a son. After Rerir and his wife ate the apple Freya gave him, his wish was fulfilled by the birth of Volsung.

Rhadamanthus (rad-u-man'-thus), G, a son of ZEUS and EUROPA and brother of MINOS. Rhadamanthus was a teacher of HERACLES and was considered extremely wise and just. After his death, he became one of the judges of HADES, where he allotted to the souls of the dead their fate.

Rhea (ree'-u), G, the daughter of URANUS and GAEA, sister and wife of CRONUS, and mother of the gods. Cronus and Rhea were the rulers of the TITANS. Their children were DEMETER, HADES, HERA, HESTIA, POSEIDON, and ZEUS. Because Cronus swallowed his children at birth to avoid the loss of his power, as it had been prophesied to him, Rhea sent Zeus to Crete to be raised and gave Cronus a stone in his place. Rhea was a goddess of fertility, and her attendants were the CURETES. She was associated with CYBELE in Asia Minor, and the Romans identified Rhea with OPS and BONA DEA.

Rhea Silvia (ree'-u sil'-vee-u), R, the daughter of Numitor, a descendant of AENEAS and mother of ROMULUS and REMUS by MARS.

Rhiannon (ree'-an-un), Ce, a goddess of fertility who was PWYLL's wife and the mother of PRYDERI. She was made to undergo punishment because she was accused of killing her infant son, who in fact had been kidnaped. Rhiannon married MANAWYDDAN after Pwyll died.

Ribhus, the (rahyb'-uhz, -huhz), I, three elves who were skillful artisans and builders of the chariots of the gods. They learned their craft from TVASHTRI, whose daughter, SARANYU, was their mother. Their father was INDRA. The Ribhus were granted immortality in recognition of their many kindnesses and their wondrous creations.

Rind (rind), Sc, the one whose love ODIN, according to the less familiar account of Saxo Grammaticus, the twelfth-century Danish writer, sought in his efforts to win revenge for BALDER's death. Rind bore Odin a son, who finally avenged Balder by slaying HODER.

Rishis, the (rish'-eez), I, mythical beings who preserved and handed down the knowledge imparted by the VEDAS. Seven in number, the Rishis were the stars of the Great Bear.

Roma (roh'-mah), R, the daughter of EVANDER, who named the city of Rome in her honor. She was the protective goddess of the city.

Romulus (rahm'-yu-lus), R, twin brother of REMUS. Romulus and Remus, sons of MARS and RHEA SILVIA, were born at Alba Longa, a town founded by ASCANIUS, son of AENEAS. Amulius, their uncle, set the infants adrift after usurping the throne, but they were saved and nursed by a wolf. Romulus was the founder and first king of Rome (April 753 B.C., according to legend), having slain Remus in a disagreement at the time of the building of the city. Romulus was deified after his death and was worshiped as QUIRINUS, a god of war.

Rongo (rawng'-oh), O, a Polynesian god of agriculture and fertility, the center of veneration at the time of the harvest celebration. Rongo was a patron deity of music and enjoyed widespread popularity. In the Marquesas he was known as ONO; in Hawaii, as LONO.

Ru (roo), O, the Tahitian god of the east wind. He was the brother of HINA, who, in their legend, sailed to the moon in a canoe.

Ruahatu (roo-ah-hah'-too), O, a Polynesian god of the sea, venerated especially in Tahiti.

Rudra (ruhd'-ru), I, a dreaded god of storm and mountain. He was also a deity of the dead and a demon skilled in archery, who brought disease with his arrows. His sons were the MARUTS, also known as Rudras.

Rusalka (roo-sahl'-kah), Sl, a deity, the spirit of any human girl whose death was caused by drowning. Although belief in the Rusalka was widespread among the Slavs, the appearance and personality of this divinity often varied according to region. In general, a northern Rusalka was pale, unkempt, naked, and corpselike in look, while her actions could be cruel and violent. A Rusalka of the southern regions, on the other hand, was attractive, friendly, kind, and of gentle disposition.

The Rusalki were divinities of both water and forest, spending the summer in the woods and returning to the water at its end. Their time was spent in frolic and mischief.

Rustum   (roo'-stum), Pe. *See* SOHRAB AND RUSTUM.

Ruti   (root'-ee), Ph, a deity of BYBLOS, the son of a god called Ra, whom the Phoenicians incorporated into their own mythology under various epithets. Ruti was sometimes represented with the head of a lion.

Saga   (sah'-gu), Sc, an Icelandic or Norse narrative of the medieval period, recounting in prose the events and exploits of an individual or family, or other group of people, as the VOLSUNGA SAGA revolves around the VOLSUNGS.

Salus   (say'-lus), R, the goddess who was the personification of health and welfare. She was identified with the Greek goddess HYGEIA.

Samhitas, the   (sum-hi-tahz'), I, the name given to the four books (the *Rig-Veda,* the *Sama-Veda,* the *Yajur-Veda,* and the *Atharva-Veda*) of the VEDAS that are generally considered to form a unit.

Sampo, the   (sahm'-paw), F, a magic object, perhaps a talisman or mill, that granted all wishes and produced food and wealth. ILMARINEN forged the Sampo and won the hand of LOUHI's daughter, the Maid of the North. Later, Ilmarinen returned to POHJOLA to steal the Sampo with the aid of VAINAMOINEN and LEMMINKAINEN, but it was broken in the skirmishes that followed, leaving only a few fragments.

Saranyu   (sah'-run-yoo), I, the goddess of the clouds in Vedic mythology. She was the daughter of TVASHTRI and mother of the RIBHUS, whose father was INDRA. Saranyu became the wife of VIVASVAT, but she left him shortly after the wedding. Another bride for Vivasvat was made in her image, and was the mother of YAMA AND YAMI and of the ASVINS.

In Hindu mythology, Saranyu is sometimes the wife of SURYA, but in some versions she is called Sanjna, daughter of VISVAKARMA.

Sarasvati   (su-rus'-vu-tee, sur'-us-), I, in early Vedic myth, a river-goddess; in later myth, the lovely wife of BRAHMA, born of his body. Sarasvati was goddess of wisdom and learning and of music and the arts. In time, she took on many of the characteristics of the goddess VACH.

Sarasvati is often depicted seated on a lotus and as having four arms. A beautiful white marble temple was built at Dilwara and dedicated to Sarasvati.

Sarpedon (sahr-pee'-dun), G, a son of ZEUS and EUROPA and brother of MINOS and RHADAMANTHUS. A hero in the TROJAN WAR, he was slain by PATROCLUS, and his body was rescued from the Greeks by APOLLO. The Lycians were thought to be descended from Sarpedon. In some versions, he was the son of ZEUS and LAODAMIA.

Sati (sah'-tee), E, 1. the first wife of KHNUM, who helped her husband protect the upper Nile and the Cataracts. She is depicted wearing on her head the white crown of the South with two horns and holding a bow and arrow. Arrows were symbols of the swiftness of the Nile's course.

E, 2. a serpent that lived in AMENTI and preyed on the dead.

I, 3. a manifestation of PARVATI as the daughter of DAKSHA. Sati loved SHIVA and chose him for her husband despite her father's opposition.

Saturn (sat'-urn), R, an early god of planting and harvest, who ruled during the GOLDEN AGE, identified with the Greek god CRONUS. The Temple of Saturn at the west end of the Roman Forum was dedicated to him and his wife, OPS. The Saturnalia, an annual festival held in mid-December in honor of Saturn, was a time of gift giving and entertainment. His name survives in the word Saturday, "Saturn's day."

Satyrs, the (say'-turz), G & R, deities of the woods and countryside —they were men with the horns and legs of goats—who were the attendants of DIONYSUS or BACCHUS. The satyrs were celebrated for their lascivious orgies, hence the word "satyr."

Savitri (sah'-vi-tree), I, 1. the sun as exemplified in its rising and setting. He was one of the ADITYAS and represented universal movement, seen in the course of the sun and the motion of the winds and seas. Savitri, the ruler of the heavens, was carried in a gleaming chariot by shining horses. His eyes and arms were golden.

2. the heroine of a famous independent episode in the MAHABHARATA who, by her pleading, persuaded YAMA, the god of death, to release her husband, Satyavan.

Scarab (skar'-ub), E, a representation of a beetle, the sacred symbol of everlasting, eternal transformation, and of immortality. The scarab was associated with the god KHEPRI and was often used as a seal, or an amulet worn for protection against evil.

Scylla (sil'-u), G, 1. the daughter of PHORCYS who was changed into a monster. GLAUCUS fell in love with her, but she spurned him. When Glaucus asked CIRCE to help him, she fell in love with Glaucus and therefore turned Scylla into a monster out of jealousy. Scylla then became an ugly six-headed creature. Out from her body grew heads of fierce dogs and serpents. She dwelt opposite CHARYBDIS on the coast of Italy at the Strait of Messina and was a menace to sailors, among them the ARGONAUTS and the followers of ODYSSEUS and AENEAS. She would swallow all within her reach. The expression "between Scylla and Charybdis" means between two difficulties of equal intensity.

2. the daughter of King NISUS of Megara. Scylla betrayed Megara to MINOS, whom she loved, by cutting a purple lock of hair from her father's head, thus enabling Minos to capture the city, whose fate depended on the lock. However, Minos refused to marry her out of contempt for her betrayal of Nisus, after which she killed herself. In some versions, she was transformed into a lark, and her father was transformed into a hawk.

Seasons, the, G. *See* HORAE.

Seb (seb), E. *See* GEB.

Sebek (se'-bek), E, a crocodile believed to be the incarnation of a god and worshiped as such. Sebek was associated with the pharaohs of the Thirteenth Dynasty, and sanctuaries were built to him during that period. He was depicted as a crocodile or a crocodile-headed man.

Sedna (sed'-nah), NA, the Eskimo spirit of the sea, whose home is in its lower reaches. On earth, she had been AVILAYOQ, the creator of men and animals. As goddess of the sea, she had control of the sea animals and the food supplied by them. When she was angry, the waters were rough and the hunting poor. She received the INNUAS of those who died from natural causes into her kingdom in the dark depths of the sea.

In Greenland, Sedna is also called ARNAKNAGSAK, and she has a number of other names which vary from region to region.

Seker (se'-ker), E, an early god of vegetation and later the deity of the necropolis of MEMPHIS and of the underworld. Seker was closely identified with OSIRIS, who was known at Memphis as Seker Osiris. Seker, who was represented with the head of a hawk, was known by the Greeks as Soucharis.

Sekhmet (sek'-met), E, a warrior-goddess who was depicted with the head of a lioness or as a lioness. She was often identified with HATHOR, who took the shape of a lioness and did battle for RA against those mortals who were rebellious against him. In the end, Ra had to come to the rescue before the human race was exterminated. Sekhmet was the wife of PTAH and mother of their son NEFERTEM.

Selene (si-lee'-nee), G, the goddess of the moon, daughter of HYPERION and THEIA and sister of EOS and HELIOS. Selene fell in love with the shepherd ENDYMION and visited him nightly as he slept. Selene was later associated with the goddess ARTEMIS. The Romans identified her with DIANA and LUNA.

Selket (sel'-ket) or **Selkit** (-kit), E, a deity of marriage and of the dead. She was the protectress of the mummified dead and guardian of the canopic jars into which the viscera were put. The scorpion was sacred to Selket, who was sometimes represented as a scorpion with the head of a human.

Selkit (sel'-kit), E. *See* SELKET.

Semele (sem'-u-lee), G, the daughter of CADMUS and HARMONIA and mother by ZEUS of DIONYSUS. Zeus loved Semele, but HERA caused her to doubt if he was really Zeus. Zeus promised to fulfill any request made. As a result, he appeared to Semele as a true god, accompanied by thunder and lightning, whereupon Semele was instantly consumed by fire and carried to the heavens by the king of the gods.

Semiramis (si-mir'-u-mis), A-B, the beautiful queen of Babylon who was said to have built that city and to have conquered a vast amount of territory.

Sengen (seng'-gen), J, the goddess of Mt. Fuji, whose sanctuary was erected on the summit.

Serapis (su-ray'-pis), E, the name given by the Greeks to the sacred bull of MEMPHIS, believed to be OSIRIS incarnate in APIS. Serapis was worshiped as the god of the Ptolemies and as the chief deity of Alexandria, the new capital established by the Greek rulers, where a large, lofty temple was erected to him. His worship spread throughout the Greek and Roman world. In the nineteenth century, over sixty mummified bulls were discovered in the Serapeum at Sakkara near Memphis. Serapis was also known as HAPI.

Seshat (sesh'-at) or **Sesheta** (-et-ah), E, a goddess who was closely linked to THOTH as the patroness of writing and literature and the recorder of historical events. She was a helpmate to Thoth in his work and was the wife most often mentioned in connection with him. As a deity of the stars, Seshat contributed her skill to builders by aiding them in the stellar alignment of new structures, especially in the planning of temples. She is depicted wearing a crescent and star with two plumes on her head.

Sesheta (sesh'-et-ah), E. *See* SESHAT.

Sestos (ses'-tahs), G, a town in Thrace, opposite ABYDOS on the north side of the Hellespont where HERO was a priestess of APHRODITE. *See also* LEANDER.

Set (set) or **Seth** (seth), E, the son of GEB and NUT and brother of OSIRIS and ISIS. His hatred of his brother led him to trick Osiris and bring about his death. A chest was made and was offered at a banquet as a present to the one who could fit into it. When Osiris, in his turn, got into it, the lid was sealed and the chest tossed into the Nile. Although it was found after a search by Isis, Set recovered the chest and cut Osiris' body to pieces. With the help of THOTH, Isis was able to restore her husband's body and bring him back to life again. Set was slain in vengeance by HORUS.

Set was sometimes called the father of ANUBIS by his sister NEPHTHYS, but he believed Anubis had been conceived by Osiris. The representation of evil, Set was identified by the Greeks with TYPHON.

Seth (seth), E. *See* SET.

Seven Against Thebes, Expedition of the, G, a war against THEBES to overthrow ETEOCLES. Because his brother Eteocles would not give the throne of Thebes to him, although each was supposed to reign in alternate years, POLYNICES went to Argos where, with the help of King ADRASTUS, he gathered an army to support him in his cause against Eteocles. The seven leaders: Amphiaraus, Capaneus, Hippomedon, PARTHENOPAEUS, TYDEUS, Polynices, and Adrastus. In the end, Polynices and Eteocles killed each other, thus ending the war. Of the seven, only Adrastus survived.

Shah Namah, the (shah nah'-mu), Pe, the "Book of the Kings," an epic poem of ancient Persian legendary history. Firdausi composed this work of almost sixty thousand verses in the tenth century. Tales of warrior and culture heroes predominate, among them the famous episode of the exploits of the hero RUSTUM and his son SOHRAB.

Shai (shay), E, a divinity who accompanied each human from birth to death, decreeing the course of his life, and appearing with the soul of the dead when he was tried and judged before OSIRIS.

Shakuru (sha'-ku-roo), NA, the name given to the sun by the Pawnee Indians. Shakuru is honored each year with a great ritual celebration, which includes dances, processions, and religious ceremonies.

Shala (shah'-lah), A-B, the consort of the god ADAD.

Shamash (shah'-mahsh), A-B, the sun-god, regarded as the bringer of light and the upholder of righteousness and law. Originally a Semitic deity, Shamash was brought to Mesopotamia by the Akkadians. With his father, SIN, the moon-god, and his sister, ISHTAR, Shamash formed a cosmic triad of some importance. Shamash had the ability to deliver oracular responses of prophecy.

Shamash's consort was AYA; KITTU and MISHARU, their children. His chief sanctuary was in Babylon, and he was worshiped also at Sippar. His Sumerian counterpart was UTU.

Shango (shang'-oh), Af, the legendary first king of the Yoruba tribe, whose palace was of shining metal and whose stables held hundreds of fine horses. His wife was OYA. After a long rule filled with the wars he so liked to wage, Shango disappeared into the earth, and was worshiped thereafter by an active priesthood and human sacrifice. Shango was the son of YEMAJA and AGANJU or, in another version, of ORUNJAN.

Shedu, the (shay'-doo), or **Lamassu, the** (lah-mas'-soo), A-B, the genii who were spirits of good, guarding against the forces of evil and acting as intermediaries between deities and man. The shedu accompanied each individual as benevolent, unseen protectors. They also stood guard before the sanctuaries and temple gates. In this capacity, they had the shape of winged bulls with the heads of men.

Shen-Nung (shen'-nuhng'), Ch, an emperor of the third millennium B.C. who brought the skills of agriculture to his people and was deified after his death.

Shesha (shay'-shu), I, a serpent with many heads. He sprang from the mouth of BALARAMA as he was dying. Shesha was king of the NAGAS. During the periods between VISHNU's incarnations, Shesha's body was his bed, and the heads formed a protective covering over the god. Shesha, also called ANANTA, was sometimes identified with VRITRA.

Shichi Fukujin, the (shee'-chee fuh-koo'-jin), J, the seven deities of luck, a group of six gods and one goddess, whose names were BENTEN, BISHAMON, DAIKOKU, EBISU, FUKUROKUJU, HOTEI, and JOROJIN.

Shina-Tsu-Hiko (shee'-nah-tsoo-hee'-koh), J, the god of wind, born of IZANAGI's breath.

Shi Tenno, the (shee' ten-noh'), J, the guardians of the four cardinal points of the compass, the protectors of the world against the demons. The guardian of the north was BISHAMON or Tamon; of the south, KOMOKU; of the east, JIKOKU; and of the west, ZOCHO.

Shiva (shee'-vu) or **Siva** (see'-vu), I, originally a god of a primitive Hindu religion and adopted into the Brahmanic pantheon as a representation of destruction and disasters similar to his Vedic predecessor RUDRA. Shiva's wife was PARVATI, who was known also by other names, each representing a different manifestation of the goddess.

When VASUKI was pulled by the DEVAS on one side and the ASURAS on the other as they churned the sea, it was Shiva who saved the creatures of the earth by drinking the venom that came pouring from the king of the snakes in his effort.

In human form, Shiva is often depicted with three eyes and four arms, wearing snakes as ornaments and a string of skulls around his neck. He was also called NATARAJA in his role as lord of rhythm and dance. With BRAHMA and VISHNU, Shiva was one of the triad of gods called the TRIMURTI.

Shoden (shoh'-den), J, the name given by the Japanese to the Vedic god of wisdom, GANESHA.

Shou-hsing (shoh'-shing'), Ch, the god of long life, highly revered for his power to bestow the gift of longevity. He recorded the destined date of a person's death, but could sometimes be persuaded, by honor and sacrifice, to alter his figures favorably. Shou-hsing is generally depicted carrying a staff and holding a peach of immortality. He is an old white-bearded man with a bulbous bald head. Closely connected with the god of long life were the god of salaries and the god of happiness, who were often depicted with him.

Shu (shoo), E, the god of air and light, who upheld the vault of heaven. Shu was the son of RA and twin brother of TEFNUT. These twins, the first couple of the ENNEAD, were the first divinities brought forth by Ra. Shu was the father of GEB and NUT by Tefnut. He became lord of the earth after his father Ra and was later succeeded by Geb. Shu was generally depicted with an ostrich plume on his head and sometimes as the support of the vault of heaven.

Sibyl (sib'-il), G & R, a prophetess, the most famous of which was the CUMAEAN SIBYL. The sibyls were generally either quite young or very old women who lived in or near caves and uttered advice and prophecy in ambiguous wording under the often frenzied inspiration of the gods.

Siddhartha (si-dahr'-tu, -thu), I, the name of the son born to MAYA. He became the BUDDHA, with Siddhartha as one of his epithets.

Siduri (see-doo'-ree), A-B, a goddess who lived by the sea in the midst of a beautiful garden strewn with gems. When she could not

176

deter GILGAMESH from his desire to find UTA-NAPISHTIM, Siduri directed him to elicit the help of URSHANABI.

Siegfried (seeg'-freed), T, the strong and handsome hero of the NIBELUNGENLIED, son of SIEGMUND and SIEGLINDE. When Siegfried killed FAFNIR with his father's magic sword to gain the gold the dragon guarded, he was sprayed by Fafnir's blood and thus became invulnerable except between his shoulders, where a leaf settled. Siegfried overcame the NIBELUNGS and carried off their gold. He also learned the language of the birds and gained the ring cursed by ALBERICH. Siegfried rode through the circle of flame to rescue BRUNHILD and gave her the ring.

Forgetting Brunhild, due to a magic potion, Siegfried married KRIEMHILD and then took on the appearance of his wife's brother, GUNTHER, in order to win Brunhild for him. Siegfried met his death at the hand of HAGEN, an act instigated by Brunhild.

Sieglinde (seeg-lin'-du), T, SIEGMUND's wife and the mother of SIEGFRIED.

Siegmund (seeg'-muhnd), T, the king of the Netherlands, husband of SIEGLINDE and father of SIEGFRIED, hero of the NIBELUNGENLIED. Siegmund died before Siegfried was born, but he left his son his magic sword.

Sien-Tsan (si-en'-tsahn'), Ch, the goddess and patroness of the art of cultivating silk. In her mortal life, she had been the wife of the emperor SHEN-NUNG, who was also deified.

Sif (sif), Sc, the faithful wife of THOR. When LOKI cut off her hair as a prank, the DWARFS replaced it with hair made of gold, thus saving Loki from Thor's vengeance.

Siggeir (sig'-gehr), Sc, the husband of SIGNY, who killed him with the help of SINFIOTLI after he murdered VOLSUNG, her father.

Sigi (see'-gee), Sc, a son of ODIN who was a king of the Huns and the father of RERIR.

Sigmund (sig'-mund), Sc, the eldest son of VOLSUNG and LIOD and the father of SINFIOTLI by his sister, SIGNY. Sigmund's first wife was BORGHILD, who killed Sinfiotli in anger; his second, HIORDIS, mother of SIGURD. Sigmund left his magic sword, called Gram, to his son Sigurd, who was born posthumously.

Signy (sig'-nee), Sc, VOLSUNG's daughter, mother of SINFIOTLI by her brother SIGMUND. After Volsung was murdered by SIGGEIR, her husband, Signy avenged her father's death by planning the death of Siggeir with the help of her son.

177

Sigurd (sig'-urd), Sc, the valiant, handsome hero of the VOLSUNGA SAGA, the posthumous son of SIGMUND and his second wife, HIORDIS. It was Sigurd who, encouraged by REGIN, killed FAFNIR to get the treasure of ANDVARI.

Sigurd loved and promised himself to the VALKYRIE BRYNHILD. When Sigurd went to the land of the NIBELUNGS, where GIUKI reigned as king, he was given a love potion by Giuki's wife, GRIMHILD, and, forgetting Brynhild, fell in love with and married their daughter GUDRUN. Sigurd then urged Gudrun's brother GUNNAR to wed Brynhild and he himself wooed Brynhild for his brother-in-law. The time came when Sigurd was slain at the jealous instigation of Brynhild. Sigurd corresponds to SIEGFRIED in the NIBELUNGENLIED.

Sigyn (seg'-in, see'-gin), Sc, LOKI's faithful wife, mother of VALI. When the gods, after BALDER's death, bound Loki and placed stones over him with a snake spitting venom above his head, Sigyn protected her husband by catching the poison in a bowl.

Sila (sil'-ah), NA, in Eskimo myth, the air and the atmospheric phenomena that take place in it, often referred to as silap INNUA, a term denoting the personification of air and breath. Silap innua also indicated intelligence, energy, and orderly force. Because he held sway over the weather and the environment, Sila was one of the most important of the spirits.

Silenus (sahy-lee'-nus), G, an early woodland deity of Phrygia who was, in later mythology, said to be the son of PAN or HERMES and a NYMPH. He was the oldest of the SATYRS and was the teacher and companion of DIONYSUS. The plural form of his name, *sileni,* was used to refer to a group of deities often confused with the satyrs and similar to them except for the fact they resembled horses instead of goats.

Silvanus or **Sylvanus** (sil-vay'-nus), R, the god of the fields, woods, and flocks and the guardian of boundary lines. He was associated with FAUNUS and PAN.

Silver Age, the, G & R, the AGE OF MANKIND following the GOLDEN AGE. The Silver Age was a period when difficulties and discomforts appeared, and labor and toil became necessary.

Sin (seen), A-B, an early god of the moon, son of ENLIL and husband of NINGAL. Sin's bright light kept watch against evil forces in the night. When these UTUKKU succeeded in extinguishing his brilliance with the help of ISHTAR and SHAMASH, MARDUK fought off the attackers and brought back the eclipsed light of Sin.

Marduk had given Sin his function of marking monthly time with his waxing and waning. He was a knowledgeable god who shared his wisdom with the other deities, who were said to seek his advice each month.

Sin was known as NANNA in Sumer, where he was worshiped in the form of an elderly man. The seat of his worship was Ur. Sin's symbol was a crescent. In some versions, he was the father of NUSKU.

Sina (see'-nu), O. *See* HINA.

Sinfiotli (sin'-fyawt-lee), Sc, the son of SIGMUND and his sister, SIGNY. Sinfiotli helped his mother to avenge VOLSUNG's murder by slaying her husband, SIGGEIR. Sinfiotli, in turn, was later poisoned in revenge by Sigmund's first wife, BORGHILD, after he killed her brother.

Sinteotl (seen-tay-oh't'l), Az. *See* CINTEOTL.

Sinvat (sin'-vaht), Pe, the bridge to the kingdom of the dead.

Sirens, the (sahy'-renz), G, the nymphs of the sea who lived on an island off the coast of Italy and lured sailors to their destruction with their irresistible singing. They were generally depicted with wings and with the lower part of their bodies like that of a bird.

Sisupala (si-su-pah'-lu), I, the third incarnation of RAVANA, a king's son, born with three eyes and four arms, but with the prophecy of restoration to normalcy on the knees of a man destined to be his slayer. When KRISHNA, an incarnation of VISHNU, was visiting the royal family and took the child Sisupala on his knees, the third eye and two extra arms disappeared, leaving the child's fate clear.

Years later, at a sacrificial celebration, Sisupala argued against Krishna's right to receive priority over the other kings present. Sisupala's anger grew and his insults multiplied until the flaming disk, the deity's weapon, arose to cut him apart, and Sisupala's soul entered the god's feet.

Sisyphus (sis'-u-fus), G, the son of AEOLUS and king of Corinth. Sisyphus was the brother of ATHAMAS and father of GLAUCUS by MEROPE. When ZEUS wished to put him to death because he had informed on Zeus for having abducted AEGINA, Sisyphus overcame and bound death, but HADES claimed Sisyphus and he was punished in the UNDERWORLD by having to roll a stone, which continually rolled back, up a hill forever.

Sita (see'-tah), I, an AVATAR of VISHNU's wife, LAKSHMI, as the wife of RAMACHANDRA. Sita was abducted by RAVANA and taken to LANKA, where he held her captive, leading to war between India and Lanka. After Ravana was slain by RAMA, Sita laid herself upon a funeral pyre to prove her chastity had remained unstained. She was untouched by the flames.

Sitragupta (si-tru-gup'-tu), I, the son of INDRA and INDRANI.

Siva (see'-vu), I. *See* SHIVA.

Skadi (skah'-dee), Sc, the daughter of the GIANT THIAZI. Skadi intended to attack the AESIR to avenge her father's death, but the gods, unwilling to fight a woman, told her to choose a husband from among them, and they stood with their feet showing below a curtain. Skadi believed she selected BALDER, but her choice had fallen upon NIORD's feet. She became Niord's wife and the mother of FREY and FREYA, but she soon returned to live and hunt in her native mountains.

Skanda (skun'-du), I. *See* KARTTIKEYA.

Skidbladnir (skeed'-blahd-nir), Sc, FREY's magic ship, built by the DWARFS. It could be folded to a very small size but was big enough to carry all the gods. Skidbladnir always had favoring winds and sailed a true course.

Skirnir (skeer'-nir), Sc, FREY's servant, whom he sent to WOO GERDA. Skirnir had Frey's sword to help him, but Gerda did not succumb to either pledges or threats until she was promised imminent old age.

Skrymir (skree'-mir), Sc, a GIANT whom THOR and LOKI and THIALFI met in a forest when they were traveling to UTGARD, land of the giants. His power, actions, and invulnerability mystified them completely. They later learned that Skrymir had in reality been UTGARD-LOKI, exercising his magic tricks.

Skuld (skuld), Sc, one of the three NORNS. Skuld personified the future. She was evil and was the one who destroyed the web of fate.

Sleipnir (slayp'-nir), Sc, ODIN's eight-legged horse, the foal of SVADILFARI and LOKI, who had taken on the form of a mare. He was a swift stallion, and nothing could stand in his way. Odin's son HERMOD rode Sleipnir to the realm of HEL after BALDER's death to gain his release.

Sohrab (so'-rahb) **and Rustum** (roo'-stum), Pe, the son and father who figure in the most famous episode in the SHAH NAMAH. Rustum was a hero of many exploits, whose strength and skills were manifested even in his childhood. A son, Sohrab, was born of his union with the daughter of a neighboring king, but the mother, fearing that Rustum, who had already deserted her for a hero's life, would take the boy from her, sent word that the child was a girl.

Sohrab, grown to be a young man of great valor, formed a plan to conquer Persia. When the two armies faced each other in battle, a challenge to single combat was made. Rustum, concealing his identity, faced Sohrab, a youth unknown to him. They fought furiously into a third day, until Rustum threw and mortally stabbed his rival, and learned the tragic truth from his dying son.

This legend has been impressively retold by Matthew Arnold in his narrative poem *Sohrab and Rustum* (1853).

Sol (sahl), R, the sun-god, identified with HELIOS.

Soma (soh'-mu), I, 1. a sacred plant and the juice extracted from it, which gave strength, wisdom, and immortality to those who partook of it. Soma corresponds to the Persian HAOMA of the AVESTA.

2. a god, who was the personification of the soma juice. Soma took numerous shapes, but he was chiefly an earth-god and healer. In later myths, Soma was most often the embodiment of the moon.

Song of Ullikummi, the (uh-lee-koo'-mee), a long poem recounting KUMARBI's plan to elevate the monster ULLIKUMMI to the position of king of the gods by overthrowing TESHUP. It is a Hurrian myth that had been translated into Hittite. The text, dating from about 1300–1200 B.C., is from the royal library at the Hittite capital, Hattusas, the modern Boghazkoy.

Sophocles (sahf'-u-kleez), an Athenian tragic poet of the fifth century B.C. who wrote over 120 plays. The seven extant tragedies are: AJAX, on the subject of his death; ANTIGONE, showing the conflicting claims of government and religion; OEDIPUS *Rex,* called a perfect tragedy by Aristotle: *Oedipus at Colonus,* dealing with his death; ELECTRA, treating the theme of matricide; PHILOCTETES, dealing with the effort to sway him to join the Greeks at Troy; and *Trachiniae,* concerning the death of HERACLES.

Sparti, the (spahr'-tahy), G, the men who arose fully armed from the dragon's teeth sown by CADMUS. The five who survived the battle among them became the ancestors of the nobility of THEBES.

Sphinx (sfingks), E, 1. a mythical creature with the body of a lion and a male human or an animal head, represented in colossal statues as a combined image of the sun-god RA and a pharaoh. The most famous of the sphinxes is the great Sphinx at GIZEH, sculptured from solid rock during the Old Kingdom period. It is in a couchant position and bears the headdress of a pharaoh. Excavations brought to light a small temple standing between the two forelegs. Avenues of sphinxes were used as approaches to temples and tombs in the belief that these creatures would act as invincible guardians.

G, 2. a creature, part woman, part bird, and part lioness, sent by HERA as a plague on THEBES, to punish the city because of the activities of LAIUS. The Sphinx posed a riddle and hurled from a rock all those who could not answer it. The riddle: "What animal walks on four feet in the morning, on two at noon, and on three in the evening?" Told that the Sphinx would destroy herself upon receiving an explanation of the riddle, CREON promised his crown, as well as his sister JOCASTA, to any man who could thus deliver the city from the monster. OEDIPUS solved the riddle by replying: "Man, who crawls on all fours at the beginning of his life, then walks on two feet, and needs the help of a cane at the end of his life." The Sphinx immediately destroyed herself, and Oedipus unwittingly went on to fulfill the prophecy that he would marry his own mother.

Sri (shree), I, the name of LAKSHMI when she was incarnated as the wife of RAMACHANDRA, an AVATAR of VISHNU.

Stribog (stri-bawg'), Sl, the god of the winds and storms and of the cold. His statue was said to stand at Kiev.

Stymphalian Birds, the (stim-fay'-lee-un), G, the birds that shot out their feathers and had beaks and claws of bronze and fed on human flesh. It was one of the LABORS OF HERACLES to rid ARCADIA of these birds, which lived near Lake Stymphalus. ATHENA gave Heracles a rattle of brass, with which he routed the birds and killed them.

Styx (stiks), G, 1. the river surrounding HADES, separating it from the upper world.
  2. a daughter of OCEANUS and TETHYS, and the protectress of the river Styx. She helped the Olympians against the TITANS, and the gods, therefore, swore their oaths by her as well as by the river.

Summanus (su-may'-nus), R, an early god of thunder, associated especially with nocturnal thunderstorms.

Sun Hou-Tzu (shun' hoo'-dzoo), Ch, a monkey, either a fairy or a god, who was the ruler of the monkeys and carried a magic wand. When he was taken in chains to the land of the dead, Sun Hou-Tzu found and tore up the page on which his name was recorded, stating he was no longer subject to death, and the king, Yen-Lo-Wang, conceded to his declaration.

Supai (soo'-pahy), SA. See SUPAY.

Supay or **Supai** (soo'-pahy), SA, in Incan mythology, the god of the dead, who ruled over those spirits that did not go to the land of the sun but were confined within the dark earth. Supay demanded human sacrifices, especially children, to populate his kingdom.

Surt (surrt, suhrt), Sc, the sovereign and guardian of the realm of MUSPELHEIM, land of fire. At RAGNAROK, Surt overcame FREY and brought about the destruction of the world by flame.

Surya (soor'-yu), I, the chief sun-god, who dwelt within the sun, or a divinity of the rising and setting sun. In later mythology, after VIVASVAT declined in importance, Surya was said to be SARANYU's husband. Surya formed a triad, with INDRA and AGNI, of Vedic gods.

Susanowo (soo'-sah-naw'-waw), J, the sea-god and also a god of fertility, thunder, and rain. Susanowo was born of his nose when IZANAGI was bathing in the sea to cleanse himself of the impurities of the realm of the dead.

Susanowo went with good will to visit his sister AMATERASU, goddess of the sun and ruler of heaven, but, when she mistrusted his intent, he challenged her to create girls, saying he would create boys. Three goddesses were born of Amaterasu's breath after she broke Susanowo's sword and ate the pieces. Five gods came to life from her brother's breath, when he bit into the jewels of Amaterasu's necklace, and one of these was the ancestor of the royal family of Japan.

Overcome by his achievement, Susanowo went on a rampage of destruction, and the world was covered with darkness when his sister took refuge in a cave. The gods inflicted bodily punishment on Susanowo, forcing him from their kingdom. Susanowo then went to live on earth, in Izumo province. Susanowo exemplifies the gods of the province of Izumo.

Suttung (suht'-uhng), Sc, a GIANT who stole the mead of inspiration, a mixture of the blood of KVASIR and honey, and enclosed it in a mountain. ODIN succeeded in retrieving it and carried it off to ASGARD.

Svadilfari (swahd-il'-fa-ree), Sc, a fine horse belonging to a GIANT, who was to receive the sun and the moon and FREYA as his wife, if he could construct a wall during one winter. This fine stallion, named Svadilfari, sired SLEIPNIR, ODIN's eight-legged horse, by a mare that was in reality the transformed shape of LOKI, who had enticed Svadilfari away from the giant, causing him to forfeit his promised payment.

Svantovit (svahn-toh-vit'), Sl, a warrior-god and god of plenty. The center of his cult was at Arcona on the Baltic island of Rügen. A huge four-sided statue in the temple there showed him with four heads, one looking out from each side. In his hand he held a horn which foretold, by the quantity of harvest wine remaining in it, whether the coming year would be bountiful and prosperous or lean and difficult. In addition, Svantovit's white horse, also worshiped in the temple, predicted the course of future events by the manner in which it made its way between lines of spears implanted in the ground.

Svantovit sometimes took on some of the characteristics of SVAROG and was thought of as the father of the sun.

Svarog (svah'-rawg), Sl, the sky-god, lord of the universe and progenitor of the Slavic deities. Svarog represented the heavens. His son was the god DAZHBOG, the sun personified.

Svarozhich (svah-roh'-zhich), Sl. *See* DAZHBOG.

Svyatogor (svyah-taw'-gawr), Sl, a legendary hero and a friend of ILYA-MUROMYETS. When his wife committed adultery with Ilya-Muromyets, Svyatogor slew her. Exceedingly strong, Svyatogor boasted that he could lift any weight, even the world, but one day, as he tried to pick up a little bag he found on the ground, he sank into the earth under its weight. The bag, holding the earth's weight, had defeated the braggart hero and taken his life.

Swarga (swur'-gu), I, the heaven of INDRA. Its great city, Amaravati, located on Mt. MERU, was built by the architect of the gods, VISVAKARMA.

Sychaeus (si-kee'-us), R, the husband of DIDO, who was slain by her brother PYGMALION for his wealth.

Sylvanus (sil-vay'-nus), R. *See* SILVANUS.

Symplegades, the (sim-pleg'-u-deez), G, the Clashing Rock at the entrance to the Black Sea which continually floated apart and crashed together, crushing everything in the narrow passage between. At the advice of PHINEUS, the ARGONAUTS first sent a dove through and then rowed hard, so that only the stern of their ship was touched by the rocks, as the tail feathers of the dove had been. The Symplegades became permanently fixed in place, after the Argonauts had sailed through successfully.

Syrinx (sir'-ingks), G, a nymph who was pursued by PAN. Pan clasped some reeds instead of her, and, hearing a sound in the reeds, shaped them into pipes. These were the Pipes of Pan or shepherd's pipes, also called the Syrinx.

Ta'aroa (tah-ah-roh'-ah), O, the name given to TANGAROA in the Society Islands. In the beginning, there was only darkness, until Ta'aroa created the world from a primeval egg, which became the sky and the earth. The war-god ORO was his son.

Taaut (tah'-out), Ph, the counterpart of the Egyptian god THOTH.

Tablets of Fate, the, A-B, upon which was written the destiny of the world. They were called DUP SHIMATI. The god who had the tablets in his possession became all-powerful. They were given to KINGU to mark his power.

Tacitus (tas'-i-tus), a Roman historian of about A.D. 55–120, whose

184

works furnish us with information on mythological topics, including the legends of the Teutonic peoples in particular.

Tahmuras (tah-muhr'-us), Pe, the son of HUSHENG and the successor to his father's work as well as his throne. He continued the progress and refinement of civilization. When the DEVAS revolted against his rule, he led his men in battle, overpowering the rebels with magic and his mighty club. They promised to teach the king a new skill in return for his mercy, and thus Tahmuras learned to write and acquired great knowledge. He was the father of JAMSHID, otherwise known as YIMA.

Taishaku (tahy-shah'-koo), J, the Japanese name of the Vedic god INDRA.

T'ai Shan (tahy' shahn'), Ch, the Great Emperor of the Eastern Peak, the god of T'ai-shan, a mountain in northern China, delegated by the Jade Emperor, TUNG WANG KUNG, to oversee the lives and activities of mankind and all the creatures on earth. He determined the course of men's lives, assisted by a large bureaucracy to handle the details, records, and statistics. In time, T'ai Shan assumed control over death as well as life. A large and splendid temple was erected to T'ai Shan in Peking.

Take-Mikazuchi (tah-kay'-mee-kah'-zoo-kee), J, a god of thunder, sent by the gods to force the submission and abdication of ONAMUJI in order to make way for NINIGI's ascension to the throne of Izumo province.

Takshaka (tuk'-shu-ku), I, a snake, king of the NAGAS. When a king by the name of Parikchit gave offense, by chance, to a wise old hermit, the man's son called on Takshaka for revenge. There was no escape for the king until, caught in Takshaka's coils, he met his death.

Another myth relates Takshaka's theft of a pair of jeweled earrings from a young man to whom they were entrusted by the queen, consort of Parikchit's son. Aided throughout by INDRA, the messenger ultimately retrieved the earrings.

Talos (tay'-lahs), G, 1. a man formed out of bronze by HEPHAESTUS for the purpose of guarding the kingdom of MINOS. When the ARGONAUTS landed on Crete, MEDEA brought about the death of Talos with the aid of CASTOR AND POLLUX.

2. the nephew of DAEDALUS, who was skilled as an inventor and architect and was, as a result, slain by Daedalus out of jealousy.

Tamagostad (tam-u-goh'-stahd), the principal god in the myths of the Nicaraguan Indians, worshiped as the creator of the world. His dwelling place was in the heavens.

Tamakaia (tah-mah-kahy'-u), O, in the legends of the New Hebrides, the creator, with MAUI-TIKITIKI, of the world.

Tammuz (tah'-muhz, tam'-uz), A-B, the god of crops and vegetation who died each winter and was reborn each spring. He became the husband, or lover, of ISHTAR, who went to the underworld to bring him back to earth after his death. Tammuz was the ruler of URUK. He was called DUMUZI by the Sumerians.

Tamon (tah'-mohn), J. *See* BISHAMON.

Tane (tah'-nay), O, a Polynesian sky-god, held in high esteem, especially in Hawaii, where he was called KANE, and in the Society Islands. Tane's parents were RANGI and PAPA. When darkness lay over the earth and all living things were stifled by the closeness of their embrace, it was Tane who separated them and raised his father to a lofty position. After his father was lifted up, Tane took stars and set them in the sky as his ornamentation. He adorned his mother with trees and plants.

Tane was also a god of fertility and protective deity of the birds and forests, and those who worked with wood. According to New Zealand legend, Tane was the creator of HINA, whom he shaped from the sands of HAWAIKI.

Tangaloa (tahng-ah-loh'-ah), O. *See* TANGAROA.

Tangaroa (tahng-ah-roh'-ah) or **Tangaloa** (-loh'-), O, a sea-god, the supreme deity of most Polynesians. After the flood, Tangaroa created the world again and became the progenitor of the gods and the human race. In most Polynesian myth, Tangaroa was the son of VATEA and PAPA and the twin of RONGO. In some, however, he was the elder of the two brothers, but forced to give way to Rongo because of Papa's preference for her younger son.

In Samoa, he was called Tangaloa and considered to be a sky-god. Legend there tells it was he, not TANE, who fished up the islands from the depths of the sea following the Deluge.

In New Zealand, Tangaroa was not the chief god, but shared his place of importance and his part in the creation with others. He was the Maori patron god of fishermen.

In Tahiti, he was generally believed to be a hero who was deified for his great exploits.

Tangaroa was given the name KANALOA by the Hawaiians.

Tanit (tah'-neet), Ph, a goddess of the Phoenician colony Carthage who was identified with the goddess ASTARTE. Tanit was a goddess of the heavens and of fertility and of the moon and was, with BAAL-HAMMON, the chief deity of the city. There is evidence that children

186

were offered as sacrifice in rites carried out in the worship of Tanit. She was also called Tanit Pene Baal.

Tantalus (tan'-tu-lus), G, 1. the son of ZEUS and king of Phrygia. Tantalus was the father of NIOBE and PELOPS. To test the gods, he invited them to a feast and served them the dissected body of Pelops. All but DEMETER refused the human flesh. HERMES restored Pelops to life, and Demeter gave him an ivory shoulder in place of what she had eaten. Tantalus was punished in HADES by an eternally insatiable thirst and hunger. He stood in water that receded, when he tried to drink it, and with fruit trees around him, but just out of reach. From this legend comes the word "tantalize."

2. a king of Elis in the Peloponnesus who was CLYTEMNESTRA's first husband.

Tantris (tan'-tris), Ce, the name taken by TRISTRAM when, pretending to be a minstrel, he went to Ireland to have his wound healed by ISEULT.

Tao (dou, tou), Ch, the universal energy and primeval cosmic force.

Tapio (tah'-pee-oh), F, the name of a forest spirit, a deity with power over those who hunted and walked in the woods and over the wild animals of the forest, where the bear was highly revered.

Tapiola (tah-pee-oh'-lu), F, the forest realm of TAPIO.

Tarpeia (tahr-pee'-u), R, a vestal virgin who offered to show the attacking Sabines the way into Rome in return for what they wore on their arms. Tarpeia had reference to their bracelets, but the Sabines, who entered Rome with the help of her treachery, killed Tarpeia with the shields on their arms and hurled her body from a rock at the edge of the Capitoline Hill. The rock was afterward known as the Tarpeian Rock and was the place from which traitors were thrown to their deaths.

Tarquiup Innua (tahr-kwi-oop' i-noo'-ah), NA, in Eskimo legend, the spirit that lives in ALIGNAK, the moon, and has power over animals, including the outcome of hunting, and over the fertility of mankind and the animal world.

Tartarus (tahr'-tu-rus), G, the lowermost region of HADES, where the wicked were punished. It was here that ZEUS confined the TITANS.

Tashmetum (tahsh'-mee-tuhm), A-B, the wife of NABU, credited with assisting him in the invention of writing.

Tat (taht), E, a magical knot, known as the "Knot of ISIS," a fetish connected with that goddess.

Taueret (tou'-u-ret) or **Opet** (oh'-pet) or **Apet** (ah'-), E, a

187

goddess who protected women in childbirth and their offspring during their infancy. The chief seat of her worship was THEBES. Taueret was portrayed as a hippopotamus, standing upright on her hind feet.

Tawenduare (tah-ween-du-ah'-ree), SA, among the Tupi-Guarani Indians, the god of daylight, the constant foe of his brother ARIKUTE, god of night, and always the victor in their struggle.

Tawhaki (tah'-hwah-kee), O, a Polynesian hero, a figure in many legends. In New Zealand, Tawhaki was a Maori god of thunder and clouds and was sometimes called the ruler of the kingdom of the dead.

Tawhiri (tah-hwee'-ree), O, the Polynesian god of storms, a son of RANGI and PAPA. Tawhiri was the father of thirteen children, of whom two were strong winds and eleven were clouds of various types.

Tawiscara (tah-wis-kah'-rah), NA. *See* IOSKEHA AND TAWISCARA.

Taygete (tay-ij'-i-tee), G, one of the PLEIADES. She was the mother of LACEDAEMON by ZEUS.

Tefnut (tef'-noot), E, the daughter of RA and mother of GEB by her twin brother, SHU. Shu and Tefnut were the first couple of the ENNEAD. Tefnut, goddess of dew and rain, helped Shu in his task of supporting the firmament. She was represented as a lioness or lioness-headed.

Teiresias (tahy-ree'-see-us), G. *See* TIRESIAS.

Telamon (tel'-u-mahn), G, the son of AEACUS, brother of PELEUS, and king of Salamis. Telamon was a friend of HERACLES, who gave HESIONE to him as his wife. Telamon and Hesione became the parents of TEUCER and AJAX the Great.

Telemachus (tu-lem'-u-kus), G, the son of ODYSSEUS and PENELOPE. When Odysseus did not return from the TROJAN WAR, Telemachus sought information about his father in Pylos, Sparta, and elsewhere, with little success. Upon his return to Ithaca, Telemachus found Odysseus at home and together they slew Penelope's suitors. He later married CIRCE (in some versions, it was the daughter of Circe).

Telephassa (tel-u-fas'-u), G, the wife of AGENOR and queen of Phoenicia. Telephassa was the mother of CADMUS, EUROPA, CILIX, and PHOENIX. After Europa was carried off by ZEUS in the shape of a bull, Telephassa left Phoenicia with Cadmus and died soon after in Thrace.

Tell el Amarna (tel' el u-mahr'-nu), E, the modern name of Akhetaten in Middle Egypt, site of the new capital established by

Amenhotep after he embraced the cult of ATON and changed his name to Akhenaton. The city was dedicated to the glory of the sun, Aton.

Tellus (tel'-us), R, goddess of the earth, marriage, and fertility. Her Greek counterpart was GAEA.

Tempe (tem'-pee), G, a valley in Thessaly, generally referred to as the Vale of Tempe, through which the PENEUS River ran. The Vale of Tempe, located between Mt. OSSA and Mt. OLYMPUS, was renowned for its scenery and pastoral beauty.

Tengu, the (ten'-nguh), J, playful and sometimes evil spirits who live in the treetops, especially among the mountains. These demons are depicted as small, birdlike men.

Teotihuacan (tay-oh-tee-wah-kahn'), Az, the "City of the Gods," site of the great pyramids of the Mexicans and the largest of the ancient cities. The region was inhabited by about 400 B.C., and a city was built there by Nahua-speaking peoples before the arrival of the Toltecs, who invaded the area in about A.D. 650, sacking and burning Teotihuacan. Great temples and palaces, in addition to extensive dwellings, were erected there. The most outstanding are the Temple of QUETZALCOATL, a huge complex, the Pyramid of the Moon, and the great Pyramid of the Sun, over two hundred feet high.

Terah (teer'-u), Ph. *See* ETERAH.

Terminus (tur'-mu-nus), R, the god of boundaries. The boundaries were marked by stones, called *termini,* that were sacred to JUPITER.

Terpsichore (turp-sik'-u-ree), G, the MUSE of dancing. She was represented with a lyre.

Teshup (tay'-shuhp), a Hittite god of rain and storm, whose cult spread to all the surrounding lands. Tashmishu, his brother, aided him in his struggle to overpower ULLIKUMMI, created by KUMARBI to take vengeance on Teshup. The god EA came to Teshup's aid, rendering Ullikummi powerless by cutting the stone monster from the strength of the giant UPELLURI's shoulder. In the ensuing battle against Kumarbi, Teshup appears to have successfully defended his position as king of the gods, although this part of the text is fragmentary.

Tethys (tee'-this), G, a TITANESS, the daughter of URANUS and GAEA. Tethys was the sister and wife of OCEANUS and was the mother of the OCEANIDS.

Teucer (too'-ser), G, 1. the son of TELAMON and HESIONE and half brother of AJAX the Great. Teucer was an outstanding hero of the

TROJAN WAR, noted for his skill as an archer. Exiled from Salamis, because Telamon blamed him for the death of Ajax, Teucer went to Cyprus, where he became king.

2. the first king of Troy. The Trojans were thus often called Teucri.

Teyrnon (tayr'-nun, teer'-), Ce, an early Celtic god who became a mortal. He brought up the kidnaped child of PWYLL and RHIANNON as his adopted son until the child was restored to them.

Tezcatlipoca (tes-kaht-li-poh'-kah), Az, the chief deity in the Aztec hierarchy, the personification of life and air. He was a sun-god, ruler of the sun of the first universe, as well as a god of the darkness and the north. Tezcatlipoca was in constant struggle with the Toltec god QUETZALCOATL, first overcoming him, then overcome by him.

Tezcatlipoca was symbolized by a mirror of dark obsidian, believed to reflect the actions of man and the future. He often is depicted with one foot, because the other was lost when the doors of the underworld closed on it, or, in another version, was bitten off by the huge monster that was the earth, when he brought it up from the primeval waters.

Thalia (thu-lee'-u), G, 1. the MUSE of comedy, represented with a comic mask.

2. one of the three CHARITES. Thalia's name meant "blooming" or "bounteous."

Thanatos (than'-u-tahs), G, a child of NYX and the twin brother of HYPNOS. He was the personification of death.

Thaumas (thau'-mus), G, a son of PONTUS and GAEA, the husband of the OCEANID ELECTRA, and father of the HARPIES and IRIS.

Thebes (theebz), E, 1. a city on the Nile in Upper Egypt, once an ancient capital of Egypt and an important religious center but now in ruins. It was the center of the cult of the Theban triad of deities, the god AMON, his wife MUT, and their son KHONS.

G, 2. a city in Boeotia, called Cadmea at first, taking its name from its legendary founder, CADMUS. Thebes was the home of TIRESIAS, HERACLES, and many other mythical figures, and the scene of the tragedies revolving around the descendants of Cadmus, the most noteworthy of whom were OEDIPUS and his family.

Theia (thee'-u) or **Thia** (thahy'-u), G, 1. a TITANESS, sister and wife of HYPERION, mother of EOS, HELIOS, and SELENE. She was often identified with TETHYS.

2. a daughter of CHIRON who was ravished by AEOLUS and, after being transformed into a mare by POSEIDON, gave birth to a horse.

Themis (thee'-mis), G, one of the TITANS, daughter of URANUS and GAEA. Themis was the goddess of law and justice and was depicted

with scales and sometimes with a cornucopia. She was the mother by
ZEUS of the HORAE, and the FATES. In some versions, she was the
mother of PROMETHEUS, and of ASTRAEA.

Theseus (thee'-see-us), G, the son of AEGEUS, king of Athens, and
AETHRA. Theseus was born at Troezen in the Peloponnesus, where
Pittheus, father of Aethra, was king. When he grew to young manhood, Theseus lifted the stone under which Aegeus had left his sword
and shoes before he returned to Athens. On the way, he encountered
many adventures in which he proved himself a hero. When he
reached Athens, MEDEA, now the wife of Aegeus, tried to do away
with him, but his father recognized the sword, and Theseus was
spared. Theseus took part in the expedition of the ARGONAUTS, the
CALYDONIAN BOAR hunt, and the battle of the LAPITHAE and CEN-
TAURS. He was a close friend of PIRITHOUS, who helped him seize
HELEN of Sparta (she was later ransomed) and together they went to
the UNDERWORLD, where Pirithous tried to carry off PERSEPHONE.
HADES fixed the two friends to a rock, but HERACLES rescued Theseus,
who returned safely to the upper world. Theseus went to Crete
where, with the help of ARIADNE, who gave him a thread with which
to find his way out of the LABYRINTH, he killed the MINOTAUR and
released Athens from the sacrifice of the seven maidens and seven
youths MINOS had been demanding. Theseus escaped with Ariadne
but left her on the island of NAXOS. As he approached Greece, he forgot to replace the black sails of his ship with white ones, as he had
told his father he would do if he had been successful, and Aegeus,
thinking his son was dead, cast himself into the sea. After the death
of his father, Theseus became king of Athens. He had seized ANTIOPE,
also called HIPPOLYTE, the queen of the Amazons, as his wife. The
Amazons, therefore, attacked Athens but were defeated by Theseus.
He was the father of HIPPOLYTUS by Antiope. When he later wed
PHAEDRA, she fell in love with Hippolytus, but he spurned her. She
therefore caused Theseus to doubt his son's integrity by implicating
him and then killing herself. This led to the death of Hippolytus, who
was thrown from his chariot as he was leaving Athens in exile.
Theseus himself left Athens and spent the end of his life on the island
of Scyros, where he was slain by the king, Lycomedes.

Thetis (thee'-tis), G, a NEREID, the daughter of NEREUS and DORIS.
It was at the marriage of PELEUS and Thetis that ERIS threw the
golden apple that led to the JUDGMENT OF PARIS. Peleus and Thetis
were the parents of the hero ACHILLES, to whom she tried to give immortality by dipping him in the river STYX, but she held him by the
heel, thus inadvertently denying him invulnerability.

Thia (thahy'-u), G. *See* THEIA.

Thialfi or **Thjalfi** (thyahl'-vee), Sc, THOR's servant, who accompanied him and LOKI to UTGARD. There, in UTGARD-LOKI's domain, Thialfi, the swiftest runner among men, was defeated by HUGI, an impersonation of thought.

Thiazi or **Thjazi** (thyahyt'-see), Sc, a GIANT who carried LOKI off to JOTUNHEIM and set the apples of eternal youth as the ransom price. Loki made it possible for Thiazi to seize IDUN and the apples, but the gods of ASGARD, now aging for want of their rejuvenating apples, demanded Idun's release. Loki, transformed into a falcon, changed Idun into a nut and returned her to Asgard. Thiazi, turned into an eagle, flew after them, but the gods burned his wings and killed him when he fell.

Thiazi's daughter was SKADI, wife of NIORD and the mother of FREY and FREYA.

Thisbe (thiz'-bee), G, the maiden of Babylon who loved and was loved by PYRAMUS.

Thjalfi (thyahl'-vee), Sc. *See* THIALFI.

Thjazi (thyaht'-see), Sc. *See* THIAZI.

Thobadestchin (thoh-bad-est'-chin), NA. *See* NAGENATZANI AND THOBADESTCHIN.

Thokk (thawk), Sc, an aged GIANTess, the guise LOKI assumed when he refused to weep for BALDER, thus preventing his release from HEL.

Thor (thawr), Sc, the sky- and thunder-god, said to have been born of Mother Earth. Thor was worshiped especially by sailors and farmers as the god of storms and rain, and by those who migrated to Iceland. He was generally depicted as red-bearded, extremely strong, and kindly toward mankind, but a bitter enemy of the GIANTS and all demons who threatened the order of the world. Thor's best-known attribute was his magic hammer, MIOLNIR, an infallible weapon, with which he broke up the ice of winter and made the return of the spring season possible each year. Thor also possessed iron gloves and a belt that easily doubled his strength. His chariot was drawn by goats. They furnished him with food and were instantly restored to life by his hammer.

In the Scandinavian pantheon, Thor was second only to his father, ODIN. Fishing from HYMIR's boat, Thor brought the MIDGARD SERPENT up from the sea, but Hymir cut the line before he could kill it. When RAGNAROK arrived, Thor and the Midgard Serpent destroyed each other. Thursday, "Thor's day," was regarded as a propitious day for marriages. Thor corresponds to the Germanic god DONAR.

Thoth (thohth, toht), E, the god of wisdom, learning, and writing, as well as the moon-god. Thoth was a scribe of the gods. He was the protector of HORUS and later followed him as ruler of the earth. Thoth also appears at times as the helper of Horus' enemy, SET. He was reputed to have caused the birth of the early deities from NUNU by the sound of his voice. The invention of both mathematics and hieroglyphics was ascribed to him. With his consort MAAT, Thoth weighed the hearts of the dead as they were tried before OSIRIS.

Thoth was represented as either an ibis or an ibis-headed man, or as a baboon, and sometimes with the head of a dog. His cult was centered at HERMOPOLIS, and the first month of the Egyptian year was named for him. In Hellenistic times, the Greeks identified Thoth with HERMES. Thoth was also known as AAH.

Thrym (throom), Sc, a GIANT who stole THOR's hammer, MIOLNIR, and demanded FREYA as ransom. Thor, in the guise of Freya and accompanied by LOKI, recovered his hammer by deceiving and then killing Thrym.

Thunderbird, the, NA, a great mythical bird, similar to an eagle, who, in the legend of some western Indian tribes, is the spirit that causes lightning and thunder and produces the rain for their crops.

Thyestes (thahy-es'-teez), G, the son of PELOPS and HIPPODAMIA and brother of ATREUS. Thyestes was exiled with Atreus by Pelops because they had killed their half brother CHRYSIPPUS at the instigation of Hippodamia. He became the lover of AËROPE, wife of Atreus, and was punished by Atreus, who killed two of Thyestes' children and served them to their father. As a result, Thyestes laid a curse on the House of Atreus. Thyestes was the father of AEGISTHUS by PELOPIA.

Tiamat (tyah'-maht), A-B, the goddess of the primeval sea, visualized as a dragon and representing the forces of chaos and evil. She was the salt water personified, the counterpart of APSU. The gods and the world were born of Apsu and Tiamat.

After Apsu was seized by EA, Tiamat sent troops of monsters under KINGU's command to set him free. Ea enlisted the aid of MARDUK, who slew Tiamat after a terrible battle, and from the two halves of her body created the heavens and the earth.

Tiberinus (tahy-bu-rahy'-nus), R, the god of the Tiber River. When AENEAS arrived in Italy, Tiberinus gave him good advice.

Tien (ti-en'), Ch, the god of the vault of heaven.

Tien Hou (ti-en' hoo'), Ch, the Empress of Heaven. She had been a mortal girl. Once, when her four brothers were at sea, but each on a different ship, she fell into a faint. After she was revived and three brothers came back safely, they told it was the vision of their sister appearing to them that saved them from the dangers of a tempest each one had met. The brother who did not return had not seen his sister, because she had been brought out of her faint before she could reach him. Tien Hou is the protectress of sailors and patroness of the sea.

Tien-Kuan (ti-en'-kwahn'), Ch, the Agent of Heaven, a god with the power to bestow happiness and well-being. On special family occasions and before the performance in a theater, Tien-Kuan appears dressed in the robes of a mandarin and carrying a scroll filled with good wishes for those present.

Tiki (tee'-kee), O, 1. in some accounts, a god who either created the world or brought it up from the depths of the sea. In other myths, Tiki was brought into being by TANE and was the one who created HINA and became her husband. Tiki was also known as Ti'i, and in Hawaii he was called KI'I.

2. a statue or idol, usually representing an ancestor. It was often a small figure worn as an amulet, generally of carved jade.

3. a protective spirit.

Tilo (til'-oh), Af, the sky-god and a god of rainstorms and thunder in myths of Mozambique.

Tinia (tin'-ee-u), a thunder- and fire-god, chief deity of the Etruscan pantheon, whose voice was heard in thunder and who descended to earth in lightning. Wherever his thunderbolt struck became a sacred place. Tinia had functions and attributes resembling those of ZEUS, with whom he was equated, and he was sometimes identified with the Roman god SUMMANUS. He was honored with a temple in each Etruscan city and was depicted holding a triple thunderbolt.

Tinirau (tee'-nee-rou), O, a being who was both human and divine. As a mortal, he was the handsome, princelike hero of numerous legends. As a god, his province was the sea, and he was sometimes believed to be incarnate in a whale. Tinirau was the guardian deity of New Zealand.

Tintagel (tin-taj'-ul), Ce, the legendary birthplace of King ARTHUR, located on the coast of Cornwall.

Tirawa Atius (ti-rah'-wah ah-tee-oos'), NA, the GREAT SPIRIT of the Pawnee Indians, sometimes identified with thunder or the sun. Although not a personal god, he was an active character in their mythology, especially in connection with cosmogony. After the world was created, Tirawa Atius delegated a share of his power to the other gods, giving one the care of the sun, another the moon, others the stars, and so on. When their offspring peopled the earth, Tirawa saw to it that the gods taught man the arts and skills of farming, hunting, warfare, ritual, and all else necessary to tribal culture.

Tiresias or Teiresias (tahy-ree'-see-us), G, the highly revered blind seer of THEBES, struck blind by ATHENA because he saw her bathing. Athena later regretted her action and as compensation gave Tiresias the gift of prophecy, a staff to guide him, and the knowledge of the language of the birds. It was Tiresias who revealed to OEDIPUS the truth about his parentage.

Tishiya (tish'-i-yu), Pe, a name given to the personification of the Dog Star, Sirius.

Tisiphone (ti-sif'-u-nee), G, one of the ERINYES. Tisiphone was the one who brought vengeance upon those who did evil.

Titans, the (tahyt'-unz), G, the twelve children of URANUS and GAEA. Among them were OCEANUS, TETHYS, THEMIS, MNEMOSYNE, HYPERION, THEIA, CRONUS, and RHEA. The Titans, who were the personification of violence in nature, ruled before the Olympian deities. Uranus was overthrown by his children, and Cronus and Rhea then became the king and queen of the Titans. All except Oceanus took part in the war of the Titans against the Olympian deities. After their defeat, the Titans were confined to TARTARUS. In some accounts, they were allowed to live in the ISLES OF THE BLESSED.

Tithonus (ti-thoh'-nus), G, a prince of Troy, the son of LAOMEDON. Tithonus became the father of MEMNON by EOS, who granted him immortality at his request, but forgot to grant him perpetual youth. As a result, he shriveled with age, and since he could not die, he was transformed into a grasshopper by Eos.

Tiwaz (tee'-wahz), T, an early god of the sky and of war, associated by the Romans with MARS and by the Scandinavians with TYR.

Tlahuizcalpantecuhtli (tlah-wees'-kahl-pahn-tay-koo'-tlee), Az, the lord of the dawn, who was identified with QUETZALCOATL.

Tlaloc (tlah-lohk'), Az, a god worshiped in Mexico before the Aztecs conquered that region, who became one of their most important deities, the god of thunder and rain. Tlaloc was also the deity of the mountains. He lived in the mountains with the goddesses of grain and poured forth water upon the earth, causing either growth or destruction of the grain. Infants and children were sacrificed to Tlaloc, possibly to bring grain-producing rain and prevent disaster by flood.

Tlaloc was the ruler of the sun of the third universe, which was consumed by fire. He was the husband of the flower-goddess XOCHIQUETZAL, or, in some accounts, of the water-goddess CHAL-CHIHUITLICUE. He was depicted with a mask of serpents.

Tlaloques, the (tlah-lohks'), Az, the servants of TLALOC, the rain-god. They were spirits of the clouds, coming from the east with the gentle enriching spring rains; from the south bringing the summer's nourishing rain; from the west carrying the rains to prepare nature for the dormant wintertime; and from the darkness of the north bearing icy, destructive rain.

Tlazolteutl (tlahs-ohl-tay-oo't'l), Az, the very beautiful goddess of love, the earth and fertility goddess of the Aztecs. CINTEOTL, god of corn, was her son.

Tloque Nahuaque (tlohk nah'-wahk), Az. *See* OMETEOTL.

Tonatiuh (toh-nah-tee'-oo), Az, the sun-god. His home, the House of the Sun, was the home of the warriors. Tonatiuh was fed and cooled by human sacrifice. Each day he was raised to the zenith by warriors, and, in the evening, women who died in childbirth lowered him to the darkness of the underworld. Tonatiuh was also known as PILTZINTECUTLI.

Tornaq (tawr'-nak) or **Torngak** (tawrn'-gak), NA, the name given by the Eskimos to a spirit that fulfills the role of protector of a particular locality. These spirits remain at the streams, hills, or other spots with which they are associated, or wander about at will, but in any case they form a link with the ANGAKOK or shaman, acting as assistants and communicating their knowledge of the secrets of the universe and the supernatural. The tornaq can guard the individual through all adversity.

Tornarsuk (tawrn-ahr-sook'), NA, the chief of the Eskimo spirits known as the TORNAQS. His appearance varies in different areas, as does the spelling of his name. In Alaska, he is Tungrangayak, and his body is covered with eyes, making him all-seeing. In Greenland, Tornarsuk or Tornatik is a sea monster, part man and part seal. In Labrador, Torngarsoak is a huge white bear who watches over wild animals.

Torngak (tawrn'-gak), NA. *See* TORNAQ.

Totem, NA & Af, an animal, plant, or other object from the world of nature, used as a symbol of a family, clan, or group and considered sacred. Totem symbols were hung or carved and painted in bright colors on totem poles by the American Indians of the Pacific Northwest.

Tou Mu (too' muh'), Ch, the goddess of the North Star. Called the "bushel mother," she was the mother of nine sons, who were the earliest of earthly rulers. Her palace is the center of the stellar system, and all other stars revolve around it. Tou Mu holds sway over life and death, but she is beneficent and sympathetic in the use of her power. She is depicted with three eyes and eighteen arms, holding weapons, the solar and lunar disks, a dragon's head, and five chariots in her hands.

Trident (trahyd'-unt), G & R, the spear with three prongs with which POSEIDON or NEPTUNE would stir up or calm the waters of the sea and strike the earth to bring forth fountains and springs.

Trimurti, the (tri-muhr'-tee), I, the trinity of Brahmanic Hindu divinities, composed of BRAHMA, VISHNU, and SHIVA.

Triptolemus (trip-tahl'-i-mus), G, the son of Celeus, the king of Attica. In some versions, he was the son of GAEA and URANUS. As DEMETER wandered in grief over the loss of PERSEPHONE, Celeus and his wife took the goddess into their home. She restored Triptolemus to health and taught him the skills of farming and agriculture. Triptolemus later established a temple to Demeter at Eleusis, which became the seat of the ELEUSINIAN MYSTERIES.

Tristan (tris'-tun), Ce. *See* TRISTRAM.

Tristram (tris'-trum) or **Tristan** (tris'-tun), Ce, the lover of ISEULT. Born posthumously to a mother who died in childbirth, he grew up to be a master of many skills. He became a knight in the court of MARK, his mother's brother and the king of Cornwall. Tristram fought and killed MOROLD, thus freeing Cornwall of the tribute of young men who had been forced to serve the Irish king each year, but he was wounded himself. In the guise of a minstrel and under the name of TANTRIS, he went to Ireland to have his wound healed by Queen Iseult.

Later, King Mark sent Tristram to Ireland to win the king's consent to give his daughter Iseult to him in marriage. Tristram killed the dragon that was terrifying the countryside, and accomplished his mission, but on the return journey both he and Iseult drank of a love potion intended for Mark. Tristram became Iseult's lover until they separated in fear of rising gossip.

Tristram went to live in Brittany, where he married the daughter of a king. She also was called Iseult. When he was again critically wounded, Tristram sent the token ring Iseult had given him to summon her to his aid. Deceptively told that the approaching ship carried black sails, indicating Iseult was not aboard, Tristram died.

Triton (trahy'-tun), G, the son of POSEIDON and AMPHITRITE. Part man and part sea serpent, he dwelt in the depths of the ocean and blew on his conch shell horn to stir up or calm the waves.

Trivia (triv'-ee-u), R, a name for HECATE in her aspect as goddess of the crossroads.

Troilus (troh'-i-lus), G, a son of PRIAM and HECUBA who fought in the TROJAN WAR and was slain by ACHILLES.

Trojan War, the, G, the great war fought between the Greeks and the Trojans, brought on by the abduction of HELEN by PARIS, son of King PRIAM of Troy. The Trojan War forms the basis two of the greatest epics of the pre-Christian era, the ILIAD of HOMER, which begins in the tenth year of the war, and the AENEID of VERGIL, which tells of the travels of its hero AENEAS following the fall of Troy, and the founding of the Roman nation. At the JUDGMENT OF PARIS, the golden apple was awarded to APHRODITE, in return for which the goddess gave Paris as his bride Helen, queen of Sparta. Prior to Helen's marriage of MENELAUS, her father, King TYNDAREUS, had exacted an oath from all of Helen's suitors that they would come to the aid of her husband in case anything happened to her. Among the suitors were most of the major heroes and kings of the time (e.g., ACHILLES, ODYSSEUS, AJAX the Great), all of whom, under the command of Menelaus' brother AGAMEMNON, husband of Helen's sister CLYTEMNESTRA, formed the Greek host that sailed to Troy and, having failed to achieve Helen's return, fought the war that lasted over ten years and that, at its conclusion, left the city in ruins. In this war, the twelve major deities of OLYMPUS took sides. ATHENA and HERA, having been denied the golden apple, sided with the Greeks; Aphrodite sided with the Trojans; all of the other deities became involved either because of their own personal relationships to the Greeks or Trojans or because of their connections and obligations to the three goddesses involved in the Judgment of Paris; ZEUS was the only one who achieved any sense of neutrality, which involved, more often than not, his aiding one side, then the other. According to prophecy, the war would not end until the two greatest heroes were dead (Achilles on the Greek side, HECTOR on the Trojan side), which ultimately happened. At the climax of the war, the Greeks feigned a retreat from their encampment surrounding Troy and left a huge wooden horse, ostensibly as a peace offering to the besieged city. The Trojans, believing this horse was an exchange for the PALLADIUM that had been stolen by Odysseus and DIOMEDES, hauled it into the city. That night, Greek soldiers hidden within the horse set fire to the city and opened the gates to let in the rest of the Greek army, which had returned under cover of darkness, and by the next morning the city was in ruins. Priam and most of his family were dead, and the war was over (thus, the adage "Beware the Greeks bearing gifts").

Tros (trohs), G, a son of ERICHTHONIUS, husband of CALLIRRHOË, and father of GANYMEDE. Tros gave his name to Troy, the city founded by his grandfather, DARDANUS.

Ts'ai-shen (tsahy'-shen'), Ch, the widely venerated god of wealth. His birthday, which falls on the fifth day of the first month of the Chinese year, is celebrated with sacrifice and special acts of honor.

Tsao-wang (tsou'-wahng'), Ch, the hearth-god, who resides in the home, near the hearth, to keep watch over the doings of the family. He makes his report before TUNG WANG KUNG, the Jade Emperor, when he appears once a year in heaven. He is assisted in his task by his wife. When Tsao-wang has left the house on his mission to the Jade Emperor, the family offers sacrifice, and firecrackers are set off to guide his path. His way home is again indicated by firecrackers, and he is welcomed with sacrifice.

Tsui Goab (tsoo'-ee go'-ab), Af, a mythical hero of the Hottentots. He was probably a legendary hero to whom supernatural characteristics were attributed. Tsui Goab became the central figure in a cult involving the worship of a mound of stones thought to be his grave.

Tsukiyomi (tsoo-kee'-yoh-mee), J, the god of the moon and ruler of the night. The brother of the sun-goddess AMATERASU, Tsukiyomi was born when IZANAGI washed his right eye as he bathed in the sea following his return from the world of the dead.

Tu (too), O, the Polynesian war-god. Tu was of importance in the Society Islands as a deity of creation, but his powers as a god of war were largely taken over by ORO. Tu was known in Hawaii as KU.

Tuatha De Danann, the (thoo'-u-hu day dah'-nun), Ce, the gods who, after defeating the Fomorians, were sovereigns of Ireland in an idyllic age. The goddess DANU was their mother; DAGDA, their chief and leader. The name, meaning "People of Danu," refers to the lineage of deities descended from the goddess Danu.

Tuli (too'-lee), O, a bird, the messenger of TANGAROA. In the legends of Samoa and other islands of western Polynesia, it was said the god created the first of the Samoan Islands when he threw a rock into the floodwaters so Tuli could alight upon it.

Tum (toom), E. *See* ATUM.

Tung Wang Kung (tuhng' wahng' kuhng'), Ch, the Jade Emperor, lord of the sky and chief of the celestial hierarchy. He created mankind from clay. The healthy were those whose clay dried untouched by rain; the sickly, those that were damaged by moisture.

Tung Wang Kung held sovereignty over the pantheon of gods, who were strictly accountable to him. He meted out reward and punishment to the gods according to the quality of the performance of their functions, elevating some, demoting others, and sometimes discharging the incompetent. The Jade Emperor's consort was HSI WANG MU, and he lived in a palace with his family, holding court in the same manner as the ruling emperor. He is depicted seated on a throne, wearing the formal robes and headdress of a Chinese emperor.

Tuonela (twaw'-ne-lu), F, the underworld, an island lying below the earth and separated from the world of the living by the river called TUONI surrounding it. The ruler of the land of the dead, also called MANALA, was Tuoni.

Tuonetar (twaw'-ne-tahr), F, the consort of TUONI, ruler of the kingdom of the dead.

Tuoni (twaw'-nee), F, 1. the river that surrounded the world of the dead, TUONELA, separating it from the world of the living.

2. the ruler of Tuonela, the world of the dead. His queen was TUONETAR, and their daughters were goddesses of disease, evil, and suffering.

Tupan (too-pahn') or **Tupi** (-pee'), SA, the thunder-god of the Tupi-Guarani Indians.

Tupi (too-pee'), SA. *See* TUPAN.

Turnus (turn'-us), R, the king and leader of the Rutulians who hoped to marry LAVINIA and fought AENEAS and the Trojans over her. He was slain by Aeneas.

Tvashtri (twush'-tree), I, the craftsman of the gods, son of DYAUS. Tvashtri fashioned the vessel that was ever full of SOMA, the thunderbolts of INDRA, and the weapons of the gods. It was he who taught the RIBHUS the skills of their work. He was the father of SARANYU, the wife of SURYA.

Tyche (tahy'-kee), G, the personification of fortune. Her favor was constantly invoked, and her likeness on coins was often rendered with such symbols as a cornucopia for opulence and a wheel or ball for chance. Tyche was identified with the goddess FORTUNA.

Tydeus (tahy'-dyoos), G, the son of OENEUS of Calydon and father of DIOMEDES by Deipyle, the daughter of ADRASTUS of Argos. Tydeus was an outstanding hero in the expedition of the SEVEN AGAINST THEBES.

Tyndareus (tin-dehr'-ee-us), G, the king of Sparta and husband of LEDA, by whom he was the father of CASTOR and CLYTEMNESTRA. He adopted as his own the two children, POLLUX and HELEN, which Leda had by ZEUS, who had disguised himself as a swan.

Tyndaridae, the (tin-dehr'-i-dee), G, another name for CASTOR AND POLLUX, the Dioscuri.

Typhoeus (tahy-fee'-us), G. *See* TYPHON.

Typhon (tahy'-fahn) or **Typhoeus** (tahy-fee'-us), G, a snake-headed giant, the son of GAEA. Typhon and ECHIDNA bore CERBERUS, the NEMEAN LION, and the HYDRA of LERNA. When he rose up against the gods and the power of ZEUS, he was struck down with a thunderbolt and sent to TARTARUS.

Tyr (teer, toor), Sc, the son of FRIGG. In some accounts, he is the son of ODIN, while in others he is said to be HYMIR's son. Tyr was the war-god and also the deity of athletes. When the gods chained FENRIR with GLEIPNIR, Fenrir demanded a pledge that he would be released again. Tyr put his hand in the mouth of Fenrir as a bond and lost it when Fenrir realized he was not going to be unchained. At RAGNAROK Tyr was mauled to death by GARM, watchdog of NIFLHEIM, as he killed the animal.

Tyr was called Tiw by the Anglo-Saxons. He was identified with Mars, hence Tuesday, the French *mardi*, "MARS's day," is "Tiw's day."

Ueueteotl (way-way-tay-oh't'l), Az, the god of fire, both creative and destructive, who held a position of seniority among the gods. His dwelling place was the North Star.

Ugarit Tablets, the (oo-gu-reet'), Ph, the cuneiform tablets found at RAS SHAMRA, the ancient Ugarit. These tablets came from the Temple of BAAL and date from about the middle of the fourteenth century B.C., when the town was destroyed by earthquake. They give us the main outlines of their mythology and legends, but the text is fragmentary and contains numerous gaps, as well as difficulties in translation due to the characteristics of the script.

Uitzilopochtli (wee-tsee-loh-pohch'-tlee), Az. *See* HUITZILOPOCHTLI.

Ukko (ook'-oh), F, the god who, in later Finnish mythology, took the place of JUMALA as the supreme god of the air and the sky. Ukko, the thunder-god, caused the rains to fall.

Ukwa (ook'-wu), Af, in legends of the Shilluks, the grandson of Kola, the son of the sacred white cow that rose from the Nile River, when she was created by JUOK. Ukwa was wed to two priestesses of the Nile and became the ancestor of the Shilluk tribe.

Uller (uhl'-ur), S & T, the god of hunting and archers and of winter. Uller, THOR's stepson, was the son of SIF.

Ullikummi (uh-lee-koo'-mee) or **Ullikummis** (-mis), in a Hurrian legend, which spread to all of Asia Minor and to Phoenicia, the stone monster son whom KUMARBI conceived of a rock, to carry out his plan to overthrow TESHUP. Ullikummi was placed on the shoulder of the giant UPELLURI, where he continued to grow in stature and strength in spite of an attack by a band of seventy gods who tried to do away with him, and grew up to have mighty strength. He was weakened, however, when EA cut him from Upelluri's shoulder because the gods feared Ullikummi would destroy mankind as well as Teshup, and Ea was afraid lest there would be no one to offer sacrifice to the gods.

Ullikummis (uh-lee-koo'-mis). *See* ULLIKUMMI.

Ulysses (yoo-lis'-eez), R, the corrupted or Anglicized form of Ulixes, the Latin name for ODYSSEUS.

Uma (uh'-mah), I, the spouse of SHIVA in the aspect of a lovely beauty, a representation of light. In this shape, Shiva's wife crept up behind him while he was in contemplation and put her hands over his eyes. Darkness fell over the world, and all were afraid, until an eye of flame suddenly appeared in the middle of his forehead, lighting everything with its flashing fire.

Underworld, the, G & R, the dark, sunless abode of the dead, located in the west on the edge of the earth beyond OCEANUS. There was an entrance to the underworld at Lake AVERNUS near Cumae. The underworld was surrounded by the river STYX and the ACHERON, with its branches, COCYTUS, river of wailing, PHLEGETHON, river of fire, and Lethe, river of forgetfulness. HERMES conducted the souls of the dead to the underworld and CHARON ferried those who had been given proper burial and passage money across the water to the entrance, which was guarded by the three-headed dog CERBERUS, who stood at the gate. The judges of the underworld were AEACUS, MINOS, and RHADAMANTHUS, who condemned the wicked to torment in TARTARUS and assigned the good and blessed to the ELYSIAN FIELDS. Only a few mortals, among them ODYSSEUS and AENEAS, were permitted to descend to the underworld and return again to earth. An underworld of some type appears in the mythology of practically all groups of people as the home of their dead.

Unferth (un'-furth), in the poem *Beowulf*, one of HROTHGAR's court who was extremely jealous of BEOWULF.

Unkulunkulu (oon-koo-lun-koo'-loo), Af, in myths of the Bantu tribes, the primordial man, progenitor of mankind. He was born of reeds and became a culture hero who taught men skills and crafts and instructed them in tribal customs. Unkulunkulu dispatched a chameleon to tell men there would be no death. Because the chameleon loitered on his way, he then sent off a lizard with the opposite message. The lizard arrived first, and thus men became mortal.

Untamo (oon-tah'-moh), F, the uncle of KULLERVO, whose hatred for the boy's father, KALERVO, caused him to make attempts upon Kullervo's life.

Upangas, the (oo-pan'-guz), I, one of the groups of Vedic sacred writings, a source of myths and legends.

Upanishads, the (oo-pan'-i-shadz, -pah'-ni-shahdz), I, a group of treatises composed in about the eighth to sixth centuries B.C. and set down in written form about A.D. 1300. They are mainly in the shape of dialogues, expounding the thoughts and beliefs of the end of the Vedic period and the beginning of the Brahmanic.

Upelluri (uh-pell-uhr'-ee) or **Upelluris** (-is), in Hurrian legend, a giant who held up the earth and sky. ULLIKUMMI was placed on his shoulder and entrusted to him so that he might derive great strength from him.

Upelluris (uh-pell-uhr'-is). *See* UPELLURI.

Upshukina, the (up-shuh'-kee-nu), A-B, a great hall where the gods met to hold council. The IGIGI held a banquet there and gave MARDUK full powers as king and ruler of the world.

Upuaut (oo'-poo-awt), E, a god with the head of a jackal or wolf, depicted guiding the bark of the sun or leading fighting men against the enemy. Upuaut, a name meaning "opener of the way," was worshiped at ABYDOS, where he was known as KHENTI AMENTI, "Ruler of the West," in his role as deity of the souls of the dead.

Uraeus (yuh-ree'-us), E, a flame-breathing asp who protected the god RA by destroying his foes. Ra was sometimes depicted wearing on his head the disk of the sun surrounded by the uraeus, a symbol of royalty and power.

Urania (yuh-ray'-nee-u), G, 1. the MUSE of astronomy, depicted holding a globe in her hand.

2. an epithet of APHRODITE in her aspect as goddess of spiritual love.

Uranus (yuhr′-u-nus, yuh-ray′-), G, the personification of the sky and heavens. Uranus, son and husband of GAEA, was the father of the CYCLOPES, HECATONCHIRES, and TITANS. The Titans, with the exception of OCEANUS, aided by Gaea, rebelled against Uranus, because he had thrown some of his monstrous offspring into TARTARUS. Uranus was mutilated by his son CRONUS, who succeeded his father as the supreme ruler until his own eventual overthrow by his son ZEUS.

Urd (uhrd), Sc, one of the NORNS. Urd's fountain furnished the water with which the Norns kept YGGDRASIL alive. Urd personified the past.

Urdar (uhr′-dahr), Sc, the first NORN, from whom the other three fates were derived.

Urshanabi (ur-shah-nah′-bee), A-B, the ferryman who carried GILGAMESH in safety across the waters to the abode of death, when Gilgamesh sought out UTA-NAPISHTIM after ENKIDU's death.

Uruk (oo′-ruhk), A-B, a city in Sumer, located near the Euphrates River, where an annual festival in celebration of ANU and ISHTAR was held. Its biblical name was ERECH.

Ushas (uhsh′-us, uh-shahs′), I, the Vedic goddess of the dawn, who prepared the way and led the chariot of the sun across the heavens. She was the daughter of DYAUS and PRITHIVI and was sometimes considered to be the wife of the fire-god AGNI, her brother.

Uta-Napishtim (uh′-tah-nah-pish′-tim) or **Utnapishtim** (oot-nah-), A-B, a wise man who, at the instigation of EA, built an ark, in which he and his family, animals, and birds survived the cataclysmic flood that ENLIL sent upon the earth. When, after seven days and nights, the ark came to rest on a mountain, Uta-Napishtim offered sacrifice to the gods, and Enlil granted him immortality. It was Uta-Napishtim whom GILGAMESH sought out after Enkidu's death, in his attempt to gain the gift of immortality.

Utgard (oot′-gahrd), Sc, a city or a section of JOTUNHEIM and the realm of the giant UTGARD-LOKI. Utgard is sometimes identified with Jotunheim.

Utgard-Loki (oot′-gahrd-loh′-kee), Sc, the king of UTGARD in JOTUNHEIM, who challenged THOR, LOKI, and THIALFI to a number of contests of strength and endurance when they visited his kingdom. They were defeated in all of them, only to discover too late that they had been successfully tricked throughout their trials by Utgard-Loki's magic and that he had indeed faced them before as the GIANT SKRYMIR.

Uther (yoo'-thur) or **Uther Pendragon** (pen-drag'-un), Ce, a descendant of BRUT and king of England at the time of the Saxon invasions in the fifth and sixth centuries A.D. MERLIN gave Uther the appearance of IGRAINE's husband, the Duke of Cornwall, and he became the father of ARTHUR by her.

Uther Pendragon (yoo'-thur pen-drag'-un), Ce. *See* UTHER.

Utnapishtim (oot-nah-pish'-tim), A-B. *See* UTA-NAPISHTIM.

Utu (oo'-too), A-B, the Sumerian sun-god, counterpart of the Babylonian god SHAMASH.

Utukku, the (oo'-tuh-koo), A-B, genii who were spirits holding a position subordinate to that of the gods. Those called the EDIMMU were forces of evil; the SHEDU, forces of good.

Vach (vahch), I, the goddess of speech. Vach brought wisdom and knowledge of the worship of the gods.

Vaikuntha (vahy-kun'-thu), I, a city of gold and jeweled palaces, the heaven where VISHNU reigned. It was sometimes described as situated on Mt. MERU.

Vainamoinen (vai'-na-muhi-nen), F, an aged sage and magician, the hero of the KALEVALA. He was the son of ILMATER, the virgin of the air, and the sea. He fell in love with AINO, but she fled from him and, falling into the sea, took the shape of a water deity. Aino's brother, JOUKAHAINEN, attempted to slay Vainamoinen, but he was not successful. The arrow killed Vainamoinen's horse, and he was thrown into the sea, where an eagle rescued him. He then sought a bride in POHJOLA. LOUHI promised her daughter to him in exchange for the SAMPO. ILMARINEN undertook to forge it and was chosen in Vainamoinen's stead.

Later, Vainamoinen went with Ilmarinen and LEMMINKAINEN to Pohjola to steal the Sampo. En route, he made a stringed instrument, called the kantele, from the bones of a pike. With its music, he put the people of Pohjola to sleep and seized the Sampo. Lemminkainen, however, woke them with his song, and Louhi created a storm, during which the kantele was lost and the Sampo was shattered. Vainamoinen salvaged a few pieces of the Sampo and thus brought prosperity to his land. After his victory over the people of Pohjola, and the birth of MARJATTA's son, who would take his place as the powerful hero of his people, Vainamoinen built a ship which carried him away on the sea.

Valhalla (val-hal'-u, val'-), S & T, ODIN's great hall, the dwelling place of Odin and the VALKYRIES, and the place where heroes and brave warriors slain in battle resided in the afterlife. Valhalla was depicted as a palace where Odin and the heroes feasted and drank while awaiting RAGNAROK, when they would march out to fight the GIANTS seeking to destroy the earth.

Vali (vah'-lee), Sc, the son of LOKI and SIGYN. In the twelfth-century account of Saxo Grammaticus, Vali was the son of ODIN and RIND. Vali represented justice, and it was he who slew HODER to avenge the death of BALDER.

Valkyries, the (val-keer'-eez, -kahy'-reez, val'-), S & T, warrior maidens who dwelt with ODIN in VALHALLA. Odin chose the souls of warriors slain in battle who were to enter Valhalla, and the Valkyries rode into battle at his bidding to carry the fallen heroes to Valhalla and make them welcome with mead. BRYNHILD is the most famed of the Valkyries.

Valmiki (vahl-mee'-kee), a Hindu poet, considered to be the author of the RAMAYANA.

Vamana (vah'-mu-nu), I, the fifth AVATAR of VISHNU, in which he took the shape of a dwarf. Vamana drove the demon BALI into PATALA, thus freeing heaven and earth of further menace by him.

Vanir, the (vah'-nir), Sc, a race of beneficent and peace-loving gods, who were deities of fertility and protectors of the fruits of the earth and all living things. The Vanir, among whom were NIORD, FREY, and FREYA, aided their worshipers by means of divination. There were frequent struggles between the Vanir and the AESIR until the Vanir were finally admitted to ASGARD.

Varaha (vu-rah'-hu), I, the third AVATAR of VISHNU. During the Deluge demons took over the earth. Incarnated as a wild boar, Vishnu dove through the floodwaters, slew the demon HIRANYAKSHA, who was holding down the earth, and raised it to the surface. At the same time, Varaha rescued the VEDAS from the watery depths.

Varuna (vur'-uh-nu, vahr-u'-), I, an early Vedic god of the overarching sky and the waters. Varuna, an omniscient and ever present power, had supreme authority and wisdom as a god of law and justice, the witness of oaths and the guarantor of mercy and the principles of order and morality in the universe. Later, he came to be associated with the moon and was the guardian of the sacrificial SOMA stored in the moon. With YAMA, Varuna was a lord of the dead, whose kingdom was in the moon.

Vasuki (vah'-suh-ki), I, a huge snake, a ruler of the NAGAS. Vasuki served as a rope for the gods to churn the sea and, again, for Vaivasvata to moor his ship to the horn of MATSYA.

Vasus, the (vah'-suhz), I, a group of deities who were the attendants of INDRA. Among them were AGNI, PRITHIVI, and VAYU.

Vatea (vah'-tee-u) or **Atea** (ah'-), O, in the myth of some islands, the father of TANGAROA and also of RONGO. Their mother, PAPA, however, managed to make Rongo heir to the power in place of his older brother. The sun and moon were regarded as the eyes of Vatea.

Vayu (vah-yuh'), I, the god of wind, and one of the VASUS. He was the father of HANUMAN. Vayu's importance and worship declined as INDRA and the nature-gods associated with him gained in stature.

Vedas, the (vay'-duz, vee'-), I, the Sanskrit scriptures, the earliest sacred writings of India, dating from between 1200 and 800 B.C. and forming the corpus of the Hindu sacred literature. The foremost of the Vedas are four books called the SAMHITAS. These are: (a) the *Rig-Veda,* a collection of 1,028 hymns belonging to a period no later than about 1700–1500 B.C., and a rich source of myths and legends of the gods; (b) the *Sama-Veda,* a book of chants, mantras, and tunes connected with the *Rig-Veda;* (c) the *Yajur-Veda,* consisting of sacrificial formulas, prayers, and explanatory material; (d) the *Atharva-Veda,* a grouping of mantras and formulas, charms and spells, all showing evidence of the adaptation of the native Indian tribal beliefs by the Aryan settlers.

Veles (ve'-les), Sl. *See* VOLOS.

Venus (vee'-nus), R, an early Italian goddess of the spring seasons and gardens, later identified with APHRODITE, the Greek goddess of love.

Verdandi (ver'-dan-dee), Sc, one of the NORNS. Verdandi personified the present. She was kindly, and she helped URD to shape the web of fate.

Vergil or **Virgil** (vur'-jil), the Roman epic and pastoral poet Publius Vergilius Maro, 70–19 B.C. He was the author of the AENEID, the greatest of Latin epic poems, a work in twelve books centering on the wanderings of the hero AENEAS and his followers after the fall of Troy, and the establishment of their new home in Italy.

Vertumnus (vur-tum'-nus), R, the god of gardens, orchards, and of the four seasons. He was the husband of Pomona, the goddess of fruit trees.

Vesper (ves'-pur), R, the Latin name for HESPER, the Evening Star.

Vesta (ves'-tu), R, the goddess of the hearth and fireside. Vesta's sacred fire in the Roman Forum was tended by priestesses called vestal virgins. Her Greek counterpart was HESTIA.

Victoria (vik-tohr'-ee-u), R, the personification of victory, analogous to the Greek goddess NIKE.

Vidar (vee'-dahr), Sc, the son of ODIN. A deity of the AESIR, Vidar was portrayed as a strong and silent god. After FENRIR broke away from his chain, GLEIPNIR, and consumed Odin, Vidar killed Fenrir and survived RAGNAROK, becoming a god of the world that was to be born anew into a golden age.

Vigrid (vee'-grid), Sc, the enormous battlefield where the final bloody battle between the gods and the evil forces of the GIANTS and monsters took place at RAGNAROK.

Viracocha (vee-rah-koh'-chah), SA, the Incan god of water and growing things, the creator and spirit of life. Like PACHACAMAC, Viracocha antedated the Incas in Peru and was taken by them as one of their gods. He lived in the depths of Lake Titicaca. He was the creator of the sun, moon, and stars and was lord of thunder, lightning, and rain. His sister and wife was MAMA COCHA, also a deity of the water. Children and animals were sacrificed to him.

Virgil (vur'-jil). *See* VERGIL.

Vishnu (vish'-noo), I, originally a Vedic god exemplifying benevolence and associated with the sun and light. In the myths of popular Hinduism, Vishnu was believed to have had ten incarnations, the most famous of which are the AVATAR of KRISHNA, who appears in the BHAGAVAD-GITA, and that of RAMA in the RAMAYANA. His ninth avatar was in the body of BUDDHA, and his tenth and final incarnation will come in the future, in the form of KALKI at the creation of a new and better world. In later Hinduism, Vishnu is the second deity of the TRIMURTI, the other two being BRAHMA and SHIVA.

Vishnu is often represented holding a mace, shell, disk, and lotus in each of his four hands, and with blue skin, and clothed in yellow. Numerous epithets were given to Vishnu, a result of the process of assimilation of neighboring and minor gods into his cult. Vishnu's consort was LAKSHMI, the goddess of beauty.

Visvakarma (vis'-vu-kahr-mu), I, the architect for the gods, who built the city of LANKA and the great city of Amaravati in SWARGA. Visvakarma was a RISHI and the father of NALA. Many of his characteristics are often confused with those of TVASHTRI and VIVASVAT, and he was later identified with Tvashtri.

Vivanhvat (vee'-vahn-vaht), Pe, the first human to make the sacred drink HAOMA. He was rewarded with a splendid son, YIMA, and a life free from evil.

Vivasvat (vi-vahs'-vut), I, the rising sun in Vedic myth. He was the husband of SARANYU, daughter of TVASHTRI, and the father of YAMA AND YAMI and the ASVINS.

Volkh (vawlkh), Sl, a creature who had magic powers and transformed himself into various shapes, taking the form of a bird, an animal, or an insect at will. Volkh acted as protector of the city of Kiev.

Volos (vaw'-lus), or Veles (ve'-les), Sl, in early mythology, a god of beasts and wild animals, with many of the functions of a god of war. At a later period, he became a protective deity of shepherds and cattle and was viewed as more rustic and like the peasants who were his worshipers. Among the Czechs, Volos was considered to be a demon rather than a deity.

Volsung (vol'-suhng), Sc, 1. the son of RERIR and a grandson of ODIN's son SIGI. He was the father by LIOD of SIGMUND, the eldest of ten sons, and of SIGNY, by whose husband, SIGGEIR, he was murdered.

2. the name Volsung is also used to refer to any member of his family.

Volsunga Saga, the (vol'-suhng-gu sah'-gu), Sc, an Icelandic tale of the thirteenth century, relating the deeds of the VOLSUNGS and the role played by the gods and goddesses, as well as by the heroes and heroines, which corresponds to the NIBELUNGENLIED of the Teutons. The Volsung hero was SIGURD, son of SIGMUND and Hiordis. He wed GUDRUN and won BRYNHILD for GUNNAR. His death was brought about by Brynhild, seeking vengeance for his having deserted her for Gudrun.

Volsunga Saga	Nibelungenlied
Sigmund	Siegmund
Hiordis	Sieglinde
Sigurd	Siegfried
Gudrun	Kriemhild
Gunnar	Gunther
Brynhild	Brunhild

Voltumna (vawl-tum'-nu), the Etruscan mother goddess. She was the protective goddess of the Etruscan Confederation, whose assemblies were held in her temple.

Vritra (vrit'-ru), I, a huge monster, a dragon or serpent, with a great thirst for rain clouds. When INDRA and Vritra met in combat and the dragon got the upper hand, Indra fled and was advised to make peace with his enemy. VISHNU, however, intimated his help would come to Indra in the future. Vritra set forth the terms of the pact, stating he must not be attacked by day or night, or with a wooden, stone, or iron weapon, or with any object that was wet or dry, and Indra agreed.

When Indra was by the sea one day at twilight and saw Vritra nearby, a great mass of foam appeared. With this in hand, Indra killed the monstrous dragon, and all knew Vishnu was incarnate in the foam.

Vulcan (vul'-kun), R, the god of fire and metalworking, identified with the Greek god HEPHAESTUS.

Wainamoinen (wai'-na-muhi-nen), F. *See* VAINAMOINEN.

Wakonda (wah-kahn'-dah), NA, the GREAT SPIRIT of the Sioux Indians, Father of the Sky, the supreme being and the unseen power governing the world and controlling the life forces. The Pawnees call him TIRAWA ATIUS.

Wamara (wah-mah-rah'), Af, a deity worshiped by some of the tribes of Uganda. He was the father of three sons, who were gods of the sun and moon, cattle, and water. His fourth son had numerous adventures as a hero, and a grandson upheld the vault of the heavens.

Wang (wahng), Ch, the armed guard of the palace door of TUNG WANG KUNG.

Wen Ch'ang (wen' chahng'), Ch, an ancient god, emperor of literature, an honor bestowed on him by TUNG WANG KUNG, the Jade Emperor, after he had lived a number of active, eventful lives. The god of examinations, K'UEI-HSING, was his helper. Wen Ch'ang is depicted in the dress of a mandarin and is usually seated, with a scepter in his hand.

Weneg (wen'-eg), E, the scribe of the god RA.

Wiglaf (wig'-lahf), in the poem *Beowulf,* a kinsman of BEOWULF who went with Beowulf and a group of ten others to hunt out a dragon that was plaguing the countryside. When Beowulf attacked the monster, all the men fled except for Wiglaf, who helped Beowulf kill the creature before Beowulf fell mortally wounded.

Winabojo (win-u-boh'-joh), NA. *See* MANABOZHO.

Winds, the, G, the sons of ASTRAEUS and EOS. AEOLUS, king of the winds, lived on the island of Aeolia. The principal winds were BOREAS, the north wind, NOTUS, the south wind, EURUS, the east wind, and ZEPHYRUS, the west wind. Their Roman counterparts were AQUILO, AUSTER, EURUS, and FAVONIUS respectively.

Wotan (voh'-tahn), T, a god who corresponds to the Scandinavian god ODIN. The legends surrounding him are unknown because of lack of Germanic literary sources. Our only real knowledge comes from the Scandinavian myths involving Odin, his counterpart.

The same deity was called Woden or Wodan by the Anglo-Saxons and was taken to Britain when they invaded the island in the fifth century A.D. Wednesday, "Woden's day," is named for him.

Xilonen (heel-ohn'-un), Az, a goddess who was extremely lovely. When the early corn appeared and turned green, it took on divine form and was Xilonen, the counterpart of the god CINTEOTL.

Xipe (hee'-pay) or **Xipe Totec** (toh-tek'), Az, the god of spring growth, vegetation, and flowers, known as the flayed god.

Xipe Totec (hee'-pay toh-tek'), Az. *See* XIPE.

Xiuhtecutli (hee-oo-tay-koo'-tlee), Az, the god of fire, ruler of the sun of the present universe. He received offerings of live sacrificial victims, who were cast into the flames.

Xochipilli (soh-chee-peel'-lee), Az, the god of youth, love and pleasure, dancing and music. He was the twin of the flower-goddess XOCHIQUETZAL.

Xochiquetzal (soh-chee-ket'-sahl), Az, believed to be the first woman. She escaped the flood. Xochiquetzal was the goddess of flowers and love, wife of TLALOC. Their children, given the gift of speech by a dove, spoke a multiplicity of tongues, each unintelligible to the others. TEZCATLIPOCA fell in love with Xochiquetzal, taking her from the rain-god.

Xolotl (soh-loh't'l), Az, the patron and guardian of twins, considered to be the twin of QUETZALCOATL. He had the power to assume different shapes and was therefore a deity of magicians. Xolotl was a representation of the evening star, the planet Venus, as his twin was of the morning star.

Yacatecuhtli (yah-kah-tay-koo'-tlee), an ancient Mexican god of merchants and travelers. Slaves were frequently sacrificed to Yacatecuhtli, who was generally depicted with a staff.

Yakshas, the (yuk'-shuz), I, another name for the RAKSHASAS.

Yama (yam'-u, yum'-) and **Yami** (yam'-ee, yum'-), I, the first human couple, the twin children of VIVASVAT. After death, Yama and Yami became king and queen of the realm of the dead, where they prepared and maintained dwellings of bliss for those who entered their kingdom. Yama corresponds to the Persian god YIMA.

Yama-Kings, the (yahm'-u), Ch, ten kings who sit as rulers and judges of the ten courts of Hell, each of which has jurisdiction over the punishment of distinct and clearly outlined crimes committed during the offender's life. The principal Yama-King reviews the deeds of the newly arrived souls and determines whether he or one of the other judges will carry out punishment, basing his decision on the type and severity of the crime, whether it be sacrilege, arson, dishonesty, murder, or lying. It is the province of the tenth judge to determine whether the soul is to be reborn in the form of a human or an animal. The virtuous souls and those without blame may return to life on earth almost at once or may achieve a place among the immortals. Those who have sinned must undergo due punishment before receiving new earthly bodies.

Yami (yam'-ee, yum'-), I. *See* YAMA AND YAMI.

Yang (yahng, yang), Ch. *See* YIN AND YANG.

Yang-ku (yahng'-koo'), Ch, a valley in the east where the ten suns and their mother lived. Every day, each in turn, corresponding to one hour of the day, the suns crossed the sky, each one in his own chariot with the mother the charioteer, to a mountain in the west. One myth relates that, when all ten suns once appeared together, the Excellent Archer, Yi, took his magic bow and brought down all but one of the suns, saving the earth from the overpowering heat.

Yang-wu (yang'-woo'), Ch, the sun crow, a sacred bird.

Yarilo (yah-ri-loh'), Sl, a god of passion and ardent love. According to oral tradition, Yarilo was a youthful deity who, clad in white, was mounted on a white horse. He was a god of fertility and the patron of spring planting. Young girls celebrated a festival of flowers in his honor in the spring. At the end of summer, another festival, also marked by dancing and feasting, observed his passing and culminated in the performance of the god's funeral rites.

Yasodhara Devi (yu-so-dahr'-u day'-vee), I, SIDDHARTHA's wife, born on the same day he was.

Yatagarasu (yah'-tah-gah-rah'-su), J, the sacred crow of the sun-goddess AMATERASU, corresponding to YANG-WU in Chinese mythology.

Yatis, the (yat'-is, yut'-), Pe, supernatural beings with powers of evil and sorcery.

Yazata (yah-zah'-tah), Pe, one of a group of genii venerated as divine beings analogous to the physical objects and moral forces of the heavens and earth. They had many characteristics and functions similar to those of the AMESHA SPENTAS.

Yemaja (yay-mah'-jah), Af, in legends of the Yorubas, the daughter of ODUDUA and both the sister and wife of AGANJU, by whom she was the mother of ORUNJAN. Yemaja was a water deity, goddess of lakes and rivers.

Yen-Wang (yen'-wahng'), Ch, the god of the world of the dead, the chief of the YAMA-KINGS. Yen-Wang controls the manner and time of death and decides the destiny of the souls of the dead, determining the shape, human or animal, those who return to earth will take, selecting those who will receive immortality and judging the punishments for the wicked.

Yggdrasil (ig'-dru-sil, oog'-), Sc, a sacred ash tree that grew from YMIR's body and supported the universe. It had roots extending into MIDGARD, land of men; NIFLHEIM, land of the dead; and JOTUNHEIM, land of the GIANTS; and its top reached to ASGARD.

Yima (yee'-mah) or **Jamshid** (jam-sheed'), Pe, the son of VIVANHVAT, born to him in recompense for his achievement in preparing HAOMA.

When all living things were faced with destruction by flood, because of the evil deeds of the demon MAHRKUSHA, AHURA MAZDA saved Yima by telling him to mold a vast underground shelter and to take the finest specimens of all species of living creatures to dwell there, so they might survive to rebuild the earth.

Yima was the only human to possess the solar eye, giving him immortal powers to use in the creation of a life of good and bliss for all men. He was the inventor and developer of numerous skills, including weaving, and the making of iron weapons and jewelry.

Yima was a beneficent king, whose reign, favored by Ahura Mazda, brought a golden age, until, overcome by vanity and pride, and forfeiting the gift of immortality for mankind, he was taken captive by his enemies and put to death by ZOHAK.

In the SHAH-NAMAH, he is called JAMSHID, the son of TAHMURAS.

Yin (yin) **and Yang** (yahng, yang), Ch, the two ethers that came from the dividing of the original cell of primeval chaos, CH'I. Yin is female, dark, negative, and of the earth, and symbolized by a divided or broken line. Yang is male, bright, positive, and of the heavens, and symbolized by an unbroken line. Yin came to be identified with demons; Yang, to represent the gods. Yin and Yang are at the base of a doctrine of dualism, in which alternating and opposing forces brought about the creation of the universe, Yin forming the earth and Yang the sky, and shaped the fundamental nature of all living things.

Yiyi (yee'-yee), Af, among those who speak Ewe, a legendary spider, whose daughter became Death's wife. Death, who had traps in the forest, shared his plentiful supply of food with the spider Yiyi during a famine, and Yiyi, in gratitude, gave him his daughter to be his wife. One day she fell into a trap by mistake and was collected as game. When he went for him with a knife, Death chased Yiyi back to the village, and there he discovered he could get his food by killing women instead of setting traps for the forest animals.

Ymir (ee'-mir, oo'-), Sc, a primeval GIANT who lived at the beginning of the universe and was the ancestor of the race of giants. Ymir was formed from the mist rising from the ice of NIFLHEIM, melted by the warmth blowing from MUSPELHEIM. The sea, earth, and heavens were created from the parts of Ymir's body, after he was slain by ODIN and the other gods. YGGDRASIL grew from his body.

Yo (yoh) **and In** (in), J, the female and male principles, analogous to the Chinese YIN AND YANG, of the egg of chaos that split to form the earth and heavens.

Yomi (yoh'-mee), J, the realm of the dead, a kingdom of darkness lying below the earth, reached either from the edge of the sea or by a twisting, downhill road.

Youkahainen (you'-ku-hahy-nen), F. *See* JOUKAHAINEN.

Yseult (i-soolt'), Ce. *See* ISEULT.

Yum Caax (yoom kah'-ahks), M, the god of corn and agriculture. He was a handsome young deity, honored at the time of the planting and the harvesting of the maize. He was also called GHANAN.

Zagmuk (zahg'-muhk), A-B, a feast, held at the first of the year, when the gods met in the UPSHUKINA to plot the fate of mankind.

Zamna (sahm'-nah), M. *See* ITZAMNA.

Zaqar (zah'-kahr), A-B, a god who was SIN's messenger and brought dreams to men.

Zarathustra (zar-u-thoo'-stru), Pe. *See* ZOROASTER.

Zarpanit (zahr-pan'-it), A-B, the goddess wife of MARDUK.

Zarya (zur'-yu), Sl. *See* ZORYA.

Zehuti (ze-hoo'-tee), E. *See* DJEHUTI.

Zend, the (zend), Pe, a translation and interpretation of the AVESTA in the Pahlavi language.

Zend-Avesta, the (zend-u-ves'-tu), Pe, the AVESTA in combination with the ZEND.

Zephyrus (zef'-er-us), G, the west wind, son of ASTRAEUS and EOS. In the contest of HYACINTHUS with APOLLO, Zephyrus caused the discus to go astray and strike down Hyacinthus. His Roman counterpart was FAVONIUS.

Zethus (zee'-thus), G, son of ZEUS and ANTIOPE, and twin brother of AMPHION. It was Zethus who built the great stone wall around THEBES, which city he named in honor of his wife Thebe, a NYMPH.

Zeus (zoos), G, a son of CRONUS and RHEA and king of the gods and goddesses. His Roman counterpart was JUPITER. Because Cronus swallowed up all his children, Rhea gave birth to Zeus on Crete and gave Cronus a stone instead. The infant Zeus was nursed and brought up by AMALTHEA. Zeus was first wed to METIS, who forced Cronus to disgorge Zeus's brothers and sisters: DEMETER, HADES, HERA, HESTIA, and POSEIDON. The stone Rhea had given Cronus became the OMPHALOS.

When Cronus was overthrown by his children, Zeus became the supreme ruler of the heavens and of mankind, as well as of OLYMPUS, and was called the Father of Gods and Men. ATHENA sprang full-grown from the head of Zeus after he had swallowed up Metis. Zeus then made Hera his wife and queen and was the father by her of ARES, HEBE, and HEPHAESTUS. Zeus was the father of APHRODITE by DIONE, of APOLLO and ARTEMIS by LETO, of DIONYSUS by SEMELE, and of numerous other children, among them, the CHARITES, MUSES, FATES, and HORAE, and MINOS, HELEN, POLLUX, HERACLES, and PERSEUS, by various others.

The OLYMPIC GAMES were established at Olympia in honor of Zeus. DODONA, where there was a famous oracle of Zeus, was also sacred to him. Zeus, who hurled the thunderbolt to cause storms and death, was often referred to as the Cloud-Gatherer and was described as AEGIS-bearing. The eagle and the oak tree were sacred to Zeus, who was depicted with a thunderbolt or a scepter.

Ziggurat (zig'-uh-rat), A-B, a type of pyramid-temple originated by the ancient Sumerians and adopted by the Assyrians and Babylonians. It was built of brick on a rectangular base and rose in a series of terraces, each smaller than the one below, to the shrine of a deity on its summit, reached by steps winding around the outer sides.

Zipaltonal (see-pahl-toh'-nahl), a goddess of the Indians of Nicaragua who was, with TAMAGOSTAD, the chief deity and creator of the earth and all living things.

Zocho (zaw'-choh), J, one of the SHI TENNO, the guardian of the west.

Zohak (zoh'-huk), Pe, the name of the incarnation of AZHI DAHAKA. Under the influence of ANGRA MAINYU, he became an evil man and gained the throne by murdering his father. Angra Mainyu continued to control Zohak by subterfuge, until he became a formidable demon, monstrous in appearance, with serpents growing from his shoulders.

Zohak forced YIMA from power and ruled for a thousand years over a world of vice, unspeakable wickedness, and tyranny. Warned in a dream that he would be dethroned, Zohak issued a command that all the children of the land should be slain. The time came, however, when FERIDUN, hidden away by his mother at birth, grew up to vanquish Zohak and imprison him in a cave.

Zoroaster (zor-oh-as'-tur, zawr-), a Persian prophet and teacher who lived in about 600 B.C. A religious reformer, Zoroaster rebuilt and revitalized the religion of ancient Persia, setting down the basic stories and doctrines in the AVESTA. He was also called ZARATHUSTRA.

Zorya (zawr'-yu) or **Zarya** (zur'-), Sl, a lovely water priestess whose dwelling place was BOUYAN. Zorya filled the role of protectress of warriors when, in association with PERUN, she acted as a warrior-goddess.

Zu (zoo), A-B, the god of storms, who had the shape of a bird. Zu stole the TABLETS OF FATE, which were thought to have been recovered by MARDUK. He was also called ANZU.

Zurvan (zur'-vun), Pe, a god of time and destiny. In early mythology, Zurvan was the father of both AHURA MAZDA and ANGRA MAINYU. Since the first-born was Angra Mainyu and so, contrary to Zurvan's plan, became king, he gave Time to both of his sons to share and contend over, until the ultimate victory of Ahura Mazda, good, over Angra Mainyu, evil, came. Thus, the common thread of the mythology of the ancient Persians, the ever present struggle between light and dark, good and evil, was established.

BIBLIOGRAPHY

Cottie, Burland. *The Gods of Mexico.* 1967.

Davidson, H. R. E. *Scandinavian Mythology.* 1969.

Grant, Michael. *Myths of the Greeks and Romans.* 1964.

Graves, Robert. *The Greek Myths.* 1955.

Gray, John. *Near Eastern Mythology.* 1969.

Hamilton, Edith. *Mythology.* 1942.

Ions, Veronica. *Indian Mythology.* 1967.

Larousse Encyclopedia of Mythology. 1968.

Larousse World Mythology. 1973.

MacCana, Proinsias. *Celtic Mythology.* 1970.

MacCulloch, J. A., and Gray, L. H. *The Mythology of All Races.* 13 vols. 1922.

Parrinder, E. G. *African Mythology.* 1968.

Piggott, Juliet. *Japanese Mythology.* 1969.

Poignant, Roslyn. *Oceanic Mythology.* 1967.

Rose, H. J. *A Handbook of Greek Mythology.* 1959.

Werner, E. T. C. *Myths and Legends of China.* 1922.